PENGUIN BOOKS

AN AMERICAN FARMER

For many years a professor of English at New York University, Gay Wilson Allen has written biographies of William James and Walt Whitman; his biography of Ralph Waldo Emerson, *Waldo Emerson*, received the Los Angeles Times Book Award as well as the MLA Lowell Prize in 1982.

Roger Asselineau, director of American Studies at the Sorbonne, has edited works of such major authors as Irving, Faulkner, and Hemingway, and prepared a bilingual translation of Whitman's *Leaves of Grass*.

D1523928

St. John de Crèvecoeur
After a portrait by Valière, 1786
Courtesy of M. Jean St. John de Crèvecoeur

AN AMERICAN FARMER

The Life of
St. John de Crèvecoeur

GAY WILSON ALLEN
&
ROGER ASSELINEAU

PENGUIN BOOKS

PENGUIN BOOKS
Published by the Penguin Group
Viking Penguin, a division of Penguin Books USA Inc.,
40 West 23rd Street, New York, New York 10010, U.S.A.
Penguin Books Ltd, 27 Wrights Lane, London W8 5TZ, England
Penguin Books Australia Ltd, Ringwood, Victoria, Australia
Penguin Books Canada Ltd, 2801 John Street,
Markham, Ontario, Canada L3R 1B4
Penguin Books (N.Z.) Ltd, 182–190 Wairau Road,
Auckland 10, New Zealand

Penguin Books Ltd, Registered Offices:
Harmondsworth, Middlesex, England

First published in the United States of America
as *St. John de Crèvecoeur* by Viking Penguin,
a division of Penguin Books USA Inc., 1987
Published in Penguin Books 1990

1 3 5 7 9 10 8 6 4 2

LIBRARY OF CONGRESS CATALOGING IN PUBLICATION DATA
Allen, Gay Wilson, 1903–
[St. John de Crèvecoeur]
An American farmer: the life of St. John de Crèvecoeur/Gay
Wilson Allen and Roger Asselineau.
p. cm.
Reprint. Originally published: St. John de Crèvecoeur. New York,
N.Y., U.S.A.: Viking, 1987.
Includes bibliographical references.
ISBN 0 14 01.3022 5
1. St. John de Crèvecoeur, J. Hector, 1735–1813.   2. Authors,
American—Revolutionary period, 1775–1783—Biography.
3. Naturalists—United States—Biography.   4. Farmers—United
States—Biography.   5. Diplomats—France—Biography.
I. Asselineau, Roger.   II. Title.   III. Title: Saint John de
Crèvecoeur.
[PS737.C5Z54   1990]
973.3'092—dc20
[B]   89–39024

Printed in the United States of America
Set in Videocomp Baskerville
Designed by Kathryn Parise

To Monsieur Jean St. John de Crèvecoeur
for his help and sympathy
and to Franco-American Cultural Exchanges

CONTENTS

Contents

PREFACE

WE HAVE of course profited from the previous biographies of St. John de Crèvecoeur. The first, *Saint John de Crèvecoeur: sa vie et ses oeuvres* (Paris, 1883), was written by his grandson, Robert de Crèvecoeur, who had access to the abundant letters and manuscripts in the possession of the family—material since dispersed. This book is especially valuable for the section of "Correspondence."

The first American biography of Crèvecoeur was a Columbia University dissertation by Julia Post Mitchell, published in 1916. While Miss Mitchell did not attempt to analyze in depth either the man or his writings, she thoroughly investigated Crèvecoeur's wife's family in Westchester, his marriage, and the purchase of his farm at Chester, in Orange County, New York. She also did exhaustive research on Crèvecoeur's achievements and failures as consul of New York, Connecticut, and New Jersey. She was the first to assemble all the facts relating to his establishing a packet-ship service between France and the United States. In spite of the consul's strenuous efforts, this attempt eventually failed. Since Miss Mitchell has treated this episode in great detail, we have not thought it necessary to repeat at length a rather dull and monotonous story. While Miss Mitchell found it difficult to believe that Crèvecoeur served in the French army during the "French and Indian war" in Canada, we have documentary evidence that he did.

Among other works, Howard C. Rice's *Le cultivateur américain: étude sur l'oeuvre de Saint John de Crèvecoeur* (Paris, 1932) is a brilliant interpretation of the man and his writings, with more emphasis on ideas and literary art than personal details. Thomas Philbrick's brief, concise *St. John de Crèvecoeur* is a useful introduction.

We have supplemented these works with some new facts and interpretations, and paid more attention to Crèvecoeur's French background than have previous biographers.

For information and assistance of various kinds, we wish to thank the following persons and libraries in the United States: Harold J. Jonas, Goshen, New York; Arthur Golden, Nyack, New York; Everett Emerson, Chapel Hill, North Carolina; the Manuscript Division of the Library of Congress; the New York Historical Society; the Morgan Library in New York City; and the Oradell, New Jersey, Public Library.

In Europe, for information and permission to reproduce letters, manuscripts, and pictorial material, we are grateful to: the librarians of the Library of the Town of Salisbury and the Salisbury Cathedral Library; the Wiltshire County Archivist; M. Paul Jolas, Director of the Municipal Library of Mantes-la-Jolie, who supplied photocopies of the letters which Crèvecoeur sent to the Duke de La Rochefoucauld during his consulship in New York; the staffs of the Bibliothèque Nationale, the Bibliothèque de l'Arsenal, the Archives de l'Armée, and the Archives Nationales; and, above all, M. Lerch, the Director of the Archives of the Département du Calvados.

Also M. Jean St. John de Crèvecoeur, who still owns the portraits in pencil and gouache and maps drawn by Crèvecoeur while a soldier in Canada. He generously supplied us with reproductions of these and a watercolor sketch of Pine Hill.

—GWA and RA
Oradell, N.J.,
and Antony, France

INTRODUCTION

A MINIATURE of St. Jean de Crèvecoeur (see frontispiece), made in France in 1786 by an artist named Valière, shows the profile of a middle-aged gentleman (actually fifty-one years old) wearing a powdered peruke with large curls over the ears and a tail of hair hanging down his back, and a jabot decorating his shirt. The face is fair, full, and round, with a prominent nose and large eyes (said to have been brown) and a small, firm mouth. His natural hair was red, and the miniature does not show the freckles which covered his face, arms, and hands.[1] He appears to be well built. One might not guess from this portrait that he was only five feet four inches tall—though that was about average for Frenchmen at the time.

In 1786 men's fashions in France were becoming simpler, though still ornate compared with the Revolutionary period a few years later. Yet it is a little difficult to imagine this elegant gentleman as a real farmer in Orange County, New York, cultivating his own farm, plowing, cutting hay, arising at daybreak to feed his livestock. Yet that was the life he was living when he wrote *Letters from an American Farmer,* which won him fame on two continents, first in England, then in France, and finally in the United States. It is still recognized as a literary masterpiece of the eighteenth century—one of only a few from America, since American literature did not begin flourishing until half a century later.

Crèvecoeur was happy on his farm for five or six years, until his neutrality in the growing American rebellion against Great Britain brought him into conflict with his Patriot neighbors and made life unendurable for him at Pine Hill, the name he had given the house he built soon after purchasing his farm in 1769. *Letters from an American Farmer* has the reputation of depicting a utopian view of life on a colonial farm not actually on the frontier but near it. The early letters (or chapters) are almost lyrical in describing the joys of farm life, but then they turn somber and even horrifying as the author describes the persecutions inflicted on everyone who tried to remain neutral. After praising in the earlier chapters the freedom and opportunities the European immigrant found in the "New World," the farmer discovers that public opinion in this country could be as tyrannical as a despotic government in the Old World.

Although based on experience, *Letters from an American Farmer* is not actually autobiographical, but fiction in the guise of letters written to a European friend by a farmer who calls himself simply James. Crèvecoeur himself was known to his neighbors as Hector St. John, the name under which he was naturalized in 1765.[2] Taking this name may have been an attempt to disguise his French origin, and certainly he was trying to achieve an American identity. However, he was inconsistent: Four years later, when he married Mehetable Tippett, daughter of a Westchester landowner, he gave his full baptismal name, Michel-Guillaume Saint-Jean de Crèvecoeur. But later that year he bought a farm in Orange County, New York, under the name Hector St. John.[3]

Crèvecoeur's American-farmer identity, therefore, was part fantasy and part reality. The narrator of the *Letters* pretends to have inherited his farm from an English father, who was himself a second-generation American. Also he places the farm in Carlisle, Pennsylvania, instead of Chester, New York. James, the British heir, says further: "My father left me a few musty books, which *his* father brought from England with him; but what help can I draw from a library consisting mostly of Scotch divinity, the *Navigations of Sir Francis Drake,* the *History of Queen Elizabeth,* and a few miscellaneous volumes?"[4]

If there was actually a recipient of the *Letters* it was probably William Seton, a businessman in New York City, though originally from the British Isles. He was Crèvecoeur's first and best friend in North America. Primarily the correspondence (if it can be called that) was a literary device, made famous in English literature several decades earlier by the epistolary novels of Richardson, Fielding, and Sterne, and in France by Rousseau in his *Nouvelle Héloïse.* There is no evidence that Crèvecoeur read any of these works, but he was acquainted with literature, despite James's pose of ignorance, and knew something of literary traditions. In fact, he had received a very good education in France—much better than previous biographers have assumed. The Jesuit school he attended was more liberal than the later reputation of that order might lead one to suppose. It gave superior instruction not only in the humanities, including languages, but also in applied mathematics, surveying, and probably map making.

Crèvecoeur had natural talents for sketching, painting, and descriptive prose, which he cultivated in his youth and later employed as a professional map maker. His attractive watercolor sketch of Pine Hill still exists, and his commanding officer in Canada proudly sent his map of Fort George to Louis XV. He was hardly an unsophisticated backwoods farmer.

Crèvecoeur's life after he left the Jesuit school is full of mystery and contradictions which still puzzle his biographers. It seems certain that he went to Salisbury, England, to live for a few months, or maybe two or three years, with some elderly female relatives. Why he went there, and exactly when he arrived and left, is not known. By the time he turns up in Canada he speaks fluent English, which he might have learned in Salisbury; but more likely, he had already studied the language in the Jesuit school, and polished his pronunciation in England. There he fell in love with a girl, who died prematurely, and with the English language and British institutions.

Crèvecoeur's father thought he went from Salisbury to Philadelphia to work for two American merchants whom he had met in England;[5] yet no evidence of his presence in Philadelphia has been found. But there are records of his military service in the French Colonial Army in Canada in 1756–57, where his mathematical training served him well as an expert in artillery and map making, for which he won praise and promotion to first lieutenant. However, after the French defeat in Quebec, the first stage in the loss of "New France" in the seven-year war with Great Britain, he lost favor with his regiment, resigned his commission, and chose to emigrate to the British colonies instead of returning to France. It is not unlikely that his anglophilia got him into trouble with his fellow officers. But in view of his admiration for the British, why was he fighting against them and the Americans? He had not been conscripted. To this question no one has found an answer. It is one of several anomalies in his biography.

How Crèvecoeur supported himself between his arrival in New York in 1759 and his buying a farm ten years later is only partly known. He was an expert surveyor, and surveying was in great demand at that time. He may also have bought furs from the Indians to sell in New York or Albany. His friend Seton dealt in furs, though not exclusively. Crèvecoeur claimed that he was adopted by an Oneida tribe of Indians in Connecticut,[6] which suggests dealings with the Indians, and they did not employ surveyors. He also said he traveled extensively in the colonies. How much the traveling described in

Letters from an American Farmer is fiction is impossible to determine, but there seems to be no reason to doubt that he did travel widely, by foot, horseback, and canoe, sometimes with Indian guides. Certainly his writings show more detailed knowledge of American geography and the life of the settlers than those of any other writer of the period.

Though Crèvecoeur's real and vicarious experiences cannot always be separated, the main events in his life as a farmer and author are not in doubt. And these events are full of drama and pathos. After months of torment by his patriotic neighbors because he stubbornly refused to support their quarrel with Great Britain, he left his wife and two younger children in Chester under the protection of friends, and with his six-year-old son, whom he apparently intended to take with him to France, reached New York City, which almost from the beginning of hostilities had been occupied by the British army. Ironically, the British arrested him on the suspicion that he was an American spy employed by General Washington—and Washington had given him a pass through the American lines. After three very miserable months Crèvecoeur was released from prison, but during the following terrible winter he and his son nearly starved, and his health was permanently undermined.

Finally able to sail for England with his son and precious manuscripts, he was shipwrecked off the Irish coast, but saved the manuscripts. In London a publisher bought them—or, more accurately, a selection of them—for the first edition of *Letters from an American Farmer,* which became an instant success—partly because many British Whigs were sympathetic with the Americans in their rebellion. The sale of his book enabled Crèvecoeur to return to France, a year after arriving in England. There Mme. d'Houdetot, an old friend of the Crèvecoeur family, introduced him into the intellectual circles in Paris. He was lionized and urged to translate his book into French, a language he had almost forgotten after nearly three decades of speaking only English. Invited to Versailles by the king to write a long report on the North American colonies, he produced such an informative document that, some months later, he was offered a consulship in the new American republic.

For nearly two years Crèvecoeur had been unable to get any information about the wife and two children he had left in Chester, and he eagerly accepted the consulship because it would enable him to return and search for his family. He arrived in New York just as the British were evacuating the city and George Washington was marching in to repossess it. At the same time he learned that Pine Hill had been burned by Indians, his wife had died, and a stranger had taken the children to Boston. A few days later he received letters informing him that the stranger was a relative of one of five American marines he had aided on the Norman coast after their escape from British imprisonment. The story of this rescue of the Crèvecoeur children, and his trip to Boston by sleigh to rejoin them, is one of the most emotional episodes of all his adventures.[7]

Crèvecoeur worked very hard at being a good consul, and his efforts were appreciated by the leaders of the new nation, many of whom—Washington, Jefferson, Madison, and Franklin among them—became his personal friends. His most ambitious undertaking was the establishment of a regular line of packet ships between France and the United States, which he supervised. But this enterprise was never wholly successful, and finally was abandoned for lack of proper support. The confused political situation in France made it impossible for Crèvecoeur to get the reforms made which he advocated.

Someone has remarked that Crèvecoeur was a man to whom things happened. After having been trapped by some of the uglier aspects of the American Revolution, it was his fate to return to France (on his third leave from his consulship) in time to witness the horrors of the French Revolution, during which some of his closest friends were assassinated or guillotined. He himself avoided physical harm by staying out of Paris and remaining inconspicuous. But he worried about his children and his diplomat son-in-law, who was arrested twice, but was released. We have discussed those events of the French Revolution which indirectly affected Crèvecoeur and his family—and more directly his son-in-law.

After the anxieties and turmoils Crèvecoeur had experienced both in America and France, he found relief in a quiet life in the country, visiting his children and writing articles on agriculture, a field in which he was now widely recognized as an authority, for newspapers in France and the United States. Both George Washington and James Madison sought his advice on agricultural subjects.

While Napoleon was winning military victories for France, Crèvecoeur worked peacefully on a book which he hoped would be the definitive work on the United States. *Le Voyage dans la haute Pennsylvanie et dans l'état de New-York*, published in three volumes in Paris in 1801, is indeed a monumental work, but it enjoyed only a modest success in France, and has never received much attention in the United States. In 1961 Percy Adams translated an excellent selection, with an illuminating introduction;[8] and in 1963 Clarissa Bostelmann published a complete translation in two volumes called *Journey into Northern Pennsylvania and the State of New York*. Both translations are out of print.

Although most of the chapters of his book are fairly interesting to read, Crèvecoeur may have "put off" many readers by his awkward and rather silly introduction, in which he pretends to translate a water-soaked manuscript which had washed ashore in the Copenhagen harbor from a wrecked ship. Part of the manuscript is missing, he says, and he leaves some chapters of his book unfinished. The chapters pretend to be the accounts of travelers in America, the chief one being that of a visiting German. But sometimes he used the first person, as if Crèvecoeur himself were speaking—such as when he pretends to attend the dedication of Franklin College with Benjamin Franklin.

The second paragraph of Percy Adams's introduction enumerates reasons for the literary and historical importance of this book:

> . . . the book is both unique and valuable. As literature it displays Crèvecoeur more at home while writing in his native French, more sophisticated, more versatile, wandering from realistic analyses of the frontier to dramatic accounts of farmers, from romantic descriptions of Niagara Falls to poetic reproduction of Indian councils and legends. And as history the *Voyage* is in many ways Crèvecoeur's most important, certainly his most pretentious, book: It concentrates on a time later than that treated in the English works . . . and it attempts—more successfully and more in detail—to analyse motives and trends, in other words, to handle history more in the fashion of the "moderns" of the author's own century—Montesquieu, Hume, Voltaire, and Gibbon.

Thus we have in the biography of St. Jean de Crèvecoeur, alias Hector St. John, the adventurous life of a remarkable man who experienced the upheavals of two world-shaking revolutions and lived to publish two major literary works based on his knowledge of colonial life in North America in the second half of the eighteenth century. Though he was happiest as a "simple farmer,"[9] he distinguished himself as soldier, traveler, government bureaucrat, and author. Both his life and writings have a significant place in American history and deserve to be better known.

AN AMERICAN FARMER

I

Norman Child–British Youth

AFTER READING St. John de Crèvecoeur's *Letters from an American Farmer,* it is easy to imagine him sitting after dinner one winter evening in the "new parlour" of his farm. It is already quite dark outside. The north wind is howling, the snow is piling high. The cattle have been fed. The slaves have withdrawn to their quarters (for, like his neighbors, he had two or three slaves, though he is very discreet about them in his books). The children have gone to bed. His ever-busy wife is spinning (or weaving) close to the fire. It is a perfect night for Crèvecoeur. After "smoking a meditative pipe," he can start writing his third letter to his imaginary correspondent in England. "What is an American?" he asks himself. He may be "English, Scotch, Irish, French, Dutch," even German or Swedish. As for himself, strangely enough, though he writes in English and his dear Mehetable is of English stock, he is of French descent, "Normano-Americanus," as he once described himself.

The self-styled "American Farmer" was not born in America, but on foreign soil, in Normandy, near Caen, the old capital of William the Conqueror. The record of his baptism still exists.[1] Born on January 31, 1735, he was baptized the following day, at St. John's in Caen (a church which is still there, though it was badly damaged in World War II), for in those times of earnest faith and high infant mortality, babies were baptized as soon as possible after their birth. He received the Christian names Michel-Guillaume. His father was Guillaume Jean de Crèvecoeur, a squire, and his mother Dame Marie-Anne-Thérèse Blouet. His godfather was a maternal great-uncle, Michel-Jacques Blouet, also a squire, and his godmother was his grandmother on his mother's side. So he belonged to the petty nobility and to a family which was not without influence. The record specified that his godfather was Lord and Master of Cahagnolles and treasurer general of Caen, the chief town of the rich province of Lower Normandy. It is to be noted that this young Norman was not named James Hector St. John, as he was later called on American soil, but Michel-Guillaume Jean de Crèvecoeur, Jean being part of his patronym.

The Crèvecoeur family was rooted in Normandy and had been established there at least since the twelfth century, when they owned a fief at Crèvecoeur-en-Auge. In 1603, "Monseigneur Monsieur de Crèvecoeur" was "Governor in the King's name of the town and castle of Caen, mayor and bailiff of the same." Several Crèvecoeurs had been magistrates at Caen. Crèvecoeur's father was a country gentleman, well bred and reasonably well off, who spent the greater part of the year on his estate at Pierrepont,[2] some ten miles northwest of Caen, near Creully, and the winter in Caen, where life was more pleasant and comfortable. He owned a house there in the street "au Canu."[3] He even went to Paris occasionally, to cultivate his acquaintance with persons of influence like the d'Houdetots and the Liancourts. (The marquises and counts d'Houdetot belonged to the greater Norman nobility and often reached high ranks in the army. They were on friendly terms with the Crèvecoeurs because they had some property close to Pierrepont. The Liancourts were an even more distinguished family, since the dukes de Liancourt belonged to the peerage.) Crèvecoeur's mother came from a good family, but very little is known about her, except that she seems to have been well educated and a devoted wife and mother.

Crèvecoeur's childhood was thus spent in easy circumstances and in a very pleasant and prosperous region. In his *Travels in France,* Arthur Young, the famous English agronomist, wrote of having visited the region and admiring it.[4] Though his visit took place four decades later, the description he left can help us to imagine the country as it was in Crèvecoeur's time. It was a land of "pasturage" and orchards enclosed with such thick hedges of willow, oak, beech trees and thorns that one could not see through them. Being an enthusiastic agricultural expert, Young gloated over the fertility of the Pays d'Auge, which he crossed before arriving at Caen, and in Caen he marveled at the beauty "of the Abbey of the Benedictines [St. Stephen's, the parish church of Crèvecoeur's parents]. It is a splendid building," he exclaimed, "substantial, massy, magnificent, with very large apartments and stone staircases worthy of a palace."

Pierrepont itself was a charming little village consisting of only a few farmhouses with walls of studwork scattered in meadows and apple orchards at the foot of a small hill in the valley of a lazily winding river, the Thue. There was also a pond and two country seats. One, at the top of the hill, belonged to the Pierreponts, and the other was the property of Crèvecoeur's father. The latter was the more impressive and handsome. It was (and still is) a finely proportioned building of beautiful Caen limestone. A broad tree-lined avenue led up to it and it was separated from the road by tall iron railings. On the hill there still stands a small and quaint Romanesque church dating back to the eleventh century or possibly earlier. It is capped by a curious asymmetrical steeple and a tall, elegant chimney, quite an unusual feature, rising from the chancel. Inside, behind this chimney, is a small room in back of the choir, which can be reached by a stone staircase. It possesses two windows and, naturally, a fireplace. No one knows what its purpose was. It was in this little church, no doubt, that the Pierreponts and the Crèvecoeurs went to mass every Sunday, and it was in the churchyard which surrounds it that young Crèvecoeur "loved to stroll in . . . solitude . . . to examine the tombstones and to make out the moss-grown epitaphs."[5]

These were more pleasant and formative surroundings than those Chateaubriand was to know a little later not so very far from there, on the outskirts of Brittany, at Combourg. According to Arthur Young, it was "one of the most filthy places that can be seen; mud houses, no windows, and a pavement so broken as to impede all passengers; yet there is a château, and inhabited. Who is this Monsieur de Chateaubriand [the writer's father], the owner that has nerves strung for a residence amidst such filth and poverty?"

No such disparities existed in the Caen area, and instead of indulging in romantic melancholy in depressing surroundings like Chateaubriand, Crèvecoeur happily gave full play to his omnivorous intellectual curiosity. As he explained it himself in 1803: "from my early childhood, I was passionately fond of examining all the old things I found; worm-eaten furniture, old family portraits. Gothic parchments of the fifteenth and sixteenth centuries which I learned to decipher, had an indefinable charm for me. When older, I was fond of walking in the solitude of churchyards, examining graves and reading mossy epitaphs . . . I knew most of the churches in our district, the time of their foundation, the most interesting things they contained by way of paintings or sculptures. . . . On the entablature of the church-tower at Caisnet [not far from Pierrepont], (I still remember it), at the very place where the steeple started, there grew a birch-tree whose aerial position was long an object of wonder for me, and of small observations . . . some of them, which I was bold enough to set down in writing, pleased my mother."

This is an important reminiscence showing that Crève-coeur's taste for studying and writing appeared very early and that he was encouraged by a loving and sympathetic mother. During his early childhood, he was probably educated at home by her with the help of a tutor, most likely the vicar of the parish, as was the custom at the time. But these happy days could not last forever. Like the children of the English aristocracy, as soon as he was old enough, eleven or twelve, he was sent as a boarder to the Catholic equivalent of an English public school, a Jesuit "collège." It was to the famous Collège Royal de Bourbon,"[6] close by at Caen, that he went for what we would now call his secondary education.

It was quite a change from the comfortable life he had lived. He felt miserable and hated the school, at least at the beginning. Three decades later, he still entertained bitter memories of those years. "If you knew," he wrote to his children in 1785, "in what a sordid boarding-school, in what a dark and cold hovel I was confined when I was your age [they were then respectively eleven, thirteen, and fifteen], with what severity I was treated, how I was fed and clothed!"[7] He seems to have suffered above all from the cold in winter, which kept him awake in his bed in the unheated dormitory where he had to sleep under a thin blanket. He did not at all appreciate the spartan quality of his education, but, given his taste for study, he must have enjoyed the intellectual fare he was offered. The Jesuits were excellent educators and their schools had a fully deserved reputation.

The Collège Royal de Bourbon was particularly well known in Normandy. It was founded in 1608 by King Henry IV and consisted originally of three large buildings situated in the vicinity of St. Stephen's. They later formed an impressive quadrangle when the Jesuits built a church, Notre-Dame-de-la-Gloriette (which still exists) to close the central yard—and isolate their pupils from the corrupting influence of the world outside. At the end of the eighteenth century, there were over fifteen hundred young boarders, who came from the local gentry and the upper middle class of Caen.

Traditionally, the educational system of the Jesuits was above all literary. In his *Protrepticon ad magistros scholarum inferiorum (Exhortation Addressed to the Teachers of Lower Grades)*, published in Rome in 1625, the Jesuit father Francesco Sacchini declared: "Let us imagine for one moment the disappearance of belles-lettres. What would become of human life? [Apparently, in his enthusiasm, the worthy father completely forgot the existence of religion!] What a night, what darkness, what barbarity! Then would our mortal life be brief and our allotted space narrow: born yesterday and already close to death. We would be unknown to later ages . . . no more doctrinal treasures, no more scholarly sources. In short, suppress literature and you completely suppress the quality called humanity. *Denique tolles litteras ab hominibus, plane tolles humanitatem.*"[8]

Consequently, the Jesuits taught what they called "grammar"—i.e., the Latin and French languages, eloquence, style, belles-lettres—as well, of course, as catechism and ethics. Catechism theoretically came first: "The teaching of the catechism ranks first in truth, necessity, usefulness and nobleness," Sacchini said. But the Jesuits also tried to develop their pupils' sensibility and sense of beauty, for, they thought, the beauty of the physical world leads to the worship of God: "Ex divina pulchritudine esse omnium derivatur."

The originality of the Jesuits as pedagogues resided in the fact that they respected each pupil's nature and personality. At the end of the seventeenth century, Father Jouvancy, who for a time taught at the Collège Royal de Bourbon, wrote in his "De ratione discendi et docendi" ("Method of Learning and Teaching" [1691]): "Let the teacher bear in mind that every one of the pupils he has in front of him in his class-room may be a mere child as regards his age, but is fundamentally pos-

sessed of a sublime and regal dignity. Inside those small bod-
ies there hide souls which bear the mark of their divine origin
and the proofs of their celestial kinship; in their veins, there
flows Christ's blood."[8a]

Their pupils therefore were not regarded as so many little
buckets into which knowledge had to be poured, but as embers to be fanned. The instructions which were sent to Jesuit
schools in 1605 and remained valid until the expulsion of the
order from France in 1762 recommended: "No human will
must interfere between souls and God unless it be to encourage their intimacy." So the teaching methods of the Jesuits
were essentially active. Their pupils were not to absorb pas-
sively what they were taught; they were supposed to find truth
by themselves, by discussing and reasoning, "discurrendo ac
ratiocinanado per seipsum."[8b]

It was a well-balanced education, for the students' memory
was systematically trained too; they had to learn long texts by
heart every day to furnish their minds with ready-made
materials as well as with examples of what had been done in
the past. But they were also encouraged to invent and inno-
vate, especially in the highest grade, or *rhétorique,* in which
they were trained in the practice of oratory and poetry. They
took part in formal debates and had to acquire the habit of
writing daily—"nulla dies sine aliqua scriptione"—a habit
which apparently Crèvecoeur never lost.

When he was in *rhétorique,* Crèvecoeur took part in one of
these debates. Among the few documents about the Collège
Royal de Bourbon which still remain, and which are kept in
the archives at Caen, is the handsomely printed announce-
ment of

A CASE
Which will be argued in French
by rhetoricians
of the Collège Royal de Bourbon

of the Company of Jesus
of the very famous University of Caen
on Monday, July 20th 1750 at three P.M.

The program contains the argument of this debate, which was presented in the form of a play:

Argument.

Anectophile [a name of Greek origin meaning "a lover of his king"], a subject full of zeal for the Glory of his King and honored by his Master's bounties, had three friends whom the similarity of their tastes, inclinations and, above all, zealous devotion to the Prince, made him cherish equally. All three during the late war had distinguished themselves with an equal merit, though each in a different way: the first one in the King's Council, the second one as a general officer, the third one at sea as a squadron commander. Anectophile, feeling his end near, now that he had seen the fulfilment of the great Work of Peace, which had for long been the aim of his desires, wanted all his possessions, the fruit of the services he had rendered and the favors he had received, to return in a way to the Monarch, by making them reward his friends' loyalty to the Prince as well as by giving these a last proof of his love. He therefore bequeathed them all to his three friends. But in order to arouse the rivalry of the Pretenders, he divided his succession into three unequal shares and expressed the desire that the allotment should be made in proportion to their contribution, during the late war, to the Monarch's glory, which always was the main object of his zeal.

On the last page of the program, the guests could find the cast:

Will plead
For the statesman,
    Robert-François Desmares, from Caen,

8

For the general officer of the land-based troops,
   Michel-Barthélémy Gestart, from Caen,
For the squadron commander,
   Thomas de Cussy, from Caen,
Will pass judgment,
   Michel de Crèvecoeur, from Caen.

This document indicates that young Crèvecoeur was considered an excellent student by his Jesuit masters, for only the best scholars were allowed to take part in these academic festivities. It also gives us the date when Crèvecoeur left the Collège Royal de Bourbon: July 1750, before the summer recess of that year.[9]

Very likely he followed the full course of studies at the *collège*: sexta, quinta, quarta, tertia, and secunda classes and finally *rhétorique*—six years in all. On the whole, he must have responded with enthusiasm to an education that matched some of his own tastes. It is unlikely he was ever condemned to sit on the bench of laziness, "negligentiae scamnum," one of the few punishments used by the Jesuits, who did not believe in corporal punishment. Instead, they took stock in positive methods, preferring to encourage emulation among their pupils, rather than punishing them, even at the risk of developing their vanity. They were often criticized for this.

Indeed, the teaching of the Jesuits was marked by its optimism. Unlike the Jansenists and the Calvinists, who emphasized Satan's power over mankind and the likelihood of eternal damnation for most men, the Jesuits insisted on the possibility of salvation for all sinners thanks to God's infinite mercy and his free gift of grace. Crèvecoeur's faith in the fundamental goodness of man may well have been inculcated in him by his Jesuit masters, while he was still in his teens, rather than derived at a later date from Rousseau or some other *philosophe*.

Though the emphasis was on literature, the study of science and modern languages was not neglected in Jesuit schools in the middle of the eighteenth century. The Jesuits were known for their practical-mindedness and adaptability. In large commercial cities, they adapted the curriculum of their schools to prepare those of their pupils who would later engage in trade and become wealthy merchants.

These two courses of studies, a traditional and classical one based on the study of Latin and Greek, and a modern one combining the indispensable study of Latin with a vocational training, existed side by side. A little later, Chateaubriand's parents were to hesitate between the two. His mother, he wrote in his *Mémoires d'Outre-Tombe*, "suggested I should go to a school where I should learn mathematics, drawing, the handling of weapons and English; she did not mention Latin and Greek in order not to frighten away my father," for his father wanted him to become a sailor or an officer in the army while his mother destined him for the church. Crèvecoeur's parents probably had thoughts similar to those of Chateaubriand's father, so he did not study Greek, though, of course, he learned Latin. In his works, he never quotes a Greek word or author, but occasionally quotes Latin phrases—always correctly.[10] Though he did not learn Greek, he must have learned English, because of the proximity of England just as he would have learned Italian, Spanish, or Syriac if he had been at Marseilles. Here, however, we can only speculate, for it is impossible to know his *cursus studiorum* with any certainty. Though some of the records of the Collège Royal de Bourbon have survived, those of Crèvecoeur's class have disappeared.

Yet one can be almost certain he studied mathematics. A chair of mathematics and hydrology had been established at his *collège* in 1704 and existed while Crèvecoeur was a pupil. It was occupied by a distinguished mathematician, Father Yves André, whose works were published in 1767. The course seems to have been essentially practical and especially meant for the pupils who intended to become officers in the navy or the merchant marine or land surveyors and cartographers. It is quite likely, therefore, that Crèvecoeur took it. The students were trained to survey land and draw maps, and they learned to use such necessary instruments as alidades, plate levels, and verniers. So Crèvecoeur did not improvise his professions of land surveyor and cartographer in America. He had learned these trades at the Collège Royal de Bourbon.[11]

Crèvecoeur's immigration to Canada may also have been a consequence of his Jesuit education, for some of his masters had been to New France or aspired to go there as missionaries. A former master, Father Jean Bréboeuf had won fame after being martyred by the Iroquois in 1649.

Crèvecoeur was a good pupil of his Jesuit masters in all respects but one, and it was a lapse which they would not have condoned. The religious teaching of the Jesuits had practically no effect on him. After he left school, he was a Catholic in name only—and only when it was convenient or necessary. He married a Protestant and had his children baptized all at the same time when his oldest child was already six. The Catholic custom, on the contrary, was to baptize children immediately after their birth. Like the *philosophes*, and the unfrocked Abbé Raynal in particular, he considered Christianity a mere superstition and severely criticized the intolerance of the Catholic Church whenever he had a chance. He even wrote an essay on the subject, "Liberty of Worship," in praise of religious toleration, and in another essay, "The Rock of Lisbon," went so far as to denounce the teaching methods used in Catholic schools as a form of "inquisitorial tymocracy" (a misspelling of *timocracy*). By this pedantic term, he meant a system based on emulation and the love of honors.

Though excellent educators, the Jesuits had a less noble side that Crèvecoeur may have discovered only after he arrived in Canada, where the order was extremely powerful and played an important role politically in the development of the country. In their fanatical zeal for the propagation of the faith and the aggrandizement of the Catholic Church, they were too often ready to place cushions under sinners' elbows, especially if the sinners belonged to the higher classes and occupied important positions. From the eighteenth century, the Jesuits were frequently accused of being given to intrigue and equivocation. They were so clever at adapting themselves to their environment that they managed to penetrate non-Christian countries, particularly Japan and China, and build an empire of their own in the Americas, in Paraguay, Brazil, and the West Indies, in addition to Canada. Their aim was nothing short of the conversion of the whole world *ad majorem Dei gloriam.* This ambition proved their undoing, for, in the French West Indies, they became involved in shady commercial transactions and were sued in French courts by their victims. Their enemies took this opportunity to get rid of them. Most provincial *parlements* (they were actually law courts) ordered the dissolution of the Society of Jesus in France in 1762, and the king two years later issued an edict suppressing the order, as it had already been suppressed in Spain and Portugal. This brutal decision was immediately enforced. The Jesuits had to abandon everything they owned, including their schools, and leave the country, unless they agreed to remain as ordinary parish priests.

But in the 1740s and 1750s the position of the Jesuits was secure and Crèvecoeur's studies were undisturbed. After Crèvecoeur left the *collège,* his parents sent him to England, probably to give him a chance to improve his English by constant practice. A paternal aunt of his, whose maiden name was Mutel, had two unmarried sisters living in Salisbury,[12] and Crèvecoeur went there to live with them. The exact dates of his stay in England are unknown and it has proved impossible to track him or his relatives in local archives. Though there was already a *Salisbury Journal* (then a weekly, now a daily), young Crèvecoeur was never mentioned in it. We know he left the Collège Royal de Bourbon when he was fifteen and a half.

He may have arrived at Salisbury as early as 1751 and spent at least two years there, which would account for the excellent quality of his English when he left England.

This utilitarian explanation of his sojourn there seems natural to us in the twentieth century, but in the eighteenth century such a linguistic training was not a common practice, and there was probably another reason for this decision to send the firstborn of the family abroad for an indefinite period. We know that father and son frequently quarreled in later years, and there may already have been a conflict between them at a time when young Crèvecoeur had to choose a career. His father may very well have intended him for a military career, as was often the case in the nobility. It was indeed a career which his younger brother, Alexandre, who eventually reached the rank of lieutenant colonel, did follow a few years later. Crèvecoeur may have refused to comply with his father's desire and thus was sent into exile to England as a punishment—a form of rustication. This would also explain why he probably did not return to France at the end of his stay at Salisbury: he may have persisted in his refusal to yield to his father. To a military career he preferred a mercantile one, or at least a practical career—land surveying, civil engineering, map making: careers which he would turn to in America, but which were then considered unworthy of a noble. It would have been *déroger,* and his father would not have stood for it. Moreover, his rebellion against, or at least growing indifference to, catholicism may have been another bone of contention between father and son.

Salisbury was a much smaller city than Caen.[13] A census taken by order of the corporation some twenty years later, in 1775, gave the figure of 6,856 inhabitants, whereas Caen numbered ten times as many. But Crèvecoeur must have felt at home, for it was a Caen in miniature, a cathedral city dominated by the imposing pile of the cathedral with its spectacularly high spire and its belfry (which no longer exists), just as

Caen was dominated by the abbey founded by William the Conqueror and the sister abbey founded by his wife. Like Caen, too, it was an important market town. Twice a week it filled with livestock and carts, with farmers' wives come to sell their produce, as well as with long trains of packhorses laden with bales of raw wool or bolts of finished cloth, for Salisbury was the center of a decaying but still active cloth trade and manufacture. There were huge flocks of sheep in the country-side around the city (which Hawthorne described in his *English Notebooks*), just as there were in Lower Normandy, and the wool was spun by women and children in the outlying villages and brought to Salisbury to be dyed, woven, stretched, and dried. There was also a steel foundry which produced very fine steel because of the high chalk content of the local water, or so it was said.

According to John Aubrey, in his *Natural History of Wiltshire,* Salisbury was also the home of "the best bottled ale in the nation," and a fair quantity of it was consumed on the spot on market days, for it was a rowdy city with its one hundred inns (The King's Arms, The White Hart, and others are still there). There was a large number of apprentices, carters, butchers, weavers, and clothiers to frequent them and consume the ale. They played dice, watched cockfights, loved cudgel play. Pros-titution and drunkenness flourished in the alleyways between the tenement blocks, which were haunted by pickpockets and footpads at night. The city was not well lighted and, in winter, linkboys, carrying torches, waited for travelers at the city gates to guide them to their lodgings.

The craftsmen outnumbered the rest of the population, but there was a large number of gentry, too, to which Crève-coeur's relatives must have belonged. They met in several fashionable coffeehouses, The Parade in particular in Blue Boar Row, and would occasionally go to the theater. There were two assembly rooms where balls could be given, and a particularly important ball was held every year after the final meeting of the races, attracting large crowds from as far as London. There were also fortnightly subscription concerts for music lovers throughout the winter in the new Assembly Room at the corner of New Canal and High streets in the very center of the city, which was the oldest and, architecturally speaking (except for the cathedral close), the finest part of Salisbury. It had been laid out in a grid pattern in the twelfth century when it was decided to abandon Old Sarum and build the cathedral at New Sarum in the plain. (The original name of Salisbury was Saresbury.) Crèvecoeur had a good ear for languages, but not for music. However, he may have been dragged to these concerts by his relatives, since they were no doubt great social events. He may in particular have attended the annual music festival on St. Cecilia's Day, which was always a great occasion. On October 5, 1754, the program in the cathedral consisted of Handel's overture to *Saul*, "Te Deum," "I Will Magnify Thee," "My Heart Is Inditing," and, at night, in the Assembly Room, the oratorio *Joshua*. On the next day, the festival continued with Handel performed again in the cathedral as well as in the Assembly Room at night. Handel himself may have played at one of the private concerts organized by the founder of the festival, one James Harris.

All entertainments were not as civilized as these. From time to time there were public executions, which were extremely popular. At the time of Crèvecoeur's residence, a young girl who had killed her illegitimate child was executed. The *Salisbury Journal* relished such sensational news as much as any twentieth-century tabloid, crudely and candidly calling the child her "bastard." She was hanged and her corpse exhibited on Market Place. Crèvecoeur may very well have seen it. If he still was in Salisbury at the beginning of 1755, which is quite possible, he was lucky to have escaped the press-gang which "picked up half a score able sailors and returned with them to Portsmouth." The *Salisbury Journal* reported the event in these terms without showing the least indignation, as if such an occurrence were perfectly normal—which it was in those days.

But what did Crèvecoeur really do in Salisbury? For lack of documents we are reduced to conjectures. He may have gone to school to complete his education, though he was getting a little too old for school, or was being tutored in English at home. Anyway, for an open-minded young man with such an insatiable intellectual curiosity, there were many unusual things to observe in Salisbury, all kinds of new techniques to study, from cutlery to cloth making, glove making, and even sheep raising. He probably read much too, in order to acquire as perfect a mastery of English as possible, for he loved the language and everything English, and remained faithful to this first love ever after. Figuratively speaking, he only made a marriage of convenience with America. Visiting Virginia in 1769, he missed "the verdant lawns of England, of Ireland, and Normandy," and he always admired the sterling quality of English products: "England surpasses all the world for the perfection of mechanism and the peculiar excellence with which all its tools and implements are finished. We are but children and they [the English] are our parents."[14] As we shall see, the French ambassador who inspected him when he was consul in New York detected an underlying anglophilia in all his conduct and thinking, which he strongly reproved.

England seems also to have been the place of his first encounter with love for a woman, and the two loves probably reinforced each other. If we are to believe the letter his father sent to London in the early 1770s asking the British authorities to find out whether Crèvecoeur was dead or alive,[15] he was engaged to marry the only daughter of a Salisbury merchant. Unfortunately, the girl died before the marriage could take place. Although this is all we know about this tragically interrupted love affair, one thing is certain: This letter conclusively shows that young Crèvecoeur left for America shortly after her death instead of returning home to his parents. He must have been heartbroken and the idea of carrying on in France as if nothing had happened was hateful to him. Now that he spoke English fluently and had become so much attached to the English way of life, he may also have been tempted by the prospect of making a fortune in America among English-speaking people. His prospective father-in-law may have had business interests in Philadelphia. This, at least, is what Crève-coeur's father seems to have believed. So he may have gone to Pennsylvania first rather than to Canada. His father thought he was a merchant's partner in Philadelphia and even claimed he had received a letter his son sent him from there as recently as 1767. The letter must have been rather vague, though, since it did not even say in what line of business Crèvecoeur was engaged. And what is quite surprising is that his father should have been completely ignorant of his participation in the war between France and England in Canada, though, as we shall see, some of his friends, the d'Houdetots in particular, knew of it. His father's silence about Crèvecoeur's war record can be explained by diplomatic reasons. As he needed the help of British authorities, he preferred not to mention that his son had fought with the French army, in the wrong camp in the eyes of the British.

We do not know on what date he left England or what his first destination was. We are once more reduced to hypotheses, one of which is that he went to America by way of Lisbon. In the unpublished essay "The Rock of Lisbon," he describes the capital of Portugal as it looked after the terrible earth-quake which almost destroyed it shortly before, on November 1, 1755.[16] This may have been a mere literary exercise on a theme already exploited by Voltaire in his "Poème sur le désastre de Lisbonne" (1756). But, if the essay is autobiographical, it confirms the supposition that Crèvecoeur left England on a British ship, for, since Lord Methuen's treaty in 1703, commercial exchanges between Portugal and England were extremely active.

Another hypothesis is that, whether he went to America via Lisbon or not, before or after the earthquake, he was indeed engaged in business for a time in Philadelphia. However, he must very quickly have grown dissatisfied with this unadventurous and sedentary way of life and decided to make his living as a land surveyor, thus taking advantage of the training he had received at the Collège Royal de Bourbon. He loved to travel and gradually worked his way northward to Canada. He may have arrived there as early as 1755 or 1756.

II

French Soldier Becomes American Citizen

ALTHOUGH it has never been definitely established where Crèvecoeur went after leaving England, Crèvecoeur himself stated many years later that he went to Canada at the age of twenty,[1] which would have been in 1755. There is documentary evidence that he was in the French Colonial Army two years later, and had probably been there for at least a year. A fragmentary record in the Paris War Office states that when he enlisted (date not given) he gave his place of birth as Paris instead of Caen and the date of his birth as January 6, 1738, instead of January 31, 1735, but whether he or a careless clerk was responsible for this inaccurate information we do not know. His sponsors were given as Baron Breteuil and Marquis d'Houdetot, old friends of the Crèvecoeur family.[2] Did he enlist without his father's knowledge? His father would almost certainly have been delighted to give his consent, because he is thought to have encouraged his son to pursue a military career. Both the army and the navy chose their officers from the nobility.

For a century Great Britain and France had struggled with each other for the possession of North America. Now Canada, called New France, was France's last foothold. The seven-year "French and Indian War," as the British called it, was fast approaching a climax. In January 1756 Marquis de Montcalm was appointed by Louis XV to command French troops in Canada, but the king could spare him only two battalions because he had recently sent 100,000 troops to fight in Austria, where France had a bigger war.[3]

If Crèvecoeur was already in Canada, he was not among the young cadets who sailed from Brest early one spring morning in 1756. To them the voyage to Canada was a lark, and Captain Louis Bougainville, Montcalm's aide-de-camp, recorded in his journal that they boarded the three frigates which had been converted into troop transports "with an incredible gaiety." At that time the cadet uniform was white, trimmed in blue, with black tricornered hats and black gaiters reaching almost to their knees. Since Crèvecoeur served in the battalions commanded by Montcalm he could have been one of these enthusiastic cadets. (Of course, Crèvecoeur could have traveled from Philadelphia to Montreal and joined the Canadian home-guard troops, commanded by Marquis de Vandreuil, but one objection to that hypothesis is that Vandreuil deeply resented Montcalm and transferring from his command to Montcalm's would have been a delicate operation.)

Montcalm and two of his aides, Lévis and Boumaque, sailed from Brest on April 3, 1756, to be followed a few days later by the other officers and men.[4] This voyage, begun in such high spirits and optimism, turned out to be not only uncomfortable but dangerous. The weather was stormy on the North Atlantic and the ships encountered icebergs as they approached Canada. Montcalm's ship was grazed by one but was not seriously damaged, nor were any of the others. Finally, on May 11 Montcalm wrote his wife that his ship was safely anchored ten leagues below Quebec, where it had been stopped by ice in the St. Lawrence River. The other ships, he learned, had anchored safely in the river below.

Crèvecoeur was assigned to a special group of engineers captained by Chevalier de Lévis in the Sarre regiment.[5] Although he was also trained in the use of artillery, where his knowledge of mathematics was useful, he was mainly used as a map maker. He began by mapping the region of the St. Lawrence River and its tributaries. With Indian guides he traveled up the Ottawa River by canoe and then on foot into the forest wilderness, sleeping at night on a bed of spruce boughs and subsisting on the wild game shot or caught by the Indians.

From his published writings we know what Crèvecoeur thought of the Indians, both their virtues and their vices, but he left no record of his first impressions of them. Apparently he got along very well with them in Canada, though his first contact may have been a shock, as it was to Montcalm, who wrote his wife that they were all *villeins*.[6] Every Indian brave carried a mirror to aid him in painting his face in gaudy colors and arranging feathers on his head. Some wore laced coats without shirts which they had obtained in trade. To Montcalm they looked like a masquerade of devils. But they would prove to be effective allies in battles with the English. Crèvecoeur had good reason to be grateful to them, for he could not have drawn his maps without their aid as guides and hunters.

In 1757 Crèvecoeur drew a map of Fort George and its approaches which helped Montcalm win a ferocious battle with the British.[7] He himself took part in the fighting, and was horrified to see the Indian allies scalp and butcher wounded British soldiers. Captain Bougainville, later famous as a world explorer, sent a copy of Crèvecoeur's map to His Majesty Louis XV with the comment that its designer, "an officer [second lieutenant] in the regiment of the Sarre employed in engineering, has acquired a great reputation for his bravery and talents."[8] The following year, we also learn from Bougainville that Crèvecoeur had been promoted to first lieutenant for his "special knowledge of artillery and engineering. He has served with distinction in these two fields since his coming to Canada." This was the high point of his military career.

Something happened to the promising young engineer-cartographer either during the siege of Quebec in September 1759 or during his recuperation in the hospital in October from a wound he had received in battle. On the twenty-third of October Commissioner Bernier wrote Bougainville that "certain French officers" would be sent home by way of New York on a British ship, among them Lieutenant Crèvecoeur, who "wishes only to seek his future elsewhere." This letter says further that "if he leaves [the French army] he abandons all his appointments for a mediocre sum [that is, sells his commission], and every regiment which expells [*expulse*] an officer ordinarily gives him his passage." Does the use of the French verb *expulse* mean that Crèvecoeur was forced to resign his commission? This would seem to be the implication, but no cause is given or implied.

The circumstances of the French forces in Canada suggest reasons for resentment against Crèvecoeur.[9] During the battle for the Plains of Abraham, the high rock plateau overlooking the St. Lawrence River, both Montcalm and General Wolfe, the British commander-in-chief, were mortally wounded, and afterward many French soldiers panicked, resulting in the surrender of Quebec and the loss of the war. Before his death Montcalm asked Wolfe to treat his captured soldiers humanely, and Wolfe so ordered before he himself expired. The victorious British demanded that all French troops give up their arms, and that the Canadian people swear allegiance to the British Crown, but they controlled only the region north of the Three Rivers; Montreal was still in French hands. According to the terms of surrender, all French military personnel wishing to return to France would be transported back to Europe in British ships, and the wounded would be cared for in Canadian hospitals. Some soldiers chose to settle in Canada instead of returning home. If Crèvecoeur did not wish to return to France, why did he not remain in Canada? We can only guess. Some of his fellow officers were among those deciding to remain, and perhaps he would have been uncomfortable with them. Besides, his command of English would have made it easy, perhaps, for him to settle in an English-speaking colony—for years to come Canada would be a half-French colony. In fact, Crèvecoeur's sympathy with British ways probably was a major cause of resentment against him. It is likely that he fraternized with British soldiers after the surrender.

Montreal would remain in control of the French for nearly a year after Crèvecoeur left Canada. The commander of his regiment, Lévis, continued to fight, and even after the surrender of Montreal on September 8, 1760, he wanted to withdraw to St. Helen Island, "in order to uphold there . . . the honor of the King's arms." But he was denied his wish, and eventually in the Treaty of Paris (February 10, 1763) France would give up all claims to territory in North America except Louisiana, which was secretly sold to Spain. In the last months of 1759, it may have appeared to Crèvecoeur that France could not win in Canada, and he lacked his commander's fanatical zeal. Lévis may have regarded Crèvecoeur's attitude at this time as disgraceful and a betrayal of his patriotic duty.

However, not all of Crèvecoeur's superiors were unsympathetic toward him. On November 5 Commissioner Bernier made this report to headquarters: "I have given to Crèvecoeur two hundred and forty livres," adding that he could not do less "to get rid of him. Besides he should not and could not leave without this help. He has left me an account of all his present and past debts."[10]

Crèvecoeur himself never gave any explanation for his decision to start a new life in the British colonies. The fact that he did not even inform his father where he was or where he expected to go indicates a serious alienation, and no desire for a reconciliation. He admired the British political system, with its constitutional guarantees of justice and individual rights. Before he left France certain writers, such as Voltaire, Rousseau, and a group called the Encyclopedists, were calling for radical political and social reforms, and he must have been aware of them, as he was of Abbé Raynal a few years later. Had he been a different person, he might have chosen to return to France and join the revolt against absolutism, but he disliked verbal strife almost as much as war. Had he been able to foresee the turmoil in America a decade later, he might have had other thoughts.

Political corruption was rampant in Canada, not only because the system was a transplanted feudalism, but also because the French monarch exercised his authority at a great distance with precarious communications. The Crown parceled out the land to Court favorites, and these *seigneurs* in turn divided it among their vassals in a descending hierarchy, the lowest being the *habitants,* who cultivated the soil. The fur trade was also a monopoly of the Crown, and many of the traders took advantage of their exclusive rights, cheating and amassing private fortunes.

The highest official in Canada was the governor general, appointed by the king, but Louis XV was a suspicious monarch, and he set an *intendant* to spy on the governor general. Naturally these two officials were jealous of each other and constantly tried to undermine each other's power. At the time of Crèvecoeur's tour of duty the governor was Pierre-François Regaud, Marquis de Vandreuil.[11] He had been born in Canada while his father was governor general, and had lived there most of his life. He was wary of any official born in France.

Vauderil's character had serious flaws. He was extremely vain, impulsive, and erratic in judgment; he was unsuited for military command, which his position conferred upon him. Montcalm, of course, was born in France. He was small, energetic, rapid in speech, and impatient with subordinates who were slow or unskilled in action; but he never panicked, possessed great integrity, and his troops trusted him. A further cause of friction was that Vandreuil was responsible to the marine minister and Montcalm to the minister of war. The governor bitterly resented the appointment of Montcalm as commander in Canada and never ceased trying to undermine his authority. In fact, he never admitted Montcalm's authority over his Canadian troops. It was thus impossible to coordinate the use of Canadian and French military forces.

When Montcalm won a spectacular victory at Ticonderoga, Vandreuil was almost beside himself with jealousy. He accused the general of having let many of the British troops escape, and wrote furious letters to France demanding his recall. But he did not succeed.

By the winter of 1758 the Canadian colony was on short rations and not far from starvation.[12] This was the result in part of England's success in blockading the sea routes, but also partly a consequence of the corrupt speculations of the *intendant* and two unscrupulous importers named François Begot and Joseph Cadet, whom the governor general permitted to buy supplies in France at reasonable rates and sell them in Canada for exorbitant profit. After the war Begot and Cadet were tried and convicted in France, but Vandreuil escaped punishment. Whether or not Crèvecoeur had knowledge of these dishonest operators, the general atmosphere of suspicion, resentment, and disillusionment was pervasive, and could scarcely have failed to affect his attitudes toward the war in Canada.

However, he was not disillusioned with the Canadian people themselves, if one can trust the sentiments of his essay on "The English and the French before the [American] Revolution": "Badly governed as they were," he wrote in 1790, " 'tis surprising to observe how prosperous and happy they were."[13] The Indians, he adds, still loved the name Canadian. The women were so attractive that twenty of Montcalm's officers took Canadian wives.

Crèvecoeur blamed the English colonists, especially New England, for having forced the Seven Years' War on France. But he blamed France for not having given the Canadians more self-rule. "France overlooked it [Canada] until it was too late. The very struggle they made during the last war shows what they could have done had they been established on a broader foundation." At the time he wrote this essay Crèvecoeur thought it ironic that George Washington, who as a major on the banks of the Ohio in 1754 had led the fateful assault on French hunters and traders, was in 1776 "again a generalissimo, the friend and ally of France." Of course, Crèvecoeur's reminiscences of Canada had been affected by his own sufferings since then, as a result of the American Revolution.

We know definitely that Crèvecoeur arrived in New York on December 16, 1759, on a British ship which paused only long enough to discharge him and then continued on to London with other French officers who had chosen to return home.[14] There is no record of Crèvecoeur's life for the next five or six years. So far as it is known, he knew no one in the city, but his fluent English was combined with an ingratiating personality and the manners of a gentleman. He had enough money to last for several months, and his instruction in mathematics in the *collège* in Caen included surveying, which of course he had also used in his map making in Canada. He would have been able to support himself. Knowing the Indians, he could have become a fur trader, and possibly did.

There is a record of his having applied for naturalization as a British subject under the name of Hector St. John, a request that was granted in New York City on December 23, 1765, by act of the provincial legislature.[15] Presumably he had been using this name since his arrival six years earlier. It disguised his French origin (there may have been some resentment against France because of the war in Canada, in which many volunteers from New York and New England had fought) and Hector sounded English. After this addition he needed only to translate Jean to John; St. John was not an uncommon name in England, as Crèvecoeur probably knew from his sojourn in Salisbury.

All the evidence we have of Hector St. John's activities during the 1760s indicates that he traveled extensively and supported himself by surveying. This was a period when many owners of land were becoming concerned about their titles because the original patents had only vaguely described the boundaries, which had never been established by compass and measuring chain. A good surveyor could find plenty of work, and Crèvecoeur, who had won distinction for his military maps, was doubtless a good surveyor.

A former Canadian engineer in the Sarre regiment wrote a friend after leaving the French army that Crèvecoeur had been forced to take refuge in Albany, where he "vegetated" while occupied as a surveyor.[16] Though this sarcastic report identifies one of the places where Crèvecoeur practiced his trade, there is no further evidence that he remained long in Albany. All of his writings indicate that as a young man he had an overwhelming desire to travel, and he had the stamina to do so—by boat, horseback, and canoe, with or without Indian guides. However, in his travel accounts it is often impossible to distinguish fiction from history. Even the vividness of his descriptions is no safe guide, because he, like Herman Melville later, became expert in adapting the accounts of other travelers in his first-person narratives. He may have journeyed to Charleston, South Carolina, though this is perhaps unlikely; more likely he went to Virginia, and it is not unlikely that he visited Nantucket, the subject of no less than five of his "letters." In 1766, he recalled twenty years later, he visited a tribe of Oneida Indians in Vermont,[17] then still a part of the New York colony. They adopted him into their tribe, and he was so proud of the honor that in 1801 he listed himself on the title page of *Voyage dans la haute Pensylvanie*

et dans l'état de New-York as "un Membre adoptif de la Nation
Onéida." He would certainly not have been surveying land for
the Indians, but may have been buying furs from them to sell
in New York City.

New York, with less than twenty thousand people, was
dominated by the landed gentry and officials appointed by
George III. It was not a society in which a foreigner without
wealth or title could easily gain acceptance, but Crèvecoeur
did make friends there, especially among the merchants and
some of the plantation owners in Harlem and Westchester.
One of these was William Seton, a successful merchant, originally from Scotland.[18] During this time Crèvecoeur also met
his future wife, Mehetable Tippet, of Yonkers, whose father
owned an ample estate in Westchester County, and possibly
also in Dutchess County.[19]

In 1765 William Samuel Johnson wrote Crèvecoeur, in
response to his soliciting help in selling "Books and Medicine," that he would be pleased to render any service to him
he could "were I not under the most undispensible Obligation
on all Occasions to serve Mr. Stuyvesant [possibly Peter, one
of the leading men of the city] and his Friends." Apparently
Crèvecoeur was trying to establish some sort of mercantile
business in the city.

Another document, a report written by Peter Dubois,[20] a
magistrate for the police department, for Sir Henry Clinton,
Governor, at the time of Crèvecoeur's arrest in New York in
1779 (explained in Chapter IV) contains this information:

> In his first Voyage to America, it is said, He accom-
> panied a French Nobleman as a draftsman in a Tour from
> the Mouth of the Mississippi . . . to Canada, and from
> thence went to France.
>
> About 12 or 13 Years ago he again came out to this
> Place [New York] from Portugal; it was about the times the
> Commotions were Occasioned there on account of the
> Jesuits.

He brought with him a Small parcell of Lace and wrought Ruffles and a Letter of Introduction and Credit to Mr. Samuel VerPlank, who had resided in Holland for Some Years and Married a Lady of French Family at the Hague.

His first Year was past in Excursions to the Several Provinces from Virginia to Massachusetts Bay; and in each he form'd Some Connections. In or about the year 1767 He Induced Mr. Verplank [*sic*] and other proprietors of that Immense Tract of Land Westward of Esopus [on the west side of the Hudson River] called the Great Patent, to Open a Road into the Interior part of it, and to Commit the Direction of it to him; In this he amused himself for some time, but the Expense Rising beyond the Design of the Proprietors, this work was discontinued.

In 1768 and 1769 He resided principally at New Windsor, Making Excursions from thence frequently; here he hired a Small house and Gave out he was going to Set up a Potash Manufactory, But never Carried it into Execution.[21]

These biographical details are not found elsewhere, and may not be accurate. Dubois also reports that Crèvecoeur was supplied with money by a Mr. Verplanck (not otherwise identified, but probably an importer from Holland). "Ever since he has been in this Country, it is well known he has carried on a most Extensive Correspondence to Various parts of Europe. . . . He would Receive upward of Twenty Letters by one packet [ship] from England." He is also said by Dubois to be a man of extensive knowledge, including physic (medicine), botany, and mathematics. "Indeed in the Arts and Sciences, Nothing is new to him." It does seem clear from this report that Crèvecoeur engaged in commerce and collected news from Europe. This is not unlikely.

In spite of his extensive travels, Crèvecoeur wanted passionately to know the interior of the continent, "les pays ultramontains," meaning, probably, beyond the Alleghenies. He knew it would be foolhardy to undertake such a trip alone.

By accident he met Sir Robert Hooper, who had been commissioned to survey the sparsely settled Indiana territory.[22] Accompanied by another (unnamed) Englishman, who was as eager as Crèvecoeur to see the midcontinent, Sir Robert was glad to have both men for traveling companions.

After careful preparations for the arduous trip, Sir Robert, Crèvecoeur, and the anonymous Englishman, with three *coureurs des bois* as guides and hunters to keep them supplied with game, so that they needed to take only a few staples, left New York on April 4, 1767. Traveling by land, probably stagecoach, they reached Philadelphia, then crossed Pennsylvania to Pittsburgh, where the Allegheny and Monongahela flow into the Ohio River, making the stream navigable to the Mississippi. On May 6 they left Pittsburgh in small boats and floated down the Ohio for twenty-one days.

Crèvecoeur says he spent two months in the region of St. Louis so that he might visit the recent settlements on both sides of the Mississippi; also the Kaskaskia River, thirty or forty miles east of St. Louis. In his account, which he calls "Sketch of the Route of the voyage which I made into the interior of the continent in 1767," he does not mention Sir Robert again. Presumably Hooper continued on to Indiana, and did not rejoin Crèvecoeur and the Englishman when they resumed their journey in an English ship up the Illinois River to Chicago, then on through the Great Lakes to Fort Detroit, Niagara Falls, across Lake Huron to Lake Oneida, and by the Mohawk River to Albany, finally returning to New York by the Hudson River.

This was a tremendous journey by the primitive means of transportation available at the time, requiring immense stamina and the endurance of hardships difficult to imagine today. Incidentally, the three guides are not mentioned again. It is possible that they returned by some means while Crèvecoeur lingered in the neighborhood of St. Louis. It is likely that they were Indians from one of the settlements near Albany. As for

Crèvecoeur, he had traveled 3,190 miles, by his estimate, mostly by boat or ship on rivers and lakes. He also recorded that the trip took 161½ days, from New York to New York. In the third volume of *Lettres d'un Cultivateur Américain* he tells of visiting the Ohio River and the country of Kentucky, but this was, apparently, a different trip, or more likely, a fanciful one —as other events in this "Sketch" obviously are. Furthermore, he dated it "A Louis-Ville, le 26 Août 1784."[23] At that time he was consul in New York and worrying about his health.[24] It is unlikely that he took any strenuous trips at that time, but he knew the Ohio-Kentucky region from his voyage in 1767 to "les pays ultramontains."

III

⤟⤞⤝⤟⤞⤝

Hector St. John the Farmer

ON SEPTEMBER 20, 1769, Crèvecoeur married Mehetable Tippet, usually said to have been from Yonkers, though the marriage certificate says Dutchess County. The ceremony was performed by a Protestant minister, Jean Pierre Tétard, former pastor of the Huguenot church in Charleston, South Carolina, and at the time pastor of the old Dutch Church at Fordham. More is known about him than the bride. He lived in the section still called Kingsbridge, near Fordham, and would later become professor of French in King's College (known as Columbia after the Revolution). The marriage certificate states:

> To all concerned:
> This is to certify that on the twentieth of September, 1769, in the presence of Mr. Isaac Willett and Mrs. Margaret Willett, I have united in legitimate marriage Mr. Michel-Guillaume Saint-Jean de Crèvecoeur, usually known as Mr. Saint-John, native of Normandy in old France, and Mehetable Tippet, of Dutchess County, Province of New York.

In faith of which, I have appended my signature and
seal, in West-Chester, on the day and year given above.
Signed J. P. Tétard, N. D. M.[1]

Presumably Miss Tippet's family attended her wedding,
but we know nothing about it except the words of this marriage certificate, in which her parents are not mentioned. Julia
Post Mitchell, Crèvecoeur's first American biographer,
searched the Westchester records without finding out for sure
the first name of Mehetable's father, though she suspected it
was Henry.[2] She did learn that the Tippet family had owned
land in Westchester County for over a century. They were
Loyalists and would flee to Nova Scotia a decade later during
the American Revolution, leaving their property to be confiscated. Mitchell found no record of land owned in Dutchess
County, and naming Dutchess may have been the minister's
error.

The prominence of Miss Tippet's family at the time of her
marriage is indicated by the witnesses. Isaac Willett had been
sheriff of Westchester County for twenty-eight years (he
would resign the following year). County sheriff was a position
of considerable prestige in the colonial era. The governor of
the province made the appointment, but he himself had been
appointed by the king of Great Britain.

Since only four years earlier Crèvecoeur had become an
American citizen under the legal name of Hector St. John,[3] it
is a little surprising that at his wedding he reassumed his
baptismal name. This is proof that at this time he was not
trying to conceal his French origin. Of course, he knew that
Catholic France did not recognize the legality of marriage to
a Protestant, and this would be a formidable obstacle if he ever
wished to claim his inheritance to the Crèvecoeur estate in
Normandy. Given his failure to communicate with his family,
there is no reason to assume that he ever intended to return
to France. Still, by nature he was a prudent man, and this

prudence may have prompted him to make his marriage as legal as possible.

Where did Crèvecoeur take his bride to live? He said that the first place where he lived in Orange County, New York, was "the old Greycourt,"[4] the name of a house built in 1716 for Daniel Crommeline by William Bull, the first architect of the region. Crèvecoeur is believed to have boarded here before his marriage; so it is likely that he and his bride stayed there until they could build their own house.

A recorded deed in the courthouse at Goshen shows that on December 12, three months after his marriage, Crèvecoeur bought 250 acres of land from James and Phoebe Nesbit for £350.[5] These acres were part of a large tract called the Waywanda patent, bought in 1712 by Mr. Crommeline, a French Huguenot refugee, and some friends. It included Crèvecoeur's farm at Chester, in the Greycourt Meadows, a name which still survives. His share of these meadows would become the most fertile part of his property.

A crude dirt road ran through Crèvecoeur's property in the direction of Blooming Grove (then and now a small village) and on northeast to New Windsor, an important shipping terminal for Hudson River traffic to Albany and New York City. Today that road is an asphalt highway, No. 94. On the north side of the road the ground rose gradually to a low hill covered with pine trees. When Crèvecoeur built a house between the road and the hill, he called it Pine Hill. The ground on the south side of the road was more bog than meadow, but it would prove to be remarkably fertile after Crommeline Creek, which emptied into it, was dredged and the marsh drained. Even today the black soil of Greycourt Meadows yields bumper crops, and is especially good for truck farming.[6]

Geologists believe that a glacier came to rest here during the last North American ice age. When it finally melted, rank vegetation grew and decayed in the marsh. Animals venturing into the thick muck were trapped, and their decayed flesh became part of the compost. The bones of mastodons, ancestors of the elephant, have been found beneath the layers of peat moss in this valley. Those huge animals are thought to have reached North America over the Bering landmass bridge during the Miocene epoch a million years ago. Today the Museum Village of Orange County at Monroe has a fully articulated skeleton on view, with other mastodon bones. Crèvecoeur took keen interest in the discovery of relics of prehistoric animals, and he would have been thrilled by these discoveries so close to his farm.

The usual procedure for a settler in the backwoods (Chester was that, three miles from longer-settled Goshen, both a generation or more removed from a true "frontier" community) was, as Crèvecoeur several times pointed out in his writings, to build first a temporary log cabin but a substantial barn to serve the family's basic needs while clearing the forest,[7] and in Crèvecoeur's case, draining a swamp. The barn had to be large enough to shelter the horses and oxen (animals used for plowing and hauling), to store enough hay and fodder to last from one harvest to another, and to protect such equipment as harness, saddles, and tools. A good medium-size barn would be thirty by fifty feet and cost, according to Crèvecoeur's estimate, about $120—a substantial sum at the time.

Crèvecoeur left no record of the year in which he built the house he named Pine Hill, but it is unlikely that he delayed more than a few months after he began farming. It was burned down by marauding Indians employed by the British during the American Revolution, but today another house stands on the exact site and appears to have been built on the original foundation. A watercolor sketch of his house made by Crèvecoeur in 1778 shows a two-story building with five front windows and steps leading from the ground level to a second-story piazza. The front door on the ground floor has graceful side lights, probably fueled by whale oil.[8]

The amount of equipment and number of outbuildings the beginning farmer needed were considerable, requiring both time and money to build. Among the first essentials, he had to have a two-horse wagon and at least two or three horses, and preferably several oxen also. The kind of plow needed depended upon the soil: for heavy soil, a "two-handled plough with an English lock coulter," to be drawn by two or three horses abreast, or four oxen. A one-handled plow needed fewer draft animals, and a "corn-plough" to cultivate between the rows of corn could be drawn by one horse.

Essential outbuildings included a shop, big enough to contain a loom for the wife as well as the husband's carpentry and blacksmith tools. "Were we obliged to run to distant mechanics, who are half-farmers themselves," he wrote, "we would always be behind with our work."[9] In his shop the farmer could make repairs, and his wife could weave cloth from the fleece of their own sheep, after she had carded the wool and spun it into thread. Other structures needed included a chicken house, hogpens, a smokehouse for curing meat, a Dutch cellar (a hole or cave dug into the ground for keeping roots, vegetables, and fruits over the winter), a bee house, and a "Negro-kitchen" next to the main building, where servants could cook over an open fire. (This custom of having a detached kitchen, which can still be seen in Williamsburg, Virginia, lasted after a comfortable building supplanted the original log cabin.)

Nowhere in his writings does Crèvecoeur mention his wife by name or allude to her specifically, but he frequently describes the farmer's dependence on an industrious and skillful wife: "what a useful acquisition a good wife is to an American farmer, and how small is his chance of prosperity if he draws a blank in the lottery!"[10] Though these words are attributed to the fictional James writing to his supposed European correspondent, the repetition of such thoughts leave no room for doubting what Crèvecoeur's ideal wife was. And the fact that he would always look back upon the years on his farm as the happiest of his life seems the strongest proof that he thought he had won a prize in the lottery of marriage.

His constant reference to the wife's physical skills and unceasing activity does not mean that sentiment and affection were lacking in his own marriage. Though he wrote the letters before the beginning of literary romanticism (though not long before), Crèvecoeur liked to be called a man of feeling, and at times he could even be regarded as sentimental, a man to whom tears came easily. Once when he (or the narrator) witnessed the destruction of an otter's house, he said he saw the otter shedding tears, which caused him to shed some himself.

Certainly survival on an American farm in eighteenth-century America required fully as much, if not more, industry of the wife as the husband. "Within the more limited province of our American wives," Crèvecoeur wrote, "there are many operations, many ingenious arts, which require knowledge, skill, and dexterity."[11] She knew how to cook, even if she had slave servants. She had to know what herbs to gather for medicinal use, and where to find them; how to preserve meats and vegetables; how to milk a cow and make butter and cheese; how to take care of the chickens, turkeys, ducks, and geese. It was customary for the husband to be in charge of the larger animals, and the wife the smaller ones.

If a nearby village (and the nearest village might be remote) did not have a tailor (and professional tailors were rare in the colonies), the wife not only wove the cloth for the family's garments, she made them too. Crèvecoeur says that some wives were expert at dyeing, an art learned from the Dutch and the Indians. The latter produced beautiful colors by the use of "roots and bark of our woods, aided by indigo and alum, the only foreign ingredients we use." When the husband came in from the cold on a wintry night, his wife served him spiced cider to sip while he relaxed in front of the fireplace or beside the chimney, and she sewed, knitted, or darned: ". . . our women are never idle but have something to do from one year's end to another." The old adage that "Woman's work is never done" was a literal reality.

Crèvecoeur does not mention childbearing. In this duty his wife was not deficient either. The first child was a daughter, born December 14, 1770, named América-Francés, but usually called Fanny. On August 5, 1772, Guillaume-Alexandre (Ally) was born. The third child was also a boy, born October 22, 1774, whom they named Philippe-Louis.[12] On December 27, 1776, the Reverend Jean Pierre Tétard, at the time pastor of the French Reformed Church in New York City, visited Pine Hill and baptized all three children.[13] Witnesses were Verdine Ellsworth and his wife Dorothy. Mr. Ellsworth was a large landowner and one of Orange County's most respected citizens, and his witnessing the baptism was an indication of the social standing of the Crèvecoeurs.

Crèvecoeur had not intended to wait so long to have his children baptized. Soon after the birth of América-Francés he had asked his friend Tétard to come to his home to perform the ceremony, but the minister had replied on January 6, 1771, that it vexed him to have to say that the weather was so severe, the roads so nearly impassable, and crossing the Hudson River so perilous (at that time the only way to cross was by ferry) that he would have to promise to fulfill the request as soon as the weather permitted. Once postponed, the baptism was neglected for five years. Actually the Reverend Tétard did make the trip in 1776 at nearly the same time of year, but perhaps the winter was less severe than in 1771. Fanny was now six years old, and probably her father thought that the baptism should not be put off any longer.

Traveling in winter was one of the hazards of living so far from the city. During most winters one could travel by sleigh on the thick ice of the Hudson, but the unpaved roads to the river were often impassable. This was one reason why Crèvecoeur had to make his farm largely self-sufficient. Even during the months when the roads were open, transporting farm products to the New York market was time-consuming and expensive. Beef, for example, was so cheap that it did not pay to raise cattle to sell. And buying European goods in the city was a foolish extravagance which Crèvecoeur condemned in his *Sketches.* [14]

It was necessary, therefore, for him to produce on his farm nearly everything his family needed, and make sure that he had enough food for both human and domestic animals to last from one harvest until the next, in spite of spring floods, summer droughts, and winter storms. Crows pulled up the new-planted corn, hawks caught his wife's chickens, mud turtles ate young goslings, muskrats undermined the meadow banks, birds feasted on fruits and grain before they could be gathered, and rats and mice destroyed wheat in the bin and corn in the crib, to mention some of the pests he had to contend with. Sometimes survival seemed like a race between the farmer's industry and his natural enemies.[15]

Yet in spite of these discouragements, Crèvecoeur loved farming. Even if *Letters from an American Farmer* is not actual autobiography, he certainly identified with James the correspondent, and thus we can assume that the author was speaking his own sentiments when James writes in the first letter that of all agricultural labors "ploughing is the most agreeable because I can think as I work; my mind is at leisure; my labor flows from instinct, as well as [the strength of] my horses . . ." But he does sound a bit fanciful when he declares, "Often when I plough my low ground, I place my little son on a chair which screws to the beam of the plough—its motion and that of the horses please him; he is perfectly happy and begins to chat."[16]

In describing the American farmer's pride in his soil, Crèvecoeur was attempting to personify the happiness of the recent European immigrant who had found opportunity and freedom in the country which permitted him to acquire land of his very own. The author himself had been an immigrant in 1759, though he had not actually fled from oppression in Europe—unless he regarded his father's authority as that, which is possible. And he had chosen farming not out of desperate necessity, but because he liked the country life and the activities of the farm. Tilling the soil and raising plants and animals gave him not only a livelihood but also esthetic pleasure.

That Crèvecoeur had some assistance in operating his farm seems probable, but it is not likely that he had much. He frequently complained in both the *Letters* and *Sketches* of the scarcity and high cost of labor. Of course there were many poor immigrants, but most of them wanted to buy land on credit and work for themselves. Then there were the indentured servants, poor whites of both sexes, mostly from the British Isles, who sold themselves into seven years of labor (practically slavery) for their passage to America, at the end of which they were free to do whatever they wished or could. So far as it is known, Crèvecoeur had no indentured servants.

Did he own Negro slaves? His bitter attack on Charlestonians for their cruelty to slaves (letter 9) and his frequent praise of Quakers for their antislavery doctrines and practices leave no doubt that he disapproved of the subjection of black people. But he does say in *Sketches* 4, "After being possessed of the land, one must have a team and a Negro." And in the bucolic story of the sudden snowstorm in *Sketches* 1, it is black "honest Tom" who rides "Bonny, the old faithful mare" to the schoolhouse and brings back three children stranded by the storm, two riding bareback behind and one in front of him. Another Negro named Jack brings in wood for the fireplace during the snowstorm. That evening, "The Negroes, friends to the fire, smoke and crack some coarse jokes, and well fed and clad, they contentedly make their brooms and ladles without any further concerns on their minds."[17]

In *Sketches* 4, Crèvecoeur insists that Negro slaves are not profitable in the North, and for this reason they are few in number, and, as a consequence, well treated. "The few Negroes we have are at best our friends and companions. Their original cost is very high. Their clothing and their victuals mount to a great sum, besides the risk of losing them." The admission of this "risk" casts doubt on their contentment, though in *The Black Family in Slavery and Freedom* a respected authority corroborates Crèvecoeur's assertion that slaves were treated far more humanely in the North than on Southern plantations.[18] James Fenimore Cooper, in Chapter 5 of *Satanstoe,* claimed that the northern system of slavery was strictly domestic, the black slave "almost invariably living under the same roof with the master." One evidence of the kinder treatment of slaves in the North was the way they were permitted to celebrate "Pinkster." This was "the festival of Whitsunday, or the feast of Pentecost," when the slaves were permitted to dress up and carouse freely with their friends, especially in Albany and New York City.

Some of the most charming passages in *Letters from an American Farmer* reveal the author as a naturalist, a forerunner of Thoreau a century later. Crèvecoeur marveled at the sagacity of wild animals. He liked to go into the fields and woods just as dawn was breaking so he could hear the songs of the many birds on his farm. He studied the habits of bees, protected the quail nesting in his hedges, made friends with wasps and hornets, and enjoyed nothing more than a bee hunt, which he described in considerable detail:

After I have done with sowing, by way of recreation I prepare for a week's jaunt into the woods, not to hunt either the deer or the bears, as my neighbors do, but to catch the more harmless bees. . . . I take with me my dog, as a companion, for he is useless as to this game; my gun, for no man, you know, ought to enter the woods without one; my blanket; some provisions; some wax; vermillion; honey, and a small pocket compass.[19]

After he reaches the forest, "at a considerable distance from any settlements," he heats a stone on which he melts the wax. On another stone he pours some drops of honey, which he surrounds with the vermillion. The bees are attracted by the odor of the hot wax and soon find the honey, which they try to collect and in so doing tinge themselves with the vermillion particles. Then with his compass Crèvecoeur charts the direction of their flight, and the vermillion enables him to time how long it takes them to return for more honey. Now, knowing both direction and approximate distance of their round trip, he is able to trace the bees to their hive in a hollow tree. Then he goes to the nearest settlement to secure help in cutting down the tree and securing both the honey and the bees.

The first bees he ever found were discovered by accident in the woods, before he knew the technique described above. "This was in April; I had five swarms that year, and they have been ever since very prosperous. This business generally takes a week of my time every fall, and to me it is a week of solitary ease and relaxation." The delight the author takes in describing this passage strongly implies that it is based on experience.

It is probable also that Crèvecoeur himself did not hunt for deer, bears, and other wild animals, like his neighbors, for he strongly disapproved of hunting because of the effect it had on human character, though in chapter 4 of *Sketches* he approves of killing squirrels when they become so numerous as to be "enemies of the farmer." Perhaps his opinion of hunting had been influenced by sociological theories on the origin of human society which he had encountered in his philosophical reading. An early theory was that migratory hunters preceded agriculturalists, who needed to remain relatively stationary in order to plant, cultivate, and harvest their grains and other plant food. Crèvecoeur's sympathy was naturally with those prehistoric farmers. He regretted that many of those Americans who ventured into the deep forest, far removed from established settlements, found it easy to regress to the state of hunters, and "once hunters, farewell to the plough. The chase renders them ferocious, gloomy, and unsocial; a hunter wants no neighbor. . . ."[20]

In his travels Crèvecoeur had observed people living on the real "frontier," in what Thomas Hobbes in his *Leviathan* called "a state of nature," beyond the reach of civil law, where a man's only protection was his own strength and cunning. "Back settlers" Crèvecoeur called these people who supported themselves mainly by hunting and trapping. To him these were not the admirable people, the backbone of the developing nation Frederick Jackson Turner a century later would claim them to have been,[21] but "a mongrel breed, half-civilized, half-savage. . . ."[22] Turner thought that only the bold and creative colonists dared venture into the unknown wilderness and tame it for a civilized society. Crèvecoeur, like the federalist leaders after the American Revolution, believed they were more likely to have been the failures and misfits of society, who wanted the "unlimited freedom of the woods," beyond the restraints of churches, schools, and courts of law.

But the hunters and trappers were only the first stage of the western migration, Crèvecoeur said. Gradually they would give way to the plowman, with consequent improvement in manners and character: "thus are our trees felled, in general, by the most vicious of our people, and thus the path is opened for the arrival of the second and better class, the true American freeholder, the most respectable set of people in this part of the world. . . ."[23] Perhaps Crèvecoeur, the educated, cultivated European, was somewhat prejudiced against the crude, often illiterate, and usually indigent people who became the "back settlers." But he described them as he saw them in the 1760s and 1770s, whereas Turner could only theorize about them in 1890.

Yet in spite of his gloomy observations of people who had taken to the woods, Crèvecoeur envisioned a future nation of strong and prosperous people. Most immigrants, he said, would "immediately feel the good effects of that plenty of provisions"; and "here the laws of naturalization invite everyone to partake of the great labours and felicity, to till unrented, untaxed lands!" Of course, some immigrants would bring their vices with them, causing them to fail. But for the sober, honest, and industrious the opportunities were almost unlimited. "Whenever I hear of a new settlement, I pay it a visit once or twice a year, on purpose to observe the different steps the settler takes. . . ."[24]

As these settlements grew, more and more land was cleared for cultivation. The usual method was to clear off only the underbrush for the first season of planting and to remove the bark from the larger trees in a ring extending a foot or two in breadth. The loss of bark would stop the circulation of sap and quickly kill the tree. Denuded of leaves, the dead trees would not prevent sunlight from reaching the growing corn, wheat, or other cultivated plants. Eventually the trees would be chopped down and burned in great bonfires. Thus was land brought under cultivation, and farmers took pride in the number of acres they had cleared each year.

Though Crèvecoeur also took pride in the taming of the wilderness by American farmers, he was not blind to the damage wrought by the destruction of the trees. In *Sketches of Eighteenth Century America* he attributed the droughts in certain regions to the draining of swamps and the destruction of the forests. Many brooks fed by the swamps had dried up. "Our ancient woods kept the earth moist and damp, and the sun could evaporate none of the waters contained under these shades."[25] He also noticed that in these regions the water table was sinking, and as a consequence wells had to be dug deeper than formerly to find water. Soil erosion had not yet advanced far enough to alarm him, but of course that would be the consequence of the loss of the compost formed by decaying leaves, which had taken centuries to accumulate, and could be destroyed in one generation. In *Journey into Northern Pennsylvania and the State of New York* Crèvecoeur has an early settler say: "The second generation will regret bitterly that their fathers destroyed so much!"[26]

The term *ecology* had not yet come into use, but Crèvecoeur might be called the first American ecologist.

IV

The Nightmare Years

WHILE CRÈVECOEUR was peacefully enjoying his farm at Chester, visiting new settlements or diverting himself in slack seasons with bee hunting, events were taking place in America which would profoundly change the course of his life. In 1763 the powerful Indian chief Pontiac led a rebellion of several Indian tribes in the region of the Great Lakes which Great Britain had recently acquired by her victories in Quebec and Montreal. At the same time a major rebellion had broken out in India, thus requiring Britain to maintain enlarged armies on two distant continents. This state of affairs strained the British economy almost beyond endurance. The new monarch, George III, saw no reason why the North Americans should not bear at least some of the expense of protecting them.[1]

For this reason the infamous Stamp Act was passed in Parliament, plans were made to billet British soldiers in American homes, and restrictions were placed on maritime trade. Special efforts were also begun to stop the Americans from avoiding the paying of taxes on Jamaica rum and sugar by supporting New England smugglers. Naturally, all these attempts to raise revenue were resisted, and eventually brought about the American Revolution. Actually none of these measures was very burdensome to the two million colonists, but they felt that the freedoms and protections they had enjoyed under British constitutional government were being abridged, especially since they had no representation in the English Parliament.

Not all Americans felt that way. Many of them, who came to be called Tories after the political party in England which supported the politics of King George III, thought the demands of the Mother Country reasonable and deserving of their patriotic support.[2] Crèvecoeur agreed with them. He was not personally interested in politics, but the admiration for the British way of life which had caused him to come to New York instead of returning to France continued. Of course he was now a landowner, too, though not a large one like some Tories east of the Hudson River, but he had married into one of those families. These two facts inevitably influenced his opinion of contemporary events.

One of the authorities on the history of New York during the American Revolution, Wilbur C. Abbott, says of the polarization taking place:

> Every province contained an aristocratic land-owning or mercantile element, which, in accordance with the principles of the time, held the offices and dominated politics. On the other hand there was in every province a large and growing faction of landless or moneyless, working or pioneer classes, artisans or small landholders, for the most part late comers to America and for the most part disbarred from the franchise.[3]

Crèvecoeur was late in realizing the seriousness of the dissatisfaction of the "have-nots," though he had ample opportunity to observe it. He must have been either in New York City or near it when he was naturalized in 1765. That year agitation over the Stamp Act resulted in riots, effigy burnings of King George III, and mobs clashing with British soldiers. The disturbances were led by a loose organization which called itself the Sons of Liberty, composed mostly of day laborers, small merchants, and the unenfranchised in general, who comprised nearly 90 percent of the population. They were also joined by lawyers and publishers who did not enjoy royal patronage.[4]

Acts of terrorism continued through the winter of 1765–66, though, Abbott says, "the better element took small part or none in the riotous proceedings."[5] Even news in April of the repeal of the Stamp Act did not stop the disorders, and for nearly a year New York City was "virtually at the mercy of the mob." As a consequence, "the propertied classes, like those in the sister colony [Massachusetts], were disturbed by the fear that the mob would attack them, as it had the English officials, and, irrespective of party, they endeavored to moderate or control the more violent elements."[6]

It was during the winter of 1766–67 that Crèvecoeur visited the Oneida Indians in Connecticut, and was ceremonially adopted by them. The following year he made a five-month trip to the Mississippi and the Great Lakes; he then resumed residence in Orange County late in 1769 or early 1770. But he had friends in New York City with whom he was in touch, and he was also an inveterate newspaper reader. He certainly knew what was going on, and was familiar with both sides of the dispute. The news of violence came not only from New York City. In May 1775 Ethan Allen's Green Mountain Boys seized Ticonderoga and Crown Point on Lake Champlain, where Crèvecoeur himself had fought with the French Colonial Army. In June came the news of Bunker Hill in Boston, where a small band of Americans had defeated British soldiers.

By this time the authority of the New York Legislature had been undermined and nullified by illegal "congresses," which had begun meeting first in New York and then in Philadelphia. The Continental Congress in Philadelphia in 1774 was attended by five New York delegates, who worked for a compromise with Great Britain. Another congress in Philadelphia the following month was attended by Samuel Gale, a justice of the peace from Orange County,[7] whose sister had witnessed the baptism of the Crèvecoeur children, and was doubtless known to Crèvecoeur himself. The delegates in favor of moderation were steadily losing ground to the "radicals." Local government was disintegrating, and the less than one hundred British soldiers in Philadelphia were powerless to keep order. In Boston British troops were under siege by natives. England and America were actually at war.[8]

Further confirmation of this fact came on June 15, 1775, when the Continental Congress sitting in Philadelphia appointed George Washington supreme commander of American armies. He had distinguished himself in protecting the western frontier against French and Indian attacks in 1755–56 and was the country's most respected military leader. He assumed command on July 3 in Cambridge, Massachusetts, and remained in the vicinity of Boston until General William Howe withdrew the British soldiers stationed there to Halifax, Nova Scotia, early in 1776.

The decisive year was 1776. In January Tom Paine published *Common Sense,* a propaganda tract urging an immediate break with Great Britain. Loyalists in New York prepared a rebuttal but a mob broke into the printing office and destroyed the type before copies could be printed. The Continental Congress did not need Paine to urge it to action. Early in June it appointed a Committee to Detect Conspiracies, and local committees soon began their own "witch hunts." In New York City Tories were disarmed, and suspected Tories were assaulted in the street. As many as could left the city.

Meanwhile, General Howe had landed his troops on Staten Island, while his brother, Admiral Richard Howe, brought his formidable fleet of warships to blockade the shipping lanes. On June 26 General Washington arrived to take charge of fortifying and defending the city. The Congress's Declaration of Independence on July 4 was intended to boost the morale of the American rebels, and it did succeed in increasing their confidence and determination.

However, during the second half of 1776 the Americans were badly defeated, first by General Howe on Long Island on August 22, and in subsequent skirmishes on upper Manhattan and in Westchester County. At noon on September 14 the British took possession of New York City, and held it firmly until the end of the war. Washington was forced to retire with his forces into New Jersey and did not stop until he had crossed the Delaware River. His first victory was on the night of December 25, 1776, when his troops recrossed the Delaware in rowboats during a snowstorm and surprised the Hessian and British troops encamped at Trenton.

After the capture of New York by the British, Patriots in Orange County mobilized two regiments of militia, under the command of Colonel Isaac Nicoll, to defend the mountainous highlands near the Hudson River.[9] But the men were permitted to return to their homes after Washington's victory at Trenton. However, in September 1777 Sir Henry Clinton, now commander of the army in New York City, began, with substantial reinforcements, to move up the Hudson.[10] All able-bodied men in Orange and Ulster counties were under heavy pressure from their neighbor Patriots to enlist in the American army, disregarding all their obligations to their farms and families. Crèvecoeur, forty-three, may have been a little old for military duty, but he was no doubt urged to serve the cause in some way. The extent of his persecution can be judged by the last chapter in *Letters*, "Distresses of a Frontier Man,"[11] and the final six chapters of *Sketches*,[12] which were originally part of the manuscript from which the essays in *Letters* were selected for publication in London.

In 1775, if statements in "On the Susquehanna; [and] The Wyoming Massacre" (*Sketches* 8) can be believed, Crèvecoeur made several trips into the "back country" of Pennsylvania. Between 1775 and 1778 he traveled up and down the Susquehanna, a wide, shallow river, navigable only in spring after the melting of the snow in the mountains and in autumn during the usual heavy rains.[13] The river extends from Lake Otsego and Cooperstown to Havre de Grace, Maryland, on the Chesapeake Bay, a distance of nearly 450 miles. Sometimes he rode a horse, and at other times he traveled on foot or in a canoe with Indian companions from a Seneca village on the west branch of the river.[14]

Crèvecoeur was especially interested in the region around Wyoming, originally the name of an Indian village on the eastern branch of the Susquehanna River, and renamed Wilkes-Barre by the New England settlers after the mayor of London. (Crèvecoeur spelled the name Wioming.) The first patents to grants of land in this territory were so vaguely worded that disputes arose between colonists in Connecticut and Pennsylvania over ownership. After many skirmishes, this dispute brought about a small war from 1769 to 1771, and another in 1778. In the latter year a party of Indians and Tories led by John Butler massacred several hundred Pennsylvanians, including women and children. Crèvecoeur talked with some of the survivors and was distressed by their accounts.[15] In 1909 Thomas Campbell, the popular Scottish poet, wrote a poem about this atrocity called *Gertrude of Wyoming.*[16]

In chapter 9 of *Sketches* Crèvecoeur gives the "History of Mrs. B.," a mother of eight children and one of the casualties of the dispute between the New England and Pennsylvania settlers. Her husband sold his farm in Connecticut and moved his family to the Wyoming valley. "Nothing is so easy," she told Crèvecoeur, "as to travel on a map. . . . But actually to traverse a track of one hundred miles, accompanied with eight children, with cattle, horses, oxen, sheep, etc. This is to meet with a thousand unforeseen difficulties." When they finally arrived, they were pleased with the fertility of the soil, the luxuriant grass, and the pure water. But in one of the earlier skirmishes between the Connecticut and Pennsylvania settlers, her husband was taken prisoner, the farm was plundered, and he was carried to Philadelphia. She sent the children to live with friendly settlers and she herself walked six days until she found refuge. The following summer her husband was released and returned to Wyoming to find everything in ruins. Finally he located his children and his wife, but decided he might find a more peaceful life in Wyalusing, sixty miles up the Susquehanna River.

However, they did not find peace in Wyalusing, for now, in addition to the land disputes, they found themselves caught in the pre-Revolution quarrel. This community was made up mainly of people loyal to Britain, and Patriots south of them began to make bloody raids. Again this unfortunate family lost everything. The husband and one son died of smallpox, which the wife also contracted. While she did not die of it, she wished she had.

In Chapter 10, "The Frontier Woman," Crèvecoeur tells more concisely of the miseries of another woman, who had somehow survived the night raids but felt devastated from witnessing the massacres. She exclaims, "What astonishing scenes of barbarity, distress, and woe will not the rage of war exhibit on this extended stage of human affairs!"

The Wyoming massacre was not directly caused by the American Revolution, but was another example of the social chaos of the times. At least two years earlier Crèvecoeur had lamented the effects of the tragic quarrel between his mother and adopted country:

It spread among the lower classes like an epidemy of the mind. . . . It soon swallow'd up every inferior contest, silenced every other dispute, and presented the people of Susquehanna with the pleasing hopes of their own never being decided by Great Britain. These solitary farmers, like all the rest of the inhabitants of this country, rapidly launch'd forth into all the intricate mazes of the grand quarrel, as their inclinations, prepossessions, and prejudices led them. A fatal era which has since disseminated among them the most horrid poison. . . .[17]

Crèvecoeur described his personal dilemma with eloquent pathos in the last chapter of *Letters from an American Farmer*. The persecution he had observed in the backwoods settlements on the Susquehanna he himself also experienced in his own community. He felt "divided between the respect I felt for the ancient connection [with Great Britain] and the fear of innovation, with the consequences of which I am not well acquainted." Reason told him that once established society has broken down and various factions are grappling for power, it is impossible to predict the outcome, and one did not know whom to trust.

He wanted desperately just to be left alone to live in peace, to remain neutral. But that was impossible; neither side would permit neutrality. What, then, could he do? He might flee to Canada, as his father-in-law was forced to do. Why he did not consider such a plan is rather surprising, since he knew the country and liked the people. But the only solution he considered in his writings was to go live with a friendly Indian tribe, one not allied with British agents. The name of the tribe he was considering he did not mention; probably it was not the Oneidas who had adopted him, for he said that after twenty-three miles by land carriage (about the distance from his home to the Hudson River) he could finish the trip on water, going as far as need be to reach Indian friends who would welcome him. (The Seneca Indians on the Susquehanna were friendly to him, but they were not safe either.)

This sounds like pure fantasy, though Crèvecoeur described it in great detail and considered every imaginable effect on his children and the kind of home he could provide for them far removed from white civilization. He may also have intended this desperate daydream (though perhaps the adjective implies a nightmare) as a satire on a colonial society which had lost its sanity, and was now more uncivilized than the Indians whom it regarded as savages. He could not deny that Indians were cruel to their enemies, but within their homes he had observed nothing but harmony and tolerance.

The Indian way of life would deprive Crèvecoeur's children of the comforts to which they were accustomed, but perhaps, with his own ingenuity and technical skills, he could alleviate these to some extent, and maybe even teach his Indian hosts how to improve their lives. His children would have to learn the Indian language, and they would be tempted to become hunters instead of tillers of the soil, though he would try to teach the Indians to plow and sow. He worried, too, that his children might not wish to return to white society after tranquillity had returned to the colonies.

If Crèvecoeur seriously considered acting out this fantasy, he might actually have feared the attractions of the Indian life for his children. Francis Jennings, a twentieth-century historian of the invasion of the Indian tribes by the Europeans, says that, "It was a constant crying scandal that Europeans who were adopted by Indians frequently preferred to remain with their Indian 'families' when offered an opportunity to return to their genetic kinsmen."[18]

Jennings also points out that the Indians did not destroy their environment, and Crèvecoeur had begun to observe that the colonists were rapidly doing exactly that. The eastern tribes of Indians, especially, did not depend entirely on hunting; they also cultivated small plots of land, clearing only as much of the forest as they needed. Before exhausting the soil, or tilling it in a way to cause erosion (they had no plows), they moved on to another plot, letting the forest retake the former. Of course, the Europeans finally came in such numbers that they could not have survived by this limited agriculture, though the thought never occurred to them, because they were accustomed to a system of private ownership of land, which the Indians did not have or understand.

Crèvecoeur, too, was to some extent limited by his European intellectual inheritance, but his sympathy for the Indians enabled him to understand them better than most of his American contemporaries did. When he wrote about the Indians in his travel books he may have been influenced by the growing myth in France of the "Noble Savage" as has been charged;[19] however, he had visited the Indian villages, slept in them, dined in them, and traveled on the Susquehanna with Indian guides and friends.

But whether daydream or plan, escape to a safe Indian retreat was not possible for Crèvecoeur. To have exchanged agreements by messengers traveling by land and water and to have arranged the logistics of a trip to the Great Lakes or beyond would have taken more time and resources than he had. Possibly his only alternative was to return to France, but that also would not prove to be easy. This was no time to sell his farm. And his father-in-law, on the other side of the Hudson, whose Tory sympathies were well known, had his own problems, and could not help him.

Crèvecoeur's French biographer believed he began thinking of returning to France as early as 1773 or 1774, when the undated letter was written by someone in Normandy, probably Crèvecoeur's father, asking the aid of the British Public Records Office in New York to help him locate Michel-Guillaume Jean de Crèvecoeur, near the age of thirty-eight.[20] Since he was born in 1735, the letter must have been written in 1773. The writer says he has not heard from this person since 1767, which would have been two years before Crèvecoeur's marriage. The writer does not know whether this young man is still alive, but his family is anxious for news of him, and they hope that he will get in touch with "M. L'Ambassadeur." That the Public Record Office in New York delivered this letter we know because some years later Crèvecoeur himself deposited it in the office of the county clerk in the courthouse in Goshen. Thomas Moffat, the clerk, labeled it "A true Record at the Request of Hector St. John the Eighteenth Day of June 1798." (At that time Crèvecoeur was back in France; why he wanted the document deposited in Goshen is a puzzle, though he hoped to return to America.)

A descendant of the Crèvecoeur family says that the estate in Pierrepont had been in the family in unbroken line since the Norman Conquest. By primogeniture law, the eldest son inherited his father's entire estate—though in a few parts of France this law was not enforced. Evidently Crèvecoeur's father expected Michel-Guillaume to inherit the estate, and in his old age he wanted desperately to locate his missing son. Of course his father did not know, and perhaps could not imagine, that his son had married a Protestant. In France at that time a Protestant could not inherit property. Of course Crèvecoeur himself was still (legally) a Catholic, but *his* children would be regarded as illegitimate. A present-day member of the Crèvecoeur family says that the most valuable property Michel St. John de Crèvecoeur hoped to inherit was from an uncle, who was much wealthier than his father.

No further correspondence between Crèvecoeur and his father (or family) at this time has survived. There are other documents, however, to show that by 1778 Crèvecoeur was making desperate efforts to leave Orange County. Early in the year he asked and received permission from Major General James Pattison to "send his family by a flag going up Hudson's River," meaning, presumably, that a British ship coming up the river would take his family to New York on its return.[21] By this time the city was under the complete control of a British military commander. The sixty-two-year-old General Pattison is said to have been "efficient and treated the residents of the city as well as did any of the British officials."[22]

Before General Pattison's permission could be acted upon, however, Crèvecoeur's neighbor Henry Wisner, a powder-maker, learned of it and wrote to Governor George Clinton, protesting: "The people of our county are much alarmed at the apprehensions of St. John's being permitted to go to New York."[23] What they most feared was that he might report to British authorities that a gigantic iron chain was being forged at Sterling, just over the New Jersey line, to be stretched across the Hudson River in front of West Point to prevent British ships from sailing beyond that point. Probably Mr. Wisner was also afraid that the British might learn about his powder mill and destroy it.

Evidently this letter was effective, for July arrived and Crèvecoeur had still not received permission to leave Pine Hill. Perhaps his frustration caused him to make that trip to Pennsylvania near the time of the terrible massacre at Wyoming on July 4. Several years later in Paris, Thomas Jefferson wrote a friend who was planning to write an account of the atrocity: "I have had a long conversation with M. Crèvecoeur [about Wyoming]. He knows well that canton. He was in the neighborhood of the place when it was destroyed, saw great numbers of the fugitives, aided them with his wagons, and had the story from their mouths."[24] How did he happen to be in Wyoming at that particular time? Certainly not to help his family flee from Orange County to New York City. Since he had Seneca Indian friends only a few miles away, he could have been trying to arrange a retreat for his family with them. And Jefferson said Crèvecoeur was traveling with wagons (plural). Had he carried his family and supplies with him? Possibly the massacre convinced him that the Senecas could not provide him an escape from his troubles.

What he did during the next six months is completely unknown. Later in New York City he claimed that he had been arrested, fined, and held in jail at Goshen. These experiences may have been his reward for returning from Pennsylvania—or punishment for going there while he was under suspicion. Six months later he was finally able to leave his farm, with the permission of General Washington. He was accompanied by his six-year-old son Alex, leaving his wife and two younger children with friends at Chester. When he reached the headquarters of Major General Alexander McDougall, he met no objections to his going on to New York City.[25] In the French edition of *Lettres* he recalled having found the major general grilling some slabs of beef for lunch, which he invited Crèvecoeur to share with him and his wife. In memory Crèvecoeur called it the best meal he had had in six months, and he thought General McDougall the finest "citizen general" in the hemisphere.

This would be the last good meal Crèvecoeur would enjoy for some time. He reached New York City as a destitute refugee sometime about the middle of February 1779. On the seventeenth he wrote a letter to Roger Morris, inspector of claims of refugees for relief, begging for food for himself and his son. The wording of the letter shows his embarrassment and exhaustion:

The diffusive Misfortunes of the Times is the only Introduction I have as well as the only Plea I can make for writing you this—Like Great Many others I have relinquished ye Conveniences of Life Property Servants &c, these Incidents however are now become so common that I am very conscious they are less thought of; So many sacrifices of the same kind have been made that the Calamities of each Individual seems to be drowned in the general Mass yet they are not less felt by Each Sufferer; myself & Son are now become Refugees in this Town & find myself obliged to apply to you for the Indulgce of Rations for us both from this date, the only reward of 4 Years of Contumely Receiv'd, of Fines Imposed, Empris-

onments &. the Enclosed letters from Persons better
known to you than myself will I hope Convince You that
my Request is founded on Necessity & will enable you to
judge how far I am justifyable in making this application.[26]

William Seton, Crèvecoeur's oldest friend in New York
City, now a magistrate in the king's service, also wrote a letter
endorsing the petition. Mr. Morris forwarded both letters to
Andrew Elliot in the police department. Elliot, in turn, sent
the petition, with his added endorsement, to the mayor, David
Mathews. The mayor then returned the request to Mr. Morris,
who apparently ended the bureaucratic "run-around."

How much Mr. Morris was able to help Crèvecoeur and his
son is not known. Granting any provisions of food may have
been difficult, for in 1779 the city was severely short of food,
fuel, and housing. In addition to the British army's having
increased the housing problem, the city had lost one-fourth of
all its houses in a tremendous fire in 1776, soon after the
British troops occupied the city; Loyalists blamed Patriot in-
cendiaries, but the cause was never determined. In another
fire two years later sixty-five additional houses were lost.[27]

The population of New York, estimated at twenty-five
thousand at the beginning of the British occupation, fluc-
tuated during the war years, but housing was always extremely
scarce.[28] About half of the Patriots left the city in 1776, and
at least that many Loyalists had done so before the occupation; but in February 1777 General Robertson estimated that
eleven thousand Loyalists had returned, and three thousand
more accompanied the British army when it came back to New
York after evacuating Philadelphia in 1778. The number of
British troops billeted in the city increased from around four
thousand in 1776 to nearly ten thousand in 1781. British
officers confiscated the best houses for themselves, even from
Loyalist owners, though they were promised compensation.
Houses owned by rebels were seized outright. No appeal was

possible because courts of law were not operating; everyone obeyed military orders. King's College was used as a barracks. Prison space was so scarce that the British began holding captured Americans in ships anchored in the harbor.

Food was as great a problem as housing. Although military authorities tried to keep order in the city, some of the troops raided farms on Long Island, and farmers in Westchester and New Jersey were afraid to bring their produce to city markets —which the fires had already reduced in number. Food was so scarce that by 1777 prices had risen 800 percent.[29] A black market flourished, supplied by lawless gangs who raided the countryside for cattle and hogs.[30] The British tried to import enough beef, mutton, and flour from England and Ireland to feed their troops, but the ships were often delayed in their four-to-six-week crossing, and spoilage ran high. This food was not intended for civilian consumption, and was insufficient even for the troops. Many civilians actually starved to death. Their miseries were increased when in July 1779, four or five months after Crèvecoeur's arrival, an epidemic of fever, described as "ague" and "intermittent," perhaps typhoid or a tropical disease, broke out and raged until November of the following year.[31]

Almost by accident Crèvecoeur obtained employment for a few weeks in late spring or early summer of 1779. "Having heard Mr. Antoine Van Dam, master of the port, say that he had only a very old and discolored map, I offered to make him a new one on any scale he wished."[32] Mr. Van Dam gladly accepted this offer and Crèvecoeur made him a nice new copy, for which he was paid two Portuguese dollars, though he had asked nothing.

Encouraged by this little success, he sought and obtained a commission from Trinity Church to survey its property. In his own words, "I was employed to dig among the ruins of houses constructed on the land belonging to that rich corporation for the corner markers and to establish as best I could the ancient property lines."[33] The houses on this land had been destroyed in the fire of 1776 or 1778. This work made Crèvecoeur very happy because it "would be long and useful." Next day he purchased some white handkerchiefs and affixed them to surveyor's staffs to mark the corners of the lines he was trying to establish. Some drunken sailors took them for French flags, knocked them down, cursed him, and threatened physical violence. This unpleasant episode was symptomatic of the atmosphere of suspicion and irrational fear in New York.

On July 8 Crèvecoeur was arrested and thrown into jail on the basis of an anonymous letter sent to Sir Henry Clinton, commander of the British forces in New York in the summer of 1779, which accused him of having corresponded with General Washington and of possessing maps of the harbor, presumably to be sent to the rebels.[34] Since he had sought General Washington's permission to come to New York and he had made a map of the harbor for Mr. Van Dam, a rational mind would not have found these acts treasonable. Nevertheless, Sir Henry asked General Pattison to investigate the accusation.

Two days before Crèvecoeur's arrest the rector of Trinity Church submitted a bill for the surveying done by "Mr. H. St. John."[35] It totaled eleven pounds, two shillings, and ten pence, and on August 7 the secretary of the board recorded this amount as "paid H. St. John's account," though the words more likely recorded an intention rather than actual payment, for on this date the board also voted to postpone completion of the surveying because of the extremely hot weather. It is doubtful that the secretary visited Crèvecoeur in prison, or even knew he was there.

On the day of Crèvecoeur's arrest he had been summoned by General Pattison from Flushing, where he was staying with his son in the home of an old friend, the Reverend Mr. Brown. On July 8 General Pattison wrote a long letter to Clinton, describing his examination of the accused man. Crèvecoeur told the general of his having to leave his farm and family because of his loyalty to the king, and the general seemed convinced of his innocence. He also sent for some papers which Crèvecoeur said he had left with two friends on Long Island, Judge George Ludlow and David Colden, son of the late lieutenant governor of the New York colony. Both of these were prominent men whose loyalty was beyond question. Subsequently a deputy appointed by General Pattison examined these papers, which were actually the manuscript of the future book *Letters from an American Farmer,* and reported that they showed Crèvecoeur's strong sympathy for the British government. This report satisfied General Pattison, and in his letter to Sir Henry Clinton he asked if he should not release the prisoner on bail, which friends had offered.

One might expect that after receiving this letter, Sir Henry would have ordered Crèvecoeur released. Yet in spite of all these favorable reports, and the support of prominent citizens loyal to the king, Crèvecoeur remained in the provost's custody for three months. The cause may have been bureaucratic inefficiency, or Sir Henry's indifference; others were being falsely accused every day, and cleared their names with the greatest difficulty.

Peter Dubois, who was quoted in a previous chapter (see Note 20 for Chapter II), gives a curious detail about the papers Crèvecoeur brought with him to New York:

When he came into this City, from among the Rebels, he brought with him Some Boxes in which he had curious Botanical plants and at the Bottom of those Boxes under the Earth in which the plants were, he had private Drawers or Cases in which he had papers, But upon taking them out on his arrival here, he found them Very Damp, Nearly Wet, from the Moisture of the Earth in the Box above them. Which obliged him to take them out and Dry them before a fire in his Lodgings.

Crèvecoeur was not being held in one of the worst jails, though he may have thought so, but in the "New Gaol" built in 1759 on the common, called The Fields, where city hall now stands.[36] It was in better condition than most of the military prisons, but it was in charge of Provost Cunningham, whom the historian Abbott calls "a man of ill repute," like most "such officers in all wars." "The cruelty of Provost Cunningham made his name a synonym for all that was hateful in the presence of those who were reckoned by the patriotic party as invaders of their land."

Crèvecoeur wrote two accounts of his three-month imprisonment in New York. One he published in the first volume of the expanded French edition of *Lettres d'un cultivateur américain* (1787).[37] At first he was held in a basement cell with a group of low-class men. It was dark, foul-smelling, and very unsanitary. At night rats kept him awake. In daytime he could hear the screams and curses of men being flogged in the courtyard above, and sometimes the sounds of men being hanged. Finally he asked his guard if he could be transferred to an upstairs room where men of his own class were being held. This request was granted, and he found both the quarters and his companions less depressing. In fact, some of the men, most of whom were being held on false charges like his own, became close friends. Later in *Lettres* he told their stories.[38] Some were sympathetic with the American rebels, but all had been cruelly abused. Crèvecoeur learned that the British could be as brutal as the American Patriots, and his own Loyalist sympathy was strained by the atrocities he heard in prison.

His greatest worry, however, was for his son. He had left the boy at Flushing when he was requested to visit General Pattison, unaware of the reason for the summons. He had expected to return to Ally in a few hours, so had not made any arrangements for him, or after his detention been permitted to send any message. All Ally knew was that his father had not returned from New York. Then word was brought to the distraught father that his son was ill; full information was maliciously withheld. As the weeks dragged on he became more and more frantic, at times even delirious. His companions in prison tried to calm him and prevent his doing injury to himself. One kind old man, whose wife succeeded finally in clearing his name and securing his release, promised that he would go immediately to Long Island and find Ally.

Meanwhile, unknown to him, other friends of Crèvecoeur in the city were working to secure his release. Henry Perry sent his Negro slave to the prison to tell Crèvecoeur that he had taken Ally, still ill, to his home to care for him. Then finally William Seton, the Tory magistrate, secured his freedom by putting up a thousand pounds bail for him and guaranteeing that he would not communicate with the enemy.[39] As soon as Crèvecoeur was released he rented a horse and rushed to Mr. Perry's home at Hellgate, on the East River, where he had an emotional reunion with his son, who had despaired of ever seeing his father again. Ally was so relieved to see his father that his temperature began to fall and did not return.

After spending fifteen days with Ally in the Perry home, he returned to the city (at that time Hell's Gate was not within the incorporated limits). The cruelest winter of their lives still awaited him and his son. These experiences he narrated years later in the manuscript recently published in "Documents pour l'histoire de la Normandie." In this essay he dates his release from prison as September 17, 1779.[40] He does not say in either account why he did not stay with the Perry family longer, but perhaps he saw that he would be a burden to them, and he was always an independent and proud man. His friend Mr. Seton was himself uncomfortably lodged, with a wife and six children in crowded quarters. Even they had difficulty obtaining food and clothing for themselves.

The only lodging Crèvecoeur could find was with a couple of Welsh origin, Mr. and Mrs. Jean Pickering.[41] Before the war Pickering had been a tailor in Albany. He was loyal to King George and had served as a courier for General Cornwallis. That career ended when he was detected, pursued, and shot in the shoulder; but he had managed to destroy his dispatches, expecting capture, and had escaped to British lines at King's Bridge. British officers took him to a hospital in New York, where he recovered from his wound but was not reassigned courier duty.

Crèvecoeur gladly accepted the hospitality of the Pickerings, though all they had to offer was a barn, whose first floor had formerly been used as a stable and whose loft had stored grain, straw, and hay. The Pickerings had very little furniture, but they did have an extra folding cot, probably an army cot. At night Crèvecoeur and Ally slept in the loft and in daytime joined the Pickerings below. They had obtained rations for two from the refugee committee, which the four persons shared. By the addition of olive oil, onions, and vinegar Mrs. Pickering, whom Crèvecoeur calls a Quakeress, could make almost anything edible. Sometimes friends in the city gave Crèvecoeur cabbages, turnips, and other vegetables beginning to spoil, which they all ate with gratitude.

As winter advanced the whole city suffered from the cold, the worst in many years. Even the troops were short of wood, because the supply they had accumulated on Long Island could not be brought across the East River during December and January, when the ice was too thick for boats to break through, yet not strong enough to support a sled loaded with wood. Both soldiers and civilians cut down shade and fruit trees, even ornamental shrubs, for fuel. Anything that would burn was used, including animal fat. Crèvecoeur was delighted when a group of soldiers breaking up an old ship tied up at Corlears Hook offered to pay him in wood for helping them. He was thus able to provide fuel for Mrs. Pickering to cook their food and produce enough warmth to keep them from freezing to death.

Ally suffered most from the cold. He had no winter clothing and his father could not buy any for him. Crèvecoeur wished he had an overcoat, not for himself but to cut up to make some warm garments for Ally. However, one day while Crèvecoeur was out, perhaps chopping up the old ship, a British soldier noticed the shivering boy, asked to whom he belonged, and after Mrs. Pickering had told him of Crèvecoeur's misfortunes, he asked her to take Ally's measurements for a new suit. He then promptly had a tailor make a complete outfit of warm flannel for the boy. Before Crèvecoeur was able to meet and thank this kindhearted soldier, his company was transferred to New Brunswick, New Jersey.

Lacking warm clothes himself, Crèvecoeur contracted the fever sweeping the city. He became so weak that he almost lost the will to live. The nights were worst, when he had horrible dreams and even spells of delirium. He became a nervous wreck. He finally began to improve slowly after Mr. Seton visited him, and promised that if necessary he would adopt Ally and raise him as his own son.

Warmer weather brought the sick man some relief, though he still suffered from headaches and a nervous condition from which he would never entirely recover. After he was able to leave the house (or barn), Colonel Watson, captain of the guards, invited him to dinner, but in the middle of the meal Crèvecoeur was seized with a violent trembling, similar to an epileptic fit; Crèvecoeur himself called it "épilepsie."[42] Two soldiers carried him on a stretcher to a doctor, who gave him a dose of oil of asafetida. Twenty minutes later the trembling stopped, but he still felt almost helpless, with an overwhelming lassitude.

Later in the spring of 1780, according to Crèvecoeur's

manuscript account, he did more surveying for Trinity Church. Since he had not finished the job he had undertaken for the church the previous summer, he may indeed have resumed this employment. However, in writing about himself he was frequently unreliable about dates, and this may have been the time when he did surveying of "the Field" (City Hall Park) for the city, which he mentioned in 1784 in a letter to Robert Livingston, though there he gave the year as 1779.[43]

Crèvecoeur's account of this period of his life in New York City in the manuscript version ends with his helping Mr. Pickering, with the assistance of Mr. Seton, the "notaire royal," return to England, where he eventually secured a pension for his services to General Cornwallis. Here Crèvecoeur does not mention his own departure with Ally for England on September 1, 1780. But in *Lettres* he says, "we embarked on a ship in a convoy of one hundred and ninety sails bound for England, Scotland, and Ireland."[44] Where did he get the money for his passage? It is most likely that his friend William Seton helped him, in one way or another, but since he was going in a military convoy, it is possible that the captain of the British vessel permitted him to travel free, or for a small fee. At any rate, Crèvecoeur and his son Alexandre were finally able to start the long journey to France after their harrowing experiences in New York City.

V

Back to France

ON AUGUST 2, 1781, Crèvecoeur at last reached his old home in Normandy, some twenty-seven years after leaving it. He had been a young Frenchman of nineteen or twenty at the time of his departure and he now was forty-six years old, a middle-aged American accompanied by a nine-year-old son. Though he had not forgotten his native language, he spoke it haltingly and often incorrectly, like a foreigner.

It had taken him nearly a year to go from New York to Caen, and the trip had been far from uneventful. The ship on which he had taken passage on September 1, 1780, was part of a large convoy of eighty vessels bound for England. The ships encountered such rough weather that the convoy was scattered. Crèvecoeur's ship was wrecked off the coast of Ireland. Twenty-five years later, writing to Ally, he recalled how they were saved, and in what pitiful condition they found themselves: "You were on the shore," he wrote, "with nothing on but your shirt and your breeches, hatless, without any shoes or stockings, and your father was not much better off."[1]

Crèvecoeur was dramatizing somewhat, and he forgot to mention a rather important detail: the precious trunk which contained all his papers and manuscripts had been saved too. This trunk had gone through many adventures since he left his farm. Though the Patriots were afraid lest he should communicate useful intelligence to the British forces occupying New York, they apparently let him go with all his papers, or he managed somehow to smuggle them through their lines. Anyway, they were in his possession when he arrived in the British camp. They were carefully examined while he was under arrest by two officers sent by the British authorities. Major General Pattison thus reported to Governor Sir Henry Clinton: "they found a small trunk which . . . was opened and examined in my presence, and contained a great number of Manuscripts, the general purport of which appear [*sic*] to be a sort of irregular Journal of America, and a State of the Times of some Years back, interspersed with occasional Remarks Philosophical and Political; the tendency of the latter is to favor the side of Government and to throw odium on the Proceedings of the Opposite Party [i.e., the American Patriots], and upon the Tyranny of their Popular Government,— I have therefore ordered the Trunk to be sealed up in my own Presence, to be disposed of as you shall think proper."[2]

Crèvecoeur must eventually have recovered these papers. Some of them, however, must have been lost between his departure from his farm and his sailing from New York. He himself said: "I lost so many manuscripts whilst I was in confinement, that it is no wonder errors in fact should be there [in his *Letters*]. I lost my sketches of Maryland and so on southerly. . . ." He may have destroyed some himself before crossing the lines, for fear those which too clearly showed his Loyalist feelings should, if discovered, anger the Patriots against his wife and children.

Yet, most of them must have survived the wreck of his ship off Ireland. The best proof of this is that the first thing he did after being providentially saved was to look for a publisher for his "irregular Journal of America." It was the only way he had to raise money. Major General Pattison had accurately characterized his "Journal" when he pointed out in his report that Crèvecoeur "during his leisure hours [had] amused himself with making such literary Observations as occur'd to him, but which he is convinced will upon Perusal, do him Credit in the opinion of those attached to the King's Government. . . ."[3] They would also do him credit in the opinion of the general public, Crèvecoeur thought.

So did the publishers he found in London, Thomas Davies and Lockyer Davis, to whom he sold his manuscript for thirty guineas "on May 30th—with promise of a present if the public likes the book."[4] This represented a much larger sum of money than it would now, and Crèvecoeur must have been quite satisfied with it. He now could continue his journey home, and sailed for Ostend as soon as he could. Accompanied by Ally, he arrived at the family estate at Pierrepont on August 2.

His English publishers had made a good bargain, whatever "present"—if any—they later felt bound to give to Crèvecoeur, for his book was an immediate success when it appeared the following year. They even had to print a second edition a year later, in 1783. In the "Advertisement" which they prefixed to this edition, they specified that, contrary to the promise they had made in the first edition, there would be no "equally interesting" second volume, the author being too busy "to give the world a second collection of the American Farmer Letters."

The printing of this book was such a profitable venture that, simultaneously with the English edition, there appeared one in Dublin, published by John Exshaw, and, in 1783, a Belfast publisher, James Magee, lost no time in imitating him. No one knows whether they bought copyrights from the original London publishers and Crèvecoeur received any fee or "present" as a result, though it is unlikely that he did. Despite the last chapter on the atrocities committed by British Loyalists on the frontier, his book enjoyed great popularity.

The reason for this widespread success is that, in the years which followed the War for Independence, there was great curiosity in the British Isles, and in western Europe in general, about those extraordinary colonies which had succeeded in wresting their liberty from Great Britain. Except for *Voyage dans l'Amérique septentrionale* (*Travel in Northern America*) (1780) by Marquis François-Jean de Chastellux, who had visited America during the War for Independence as a major general in Rochambeau's army, there had appeared no book on those new United States. Moreover, many people who dreamt of migrating to America craved for authentic information about that wonderful country beyond the seas. Crèvecoeur's *Letters* answered their desires. Was it not the work of a genuine American farmer from Pennsylvania who wanted above all to inform "a friend in England" about "certain provincial situations, manners and customs, not generally known" and to convey "some idea of the late and present interior circumstances of the British Colonies in North America," as the subtitle indicated? No wonder *The Hibernian Magazine,* based in Dublin, reprinted extracts from the *Letters* even before the Irish edition came out, for it was a time when Ireland was going through a severe economic depression and many Irish people were planning to emigrate to America.

On account of its appeal to prospective immigrants, the book drew fire from a patriotic librarian at the British Museum, Samuel Ayscough. After hearing that the author was French by birth and, to make matters worse, a Catholic, he attacked the *Letters* in a witty pamphlet published anonymously and entitled: *Remarks on the Letters from an American Farmer, or a Detection of the Errors of Mr. Hector St. John; Pointing out the Pernicious Tendency of these Letters to Great Britain.* He claimed that Crèvecoeur's book was a hoax meant to attract to America English farmers who had far better stay at home. They should, he contended, turn a deaf ear to the advice of someone who was neither an American nor a farmer, contrary to what the title affirmed.

Crèvecoeur was hurt by these charges. He tried to refute them in a letter dated April 14, 1783, which he sent to the *Courier de l'Europe, Gazette Anglo-Française,* published in London. To vindicate himself, he pointed out that he had as great a right to the name American as any other American citizen. After all, nearly one-fourth of those who had fought for the independence of America were not born on American soil. Consequently, he said, his French origin did not in the least detract from the genuineness of his testimony.[5] His arguments were sound, but Ayscough's pamphlet resulted in a violent polemic. *The Gentleman's Magazine* and even *The Monthly Review,* which had originally published enthusiastic reviews of the *Letters,* sided with Ayscough. As late as 1788, Benjamin Franklin thought it necessary to defend Crèvecoeur. Addressing "a prospective emigrant," he (somewhat circumspectly) certified: "As I know the author to be an observing, intelligent man I suppose the information to be good as far as it goes."[6]

Many contemporary readers of Crèvecoeur were not as vitally interested in the literal truth of his *Letters* as the "prospective emigrant" whom Ayscough and Franklin had in mind. His book was often read for its descriptions of exotic customs in a country which had just been put on the map of the world. It was regarded as a proof that "universal benevolence" and "diffusive good will" are "not confined to the narrow limits of [one's] own country; but, on the contrary, extend to the whole human race," to quote Crèvecoeur's own words.

The merit of his work in this respect was acknowledged by the first reviewers. As early as April 1782, *The European Magazine and London Review* devoted six pages to the *Letters,* praising their vividness and reprinting long extracts from the second, third, ninth, and twelfth letters. The reviewer suspected the authenticity of the book, but did not hold this against the author, since, after all, other literary hoaxes had been perpetrated before and it did not prevent Macpherson's and Chatterton's works from being valuable additions to English literature. *The Monthly Magazine* spread the review of the *Letters* over three consecutive issues and praised the book all the more readily as it was a pro-American journal and had opposed military intervention against the Thirteen Colonies. *The Gentleman's Magazine* reproduced the letter against slavery, parts of which were also reprinted by *The Westminster Magazine, or the Pantheon of Taste.* [7]

All these magazines, however, failed to mention the charm of the book—its modesty, its sincerity, its intense appreciation of all the simple pleasures afforded by country life; in short, the author's Rousseau-like, romantic love of nature—a nature different from the tamer nature of Europe. For all his pretentious pedantry, only the literary critic and editor Baron Friedrich-Melchior von Grimm felt it. He noted in his *Correspondance littéraire, philosophique et critique:* "This book, written without method and without art, but with a high degree of sense and sensibility, perfectly fulfils the object that the author seems to have proposed: that of making the reader love America. There are to be found in it minute details, very common truths and lengthy passages; but it attracts by its simple and true pictures, by its expression of an honest soul." [8]

The book did not offer a reliable description of the life of an American farmer. Even President Washington had to acknowledge that its picture of America was in some instances "embellished with rather too flattering circumstances." [9] It reads somewhat like a journal and has all the fascination of the *Journal* of John Woolman, the Quaker tailor of New Jersey, who kept a moving record of his travels in the Thirteen Colonies and in England "in the love of the Gospel," and, like Crèvecoeur, included in his love Negro slaves as well as Red Indians. In fact, Crèvecoeur may very well have read it, since it first appeared (posthumously) in 1774. But, actually, *Letters from an American Farmer* is closer to being an epistolary novel in the tradition of Richardson or Smollett—or, rather, of Rousseau, since the author was French. It is in a way an expurgated American version of the *Nouvelle Héloïse,* in which the hero, the "farmer from Pennsylvania," leads a serene and happy life in the bosom of his family, untroubled by any unholy passion. His wife's only rival is American nature. Like Rousseau's novel, the book is full of digressions on the most diverse subjects and so can also be regarded as a loose collection of essays. It is not surprising, therefore, that such later essayists as William Hazlitt and James Russell Lowell loved it. According to Hazlitt, Crèvecoeur had "the power to sympathize with nature without thinking of ourselves or others," and this, he added, "if it is not a definition of genius, comes very near to it." Besides, Crèvecoeur knew "how American scenery and manners may be treated with a lively, poetic interest," and "wrote naturally without the dread of being thought vulgar." To James Russell Lowell, the *Letters* was "a dear book with some pages in it worthy of Gilbert White's *Selborne.*"[10]

Indeed, as the more astute readers realized, the *Letters* were not a true memoir, but a work of fiction, in which Crèvecoeur deliberately used a persona. In his introductory letter he pretended to be a "farmer from Pennsylvania," an American of English descent whose grandfather had brought with him from England "a few musty books," "a library consisting mostly of Scotch divinity, the *Navigations of Sir Francis Drake,* the *History of Queen Elizabeth,* and a few miscellaneous volumes." He thus changed his nationality, abjured his religion, and renounced his status. The better to conceal his origin, he even changed his name. Born and baptized Michel-Guillaume Jean de Crèvecoeur and originally a French nobleman and a Catholic, he now became plain Mr. James Hector St. John. This was not merely a nom-de-plume; he used it in current life under ordinary circumstances, for reasons which he never really explained. The explanation, however, is probably very simple. He wanted to turn his back on his past and become a true American, and in those days a true American was almost always assumed to be of English stock.

In his book, though, which was about an ideal rather than a real America, he gave a different definition of the term *American.* To the question "What is an American?"—a question which he probably was the first writer to pose so directly —he answered, in his third letter: "These people are a mixture of English, Scotch, Irish, French, Dutch, Germans and Swedes. From this promiscuous breed, that race now called American has arisen." It is a race among which "the rich and the poor are not so far removed from each other as they are in Europe." Each person working for himself and being sure to keep the fruits of his labor, is animated with "the spirit of an unfettered and unrestrained industry" which contributes to the welfare and prosperity of all. "The American is a new man," he concluded, "who acts upon new principles; he must therefore entertain new ideas and form new opinions." "Industry, good living, selfishness, litigiousness, country politics, the pride of [a] freem[a]n, religious indifference" are his characteristics. Such is the basis on which American society was originally resting, according to Crèvecoeur, and in the remaining letters he described with a good deal of complacency and self-satisfaction the happy consequences resulting from the application of these principles in Nantucket, South Carolina, and Pennsylvania.

But his enthusiasm did not blind him to at least two vices he lucidly detected in this otherwise idyllic utopia. First, the violence which prevailed on the frontier among people who lived "beyond the reach of government" and were "often in a perfect state of war" and "no better than carnivorous animals of a superior rank." Second, the existence in the South of an aristocracy whose wealth and prosperity were based on the ruthless exploitation of Negro slaves, who, he said, "grub up the ground, raise indigo, or husk the rice exposed to the sun full as scorching as their native one; without the support of any cheering liquor." Their masters "look not upon them with half the kindness and affection with which they consider their dogs and horses." On the contrary, they occasionally punish them with unheard-of cruelty, and Crèvecoeur gives the awful example of a slave condemned to die in a cage suspended from a tree where birds and insects eat him alive after picking out his eyes. This leads to the inevitable conclusion that "man, an animal of prey, seems to have rapine and the love of bloodshed implanted in his heart" and reserves the epithet of hero for "the most successful butchers of the world." The book thus gradually darkens and the last chapter describes "the distress of a frontier man" during the war for American independence. Unable to choose between Great Britain, the land of his fathers and his American neighbors, whom he should regard as his compatriots, the frontier man of Crèvecoeur's epistolary novel decides to take refuge with a friendly Indian tribe in the West. One utopia having failed him, he will try another, for he is confident that among the Indians living in a state of nature he will find "silence and harmony," and his children will learn "sobriety, modesty and diffidence." They will all together worship "the great Manitou of the woods and of the plains and will once more be happy and live in peace." Such was the romantic hope of this incorrigible idealist.

When in August 1781 he suddenly reappeared at his father's house, he was not yet the well known author of the *Letters,* since they would not be published until a year later. He was simply the prodigal son coming home after an absence of over a quarter of a century. His father, who had made such efforts to find him, must have been overjoyed, and delighted to discover that he had a grandson who would in time inherit the family name and estate.

Actually, the right of primogeniture was not recognized in the part of Normandy where the Crèvecoeurs lived.[11] Parents there were free to divide their possessions between their male heirs as they chose, favoring either the eldest or the youngest. Crèvecoeur did have a younger brother, Alexandre, born in 1738, who was childless. Naturally, Crèvecoeur's father would favor his elder son, since he was the one through whom the continuity of the name would be secured. This situation explains why Crèvecoeur was so keen on returning to France. Besides, he had to have Ally recognized as his legitimate heir. Crèvecoeur's marriage—celebrated by a Protestant clergyman in a foreign country—might be regarded as null and void by French courts. His desire to have Ally's status acknowledged must have been one of the reasons why he wanted so much to return to France at a definitely inopportune time. It certainly was the reason why he took Ally with him instead of leaving him behind with the rest of the family.

At Pierrepont, he found himself among gentlemen farmers passionately interested in new methods. Since he had become an American farmer, he was regarded as an agricultural expert, whose knowledge of new plants was greatly appreciated by his father's neighbors and acquaintances. One of the latter was Étienne-François Turgot, a distant relative whose aunt had married Crèvecoeur's uncle. Turgot was the elder brother of Anne-Robert-Jacques Turgot, Louis XVI's former finance minister. Like the physiocrats, Étienne believed that land was the only source of wealth, and he encouraged Crèvecoeur to publish a seventy-two page treatise on the culture of potatoes: *Traité de la culture des pommes de terre et des différents usages qu'en font les habitants des États-Unis de l'Amérique.* [12] The treatise was dedicated to the Duke d'Harcourt, governor of Normandy, and appeared in Caen on January 1, 1782. It was signed Normano-Americanus, an appropriate description of Crèvecoeur's dual loyalties.

The pamphlet told the story of the potato, its acclimatization in the British Isles and its vital importance to Ireland. It explained how it was grown and used in America, and, in conclusion, recommended its introduction into Normandy. Crèvecoeur thus was a forerunner of Antoine Parmentier, a distinguished military pharmacist who is generally credited with having introduced the cultivation of potatoes into France. Parmentier's first book on the subject did not appear until 1789, though he had praised the nutritious qualities of potatoes as early as 1773. Crèvecoeur's desert and competence were recognized in his native province, and he was elected to the Caen Society of Agriculture, a kind of local academy. His expertise was all the more appreciated as there was great need for it. Despite the efforts of a few enlightened landowners who wanted to emulate the English, agriculture in Normandy and most parts of France was still backward. The poverty of the peasants and the poor quality of the crops must have struck Crèvecoeur, just as it struck Arthur Young when he traveled through France a few years later. Young noted: "Women are now ploughing with a pair of horses to sow barley. The difference of the customs of the two nations is in nothing more striking than in the labours of the sex; in England, it is very little that they will do in the fields except to glean and make hay . . . in France they plough and fill the dung-cart." "The French have no husbandry," he concluded, "only very good roads, but they owe them to abominable 'corvées,' " which obliged the peasants to devote weeks and weeks to the upkeep of the roads instead of working on their lands.

In the middle of all his agricultural and cultural activities, Crèvecoeur did not forget America and the wife and children he had left there. Shortly after his arrival at his father's, he heard that five foreigners had landed in a small boat a few miles from Pierrepont, at Ver-sur-mer, a village close to the larger village of Creully, a few miles to the northwest of Caen. Since they spoke only English, an interpreter was needed, and Crèvecoeur rushed there to help. These foreigners, he found out, were not English (and therefore possibly enemy agents), but American naval officers who had been taken prisoner by the British two years before and detained in England. They had managed to escape and cross the Channel. Crèvecoeur took them to Pierrepont, provided them with food and clothes, and helped them to go to Lorient, where they would easily find a ship bound for America.

Naturally, he told them about his family and asked them to carry letters to his wife. The difficulty was that on their return they would probably not be free in their movements, but would be assigned some new duty by Congress. Yet one of them, Lieutenant George Little, promised Crèvecoeur that he would ask a relative living in Boston, Gustavus Fellowes, to do all he could to help. As we shall see, as soon as he landed, Little sent to Fellowes all the letters he had been entrusted with, and, by this singular stroke of luck, Crèvecoeur had a chance to come to the rescue of his two remaining children indirectly before he could do so in person.[13]

Crèvecoeur did not stay in Pierrepont long. The influential M. Turgot, who had chosen to sponsor him, thought that, with all his talents, Crèvecoeur needed a larger stage. In 1781, before the end of the year, he took Crèvecoeur to Paris, to his mansion on the Île Saint-Louis, at what is now no. 30, quai de Béthune.

It must have been an extraordinary experience for the American farmer. After all those years in America, he may have felt like Chateaubriand's Iroquois visiting "the great village" of the French.[14] He had a basis for comparison, though, since he had seen London before arriving in France. Like Arthur Young, he probably very much regretted the absence of sidewalks in the French capital, which in bad weather resulted in the omnipresence of mud. For, when it rained, the water fell directly from the roofs onto the streets. The rainwater collected in gutters in the middle of the roadway, and these gutters became true rivers impossible to cross when it rained hard. Passing coaches splashed pedestrians from head to foot.

"The streets are very narrow," Young wrote, "and many of them crowded, nine-tenths dirty. . . . Walking, which in London is so pleasant and so clean, is in Paris a toil and a fatigue to a man, and an impossibility to a well-dressed woman. The coaches are numerous, and what are much worse, there are an infinity of one-horse cabriolets [. . .] driven by young men of fashion and their imitators, alike fools, with so much rapidity as to be real nuisances, and render the streets exceedingly dangerous without incessant caution."[15]

Another drawback of Paris was that it was hardly lighted at all at night, and it was not safe to wander in most districts after dark—a dangerous time when the underworld rose to the surface.

Crèvecoeur, however, did not seem to suffer from these inconveniences. As the guest of M. Turgot, he lived in his host's spacious and handsome mansion and moved exclusively among people belonging to the upper classes. He saw only—or chiefly—the bright side of Paris, the side which justified the then popular pun: "Parisius, Paradisius" (Parisian, Paradisian). The Germans for their part coined the phrase "wie Gott in Frankreich leben" (to live like God in France). The Prince de Ligne, after visiting Paris, exclaimed: "It is a glimpse of fairyland!"

Paris was a conglomeration of squalid districts like Faubourg St.-Antoine, which the Russian historian Nikolai Karamzin in his *Letters of a Russian Traveler* (1789–90) compared to the gates of Dante's Hell, and of the most elegant and luxurious quarters, which must have filled Crèvecoeur with wonder and admiration. What a change after the simple life he had led on his American farm, where his literary tastes were looked upon with suspicion! He now found himself in brilliant circles among wealthy aristocrats who treated writers and scientists as their equals and were not ashamed to show the keenest intellectual curiosity. This also impressed Arthur Young: "Persons of the highest rank pay an attention to science and literature and emulate the character they confer. I should pity the man who expected, without the advantages of a very different nature, to be well received in a brilliant circle in London, because he was a fellow of the Royal Society. But this would not be the case with a member of the Academy of Sciences at Paris; he is sure of a good reception everywhere." For his part, the Count de Ségur noted: "This mixture of courtiers and men of letters enlightened the former and gave the latter a finer taste [. . .]. We preferred a word of praise from d'Alembert or Diderot to the most exalted favor of a prince."[16]

Ever since the 1620s, when Mme. de Rambouillet held her famous *salon* and the "Précieuses" followed her example, literary *salons* had been a lively tradition in Paris. In the latter half of the eighteenth century, they were flourishing more brilliantly than ever—dominated by women, as they had been in the preceding century. "You could see there," as Count de Ségur reminisced in his *Mémoires,* "an undefinable combination of simplicity and high-mindedness, grace and reason, criticism and toleration [. . .]. People discussed calmly, hardly ever disputed, and, as a delicate tactfulness made people expert in the art of pleasing, boredom was avoided, for no one overinsisted on anything in particular. The most often applied principle was the one laid down by Boileau, which recommends 'constantly to pass from grave to light, from pleasant to severe subjects.' So people spoke successively in the same evening 'of *The Spirit of Laws* and Voltaire's *Tales,* of Helvétius's philosophy and Sedaine's or Marmontel's operas, of La Harpe's tragedies and the licentious stories of Abbé de Voisenon, of the discoveries of the Indies as told by Abbé Raynal, of Collé's songs and Mably's politics, and Saint-Lambert's or Abbé Delille's charming verse.' "[16a]

Though these pre-Revolutionary years were characterized by violent differences of opinions, there still reigned in the Parisian *salons* a remarkable social equality which greatly contributed to their charm and acted as a powerful stimulant. It electrified the conversation both of the poets, writers, and scientists who frequented them and of their aristocratic admirers.

For scientists were not forgotten in these feasts of the intellect. In this lay the main difference between seventeenth- and eighteenth-century *salons*. Fontenelle with his *Entretiens sur la pluralité des mondes* had made astronomy a popular subject. Jean Astruc, a well-known physician, was one of the mainstays of Mme. de Tencin's salon and the naturalist Buffon of Mme. Necker's. There was no *salon* without at least one scientist.

It was a cosmopolitan society, too. Bolingbroke and Chesterfield were at home at Mme. de Tencin's, Horace Walpole at Mme. du Deffand's, the Neapolitan ambassador Carraccioli at Mme. Necker's, Grimm at Mme. d'Épinay's (it was rumored she was his mistress as well as his hostess), Stanislaw Ponniatowski, the future king of Poland, at Mme. Geoffrin's, and Benjamin Franklin at Mme. d'Helvétius's. The presence of so many distinguished foreigners further contributed to the eclecticism of the *salons* and showed the openmindedness and the insatiable intellectual curiosity of the ladies who presided over them—and that of their guests.

Those who attended the *salons* loved the intoxication of talk, and lively conversation became an end in itself. "Speech," Mme. de Staël proclaimed, "is a liberal art which has no purpose and no use [. . .]. In France, conversation is not a means to communicate ideas, feelings, personal problems; it is an instrument people like to play on. It stimulates the mind like music in some nations and strong liquor in others [. . .]. The feeling of well-being which a lively conversation makes you experience does not lie in the topic discussed. The ideas and information which it contains are not its main interest [. . .]. What matters is a certain way of behaving towards one another, of pleasing each other and displaying one's wit by one's delivery, gesture and look, lastly of emitting a sort of electricity which produces sparks, relieves some of the speakers of the very excess of their vivacity and rouses the others from their painful apathy."[17]

Mme. Geoffrin, Mme. du Deffand, and Mlle. de Lespinasse were dead when Crèvecoeur arrived in Paris, but one of their successors, Mme. d'Épinay carried on the tradition and reigned at La Chevrette near Montmorency. Diderot loved to go there and shine. After marrying a wealthy cousin who soon abandoned her, Mme. d'Épinay had become the mistress of one Dupin Francueil, the son of a very rich farmer-general and receiver of royal finances, who indulged all her whims but after a time left her alone. She then had a thirty-year liaison with Grimm, who co-presided over her *salon*. Rousseau, who did not like the couple, described her as "very lean, very pale, with as much bosom as on my hand" and Grimm as "the White Tyrant [. . .] as conceited as he was vain, with his big dim eyes and his loose-limbed body." But tastes differed. To Diderot, Grimm was a dear friend, as dear as Sophie Volland, his lifelong correspondent. To his mind, Rousseau was ungrateful, for Mme. d'Épinay had lent him a cottage in her park, L'Ermitage, where he spent some very happy months. It was there in the late 1750s that he wrote his famous epistolary novel *La Nouvelle Héloïse,* after falling in love with Mme. d'Épinay's cousin, Madame d'Houdetot, Crèvecoeur's friend and protectress.

Mme. d'Houdetot was not handsome, Rousseau admitted, but "her face was both lively and sweet, and tender [. . .] she had a forest of naturally curly black hair which fell down to her knees [. . .] all her movements were full of awkwardness and grace at the same time [. . .]. As for her character, it was angelic and contained all virtues."[18] Gouverneur Morris, who met her some ten years later, saw her quite differently: "At Madame Laborde's," he noted in his diary, "I was introduced to Madame d'Houdetot, who is the *protectrice* of Crèvecoeur, who is much courted by the academicians, who was the only beloved of Rousseau and who is I think one of the ugliest women I ever saw, even without her squint, which is of the worst kind."[19] He was definitely unfair to her. Her portraits show that she squinted only very slightly, and this "coquetterie," as it is sometimes called euphemistically, hardly detracted from her charm. It is true, however, that the smallpox she caught as a child irremediably damaged her features and her complexion. Those who knew her reputation as a lover were generally disappointed when they first met her. Thus Mme. Vigée-Lebrun gave this description of her in her *Pen and Ink Portraits*: "I knew she was not pretty, but after the passion she had inspired in J. J. Rousseau, I thought I would at least find her face pleasant, but I was quite disappointed when I saw her so plain that her romance immediately faded from my mind. It must be acknowledged, however, that her nice disposition could make you forget her ugliness."[20]

Even those who looked at her most critically were susceptible to her apparently irresistible charm. This was the case in particular of a young neighbor of hers, Viscountess Allard: "It will be a comfort," she wrote, "to all plain women to learn that Madame d'Houdetot, who was very much so, owed to her wit and, above all, to her charming character the fact that she was so passionately loved and with such constancy. As Rousseau said, her movements were both awkward and graceful; her very short sight gave her uncertainty, but, as she was shapely and had had the famous Marcel as a dancing-master, she was very graceful. Her bosom was beautiful, her hands and arms pretty, her feet dainty." In spite of adverse testimony, she must have cut a very acceptable figure.

That she was quite witty is confirmed by a remark she made at a dinner after Rousseau helped himself to a peach at the bottom of a pyramid of fruit and made the whole structure collapse: "This is how you do when you attack social institutions! You pull everything down with a single gesture, but who will rebuild what you are destroying?" On another occasion, she brilliantly improvised a short speech on the three ages of man: "Without women, man would be helpless at the beginning of his life, without any pleasure in the middle and without comfort at the end."

While still in her teens, she had been married against her will to Count d'Houdetot, who, according to Rousseau, was "as ugly as the devil," and who remained faithful for nearly fifty years to the mistress he had before his marriage. Fortunately, his young bride soon encountered Jean-François de Saint-Lambert, who far surpassed her husband in looks, wit, and talents. They became lovers and remained faithful to each other until the death of Saint-Lambert—though she dutifully had three children by her husband. There was no room for Rousseau in this unbreakable triangle. Mme. d'Houdetot was a virtuous sinner who could deceive her husband, but not her lover. Yet she agreed to take walks with Rousseau in the park and the woods around L'Ermitage. They had long conversations, which gave him "a delicious thrill such as no woman had ever given him before." And that was all. His passion was bound to remain platonic. The only outlet he found for it was the passionate letters exchanged between Julie and Saint-Preux in *La Nouvelle Héloïse* (the manuscript of which he gave to Madame d'Houdetot). We owe his masterpiece to the fidelity (outside marriage) of Mme. d'Houdetot. To Rousseau, the poet in prose, she preferred the versifier to whom she had given her faith, for Saint-Lambert was a writer, too, the author of a long descriptive poem entitled *Les Saisons* in imitation of James Thomson's *The Seasons*. Voltaire, when the poem first appeared, recognized Saint-Lambert's merits as a minor poet and called him:

> *The singer of true pleasures and harmonious imitator*
> *Of the pastor from Mantua and of sweet Tibullus.*

Later, when he was in a less friendly and more candid mood, his praise would turn ironical:

Saint-Lambert that noble author whose pedantic Muse
Writes poems much praised by Voltaire whom he praises.

Count d'Houdetot was, like Crèvecoeur, a Norman by birth and owned an estate near Pierrepont. The two families were on friendly terms, and so Madame d'Houdetot heard of his return from America shortly after his arrival. She invited him to visit her in Paris. As he had heard of her *salon* and her reputation as the distinguished friend of a number of scientists and writers, he felt shy and at first hesitated to accept her invitation. "I wrote to her," he said, "to postpone until an indefinite date the honor of calling on her to present my respects and thanks, giving my poor health as an excuse." He added: "I don't know

what she observed in the style of my letter (which I wrote first in English and then translated into French as best I could), but the quaint turn of my sentences, my use of words which I then thought French, instead of inspiring her with contempt for a man who did not even know her language, still increased her desire to see me [. . .]. She wrote me a second letter still kinder than the first to tell me she consented that I should adjourn my visit till I was fully recovered. I was congratulating myself on my success; more than one month's silence made me hope she had forgotten me, when I was unexpectedly threatened with her visit. It was Girard [her factotum] who brought me her letter. Overcome by this last manifestation of her kindness, I took the decision to obey her injunction [. . .]. How that lady welcomed me! With what promptitude she guessed my thoughts and reassured me! How, thanks to her perseverance, and a number of flattering, imperceptible little things, she made a new man of me! What rapid progress in my knowledge of French and the usages of the world, etc. the desire to please this new friend made me achieve!"[21]

He succeeded so well in pleasing her that he was soon regarded as an old friend of the family. She invited him to stay in her house in Paris, "rue Saint Honoré, near Place Vendôme." He also occasionally followed her to her country place at Sannois, not far from Eaubonne, where she had formerly rented a house close to L'Ermitage and La Chevrette—and within walking distance of an estate which Saint-Lambert owned there.

Mme. d'Houdetot must have been quite pleased with the addition she had made to her *salon,* for Crèvecoeur was paraded wherever she went and introduced to all her friends. Here was a specimen of that strange new man, the American farmer. His awkward and halting French confirmed his genuineness and further contributed to his charm. He was showered with invitations by all of Madame d'Houdetot's friends and acquaintances, who included the Duke de La Rochefoucauld, the Duke de Liancourt (with whom he was to correspond so frequently during his consulship in New York), d'Estissac, Breteuil, Rohan-Chabot, Beauvau, and Madame Necker (who nearly married historian Edward Gibbon before becoming the wife of the Swiss banker). They all wanted their share of the American savage Madame d'Houdetot had so luckily captured. Crèvecoeur met a number of writers too, among them the famous mathematician and philosopher d'Alembert; Abbé Delille, the poet; Jean-François Marmontel, a clever and versatile writer; the poet, playwright, and critic Jean-François La Harpe; Jean-Baptiste Suard, the literary critic whose wife had a brilliant *salon* of her own; the German expatriate Grimm; and a well-known lawyer with literary inclinations, Dr. Jean-Baptiste Target, who became one of his best friends, "my friend Target, the best of men," as he called him. The American farmer was gradually turning into a true French *philosophe.*

VI

"Farmer" Becomes French *Philosophe*

CRÈVECOEUR'S METAMORPHOSIS in France from "farmer" to *philosophe* was actually not so extraordinary as might be thought, for from the beginning of his writings he was a *philosophe* in disguise, as the dedication of *Letters from an American Farmer* to Abbé Raynal amply proved. In it he declared himself "a sincere admirer" of Raynal's *Political and Philosophical History of the European Settlements in the Two Indies.* As "an humble American planter," he had read it in English, he said—which was probably a fact and not fiction, for, if we are to believe his friend Pierre-Louis de Lacretelle's testimony in the *Mercure de France* in 1783: "Having chosen England as his country in his youth, he threw himself whole-heartedly into the English language; it is in this language that he read and wrote."[1] At any rate, whether he read Abbé Raynal's book in French or English, he did read it "with infinite pleasure" and adopted Raynal's views on "universal benevolence." He espoused Raynal's abolitionism, his admiration for Quakers and, generally speaking, his faith in America "as the asylum of freedom, the cradle of future nations and the refuge of distressed Europeans."[2] In short, he felt with him a strange "intellectual consanguinity." It is not surprising, therefore, that he defended in his *Letters from an American Farmer* some of the ideas dear to the *philosophes* of the Diderot-Grimm-Raynal school, and this greatly contributed to the success of his book and to his popularity in Parisian *salons*. Though he had never been in Paris before, he immediately felt at home there. He was perfectly attuned to the French intelligentsia of the time. There was a kind of preestablished harmony between him and the new acquaintances he was making—and it was all due to Raynal's book.

One of Raynal's pet ideas was that of the purity and original innocence of so-called savages. Whatever cruelty they might occasionally display, in his book he always emphasizes their heroic stoicism, especially in the chapter "Government, Customs, Virtues, Vices, Wars of the Savages Living in Canada." Raynal represents them as true democrats living in a state of perfect liberty (since the decisions of their councils were not binding, and the majority never oppressed the minority) and of complete equality (since they had no personal belongings and shared everything they had). They lacked only one thing: "the felicity of loving woman."

Crèvecoeur may have heard some of these arguments in the very *salon* of Count de Buffon, the aristocratic author of the learned and elegantly written *Histoire naturelle* in forty-four volumes, twenty-four of which had already appeared by that time. He was taken—or rather exhibited—there by Turgot at the beginning of his stay in Paris, and it was at Buffon's table and in his *salon* that, in Crèvecoeur's own words, for the first time "during the long winter evenings, [he] suddenly became aware of the charms, beauties and delicate purity of our language, which, during [his] long stay in Northern America, had become strange to [him] and the practice—though not the memory—of which [he] had almost lost." He listened with wonder and admiration to "the luminously instructive" explanations of "this great painter of nature whose works [he] had just read"[3] and who tirelessly answered his questions.

During his two years in Paris Crèvecoeur was in great demand as a witness to American achievements in the New World. Everyone wanted to entertain him, especially in the summer, when members of the aristocracy left Paris and Versailles to spend the season in the castles they owned in the vicinity of the capital. He was a frequent guest at Le Marais, which belonged to Mme. d'Houdetot's brother, Alexis-Janvier La Live de la Brèche; at Méréville, where he was invited by M. de Laborde, a famous financier; at La Roche-Guyon, the estate of the Duke de La Rochefoucauld; and at Val, the property of Marshal de Beauvau, where he had a chance to apply Franklin's discovery and install a lightning conductor. He later explained in a letter to his son-in-law, Count Otto, that he used as a mast, with Franklin's approval (for he consulted him about the matter), two fine poplars carefully squared and painted green; with the rod, they were eighty-nine feet high and taller than the surrounding buildings. The conductor was installed in the presence of a large number of the marshal's friends, who afterward followed his example and had lightning rods placed on their mansions in Paris.[4]

Though Franklin was in France at the time, it seems that Crèvecoeur never had a chance to see him. Mme. d'Houdetot informed Franklin of Crèvecoeur's arrival even before she had met him herself. So, when Crèvecoeur in his turn wrote to Franklin about some other matter, Franklin answered him on September 21, 1781, in these terms:

"Sir, I should have answered your letter of the 7th but it happened to be mislaid. Inclos'd I send the letter you desire for Governor Hancock [. . .]. Madame la Comtesse d'Houdetot had warmly recommended to me a M. Crèvecoeur who had been long in America. Please inform me if you are the same person."

Crèvecoeur hastened to confirm that he was indeed the person in question. By return post, probably, on September 26, he wrote to Franklin:

Sir,

Yes Sir I am the same person whom Madame de [*sic*] Houdetot has been so kind as to mention to you—the reason for this mistake proceeds from the singularity of ye french customs, which renders their names almost arbitrary, and often leads them to forget their family ones; it is in consequence of this that there are more alias dictums [*sic*] in this than in any other country in Europe. The name of our family is St. Jean, in English St. John, a name as ancient as the conquest of England by William the Bastard.

I am so great a stranger to the manners of this tho' my native country having quitted it very young that I never dreamt I had any other than the old family name. I was greatly astonished when at my late return, I saw myself under the necessity of being called by that of Crèvecoeur. Excuse this tedious explanation, which I hope you will not think improper, as I have run the risk of remaining unknown to you, or of loosing [*sic*] the good effects which were intended by Madame la Comtesse de Houdetot in mentioning me to you. I don't mean to be troublesome, very far from it, I am much more ambitious of ye honor of your esteem than of any thing else; I flatter myself with being able to cultivate the honor of your acquaintance this winter being invited to spend [illegible] the marquis de Turgot's house, brother to the late comptroller general.[5]

By August 1782, however, the paths of Franklin and Crèvecoeur had not yet crossed, and on August 10, Mme. d'Houdetot once more wrote to Franklin about him:

This spring, my dear Doctor, I was given the hope of seeing you at Sannois some day, in that place where at least I keep the memory of the moments which you were kind enough to spend there and where I still cultivate with tender care the monuments which you left behind. [Mme. d'Houdetot was alluding to the American acacia that Franklin planted in her park with elaborate ceremony on April 22, 1781.] The losses which I have undergone and the circumstances under which I have found myself have not allowed me this year to go and tell you in your very house my eagerness to receive you again in my home and to cultivate the feelings you flattered me with before. My dear Doctor, may I invoke them on a special occasion for the sake of an American who has just arrived and must be introduced to you without delay; he is of French descent, but lived for a long time in your country under the protection of your laws, which he respects. He has come here to see his family after losing the greater part of his possessions in the present war; his name is Crèvecoeur and he is the son of a friend of more than twenty years' standing of my husband and myself. I am asking for him all the kindness and protection which may be in your power, and if circumstances allow. I cannot add anything, my dear Doctor, to the feelings of affection and veneration which you have inspired, except the regret not to be able to renew their assurance as often as I would like. It is with these feelings, my dear Doctor, that I have the honor of being for ever your humble and most obedient servant.[5a]

Though Crèvecoeur did not meet Franklin, his stay in Paris was an almost uninterrupted succession of dinners and receptions. He found this new life enjoyable and stimulating—quite a change from his years on the frontier in America. "The conversation," he wrote in his unpublished "Souvenirs de Mme. d'Houdetot" ("Reminiscences of Mme. d'Houdetot"), "was a delicious combination of anecdotes, jests, gossip of the day, comments and judgments on new books, seasoned with French wit, vivaciousness and gaiety at their most captivating. Count d'Houdetot, who was more of a soldier and a practical-minded person than a scholar, often told me on the eve of one of those dinners: 'Come now, my friend, don't take it into your head to let us down to-morrow; you'll replace me, I insist upon it! This superabundance of wit tires me. It is so often noisy. I'll go and dine with some good old friends, who, like me, care only for a good time [. . .]. Take care not to become too bookish! we already have a surfeit of such people.' "6

M. d'Houdetot's warning was timely, for Crèvecoeur was indeed turning more and more into a writer of books, especially after the success of his *Letters from an American Farmer* in England became known in Paris. His friends, Mme. d'Houdetot and Mme. de Beauvau in particular, encouraged him to publish his own French translation of the book. He protested that his French was not adequate, but Lacretelle ignored his objections and insisted in the *Mercure de France* that "no one could translate his work better than himself, for such a translation requires much less purity and elegance than originality in the choice of the subjects and in their treatment."7

Crèvecoeur allowed himself to be persuaded. In 1782, he interrupted his round of visits and receptions and spent the summer on his father's estate working at what was to be, rather than a mere translation, an entirely new version of the *Letters.* He must have worked very hard and at great speed, for, when it appeared, the French edition of the *Letters* was twice as long as the English text. However, Crèvecoeur was helped by the fact that he was not writing a new text. He was merely translating, on the one hand, nearly all the original *Letters,* and, on the other hand, "letters," or chapters, he had not used for the English edition but had brought with him from America in his famous trunk. As to the translation proper, it was much speeded up no doubt by the help given him by all his friends, Mme. d'Houdetot herself and Saint-Lambert, as well as Prince and Princess de Beauvau and perhaps Louis de Lacretelle and Dr. Jean-Baptiste Target. They revised the first draft as it came from his pen and so, as early as January 1783, de Lacretelle could publish in the *Mercure de France* a sample of the work in progress—which may even have been completed at this date. The sample was an extract from the letter about Walter Mifflin, the Quaker abolitionist.

Lettres d'un cultivateur américain should have appeared in

1783, for Lacretelle concluded his introductory note with the promise that "if the pieces which I beg you to receive rouse the public interest, the book will soon appear with some changes and additions." Its publication was delayed by an unfortunate incident: the manuscript was lost. Between January 8 and April 4, it disappeared from the office of the director of the book trade ("le directeur des librairies"), whose permission ("privilège") was necessary if the book was to be published lawfully. Crèvecoeur wrote the following explanation to the editor of the *Courier de l'Europe* on April 14:

> You announce that the Author [of *Letters from an American Farmer*] was about to produce the translation of a book published by Mr. Thomas Davis. I know that he has translated not only this volume, but two more besides, whose English originals he had kept. The fear of rousing the anger of British critics, [because of the distinctly pro-American character of the new version] a singular chain of circumstances have just deprived him of three hundred and twenty pages in-folio; he hopes that this note will warn the publisher into whose hands these sheets might fall, that the author is now busy retranscribing them and that the fruit of this legerdemain is not even one half of all that is to appear shortly.

In a letter to the editor of the *Mercure de France* dated January 20, 1784, Lacretelle told the same story and gave the same warning:

> A very regrettable and quite unexpected accident has delayed the publication of this book. The manuscript has been lost just as it was about to be printed. The author had to do his work all over again; this new work is now in the press. I beg you, Sir, to give the public this information in order to prevent foreign booksellers from making use of the first manuscript.[8]

Though the publication was delayed, Crèvecoeur did not have to do his work all over again; he had probably kept a rough draft and could restore the text within a short time. In fact, the new manuscript was ready by June or July. This delay, however, prevented him from seeing his book when it appeared, for by the end of 1784 he was no longer in France.

There were still other obstacles to overcome—obstacles that show that the loss of the first manuscript was not entirely an accident. Crèvecoeur and his friends encountered great difficulties when they applied for the license to print the book. The manuscript was submitted to the keeper of the seals ("Garde des Sceaux"), a M. Gaillard, and to the Count de Vergennes, the minister of foreign affairs. The latter was quite liberal and saw no objection to the publication of the book, but the former, a timid civil servant, found it much too bold. He was right. It was fundamentally a rather lengthy apology for political and religious freedom. It exalted values which were all right for the New World, but heretical and dangerous in France. Paris was not Philadelphia. Though Crèvecoeur did not directly attack French institutions, the book was dangerous because it praised American democracy and the toleration and happiness which prevailed on American soil.

Faced with this opposition, Crèvecoeur did not know what to do. "It is regrettable," he wrote to the Duke de La Rochefoucauld on September 3, 1783, "that ideas which are commonplaces in Philadelphia should seem so terrible in Paris. As to the excessive length of the book, the censor probably does not know that the author ploughed and worked with his hands more often than he wrote; if I am to cut out what is considered lengthy, i.e. imperfections, there will remain very little." His friends did not give up the fight, though, and they finally obtained what was called a *permission tacite,* an unofficial permission to print the book, for in eighteenth-century France authorities were much less tyrannical in practice than they were in principle. Besides, there was little coordination between the various government departments. What was forbid-den by one was sometimes allowed by another. *Les lettres d'un cultivateur américain* eventually appeared in December 1784, after Saint-Lambert, Target, and Lacretelle had found a prin-ter for it (Cuchet, rue Serpente in the Latin Quarter) and read the proofs in the author's absence.

In spite of outward resemblances and identical titles, *Les lettres d'un cultivateur américain* and *Letters from an American Farmer* differed appreciably both in content and tone. The French edition contained considerably more material than the original edition in English. Crèvecoeur had added a number of anecdotes, as he called them, and new chapters, including those on Virginia, Canada, Jamaica and the Bermudas, and Martha's Vineyard. But the main difference between the two editions was qualitative rather than quantitative. Crèvecoeur now espoused the political views of his Parisian friends who had encouraged him to publish this French version of his experiences and helped him prepare it. *Les Lettres* were more strongly pro-American and anti-British than the *Letters*.

The book opens with a rather fulsome dedicatory letter to the Marquis de Lafayette, who had come to the rescue of those American Revolutionists whom Crèvecoeur used to abhor and who had helped destroy the earthly paradise in which the American farmer used to live. Moreover, there was a chapter at the end of the first volume on all the cruel persecutions he had had to suffer in New York at the hands of the British before he was allowed to embark for France. He also compla-cently described the atrocities committed by the English and their Indian allies, and even went out of his way to stigmatize the atrocities of which the English had been guilty in Bengal at the other end of the world. Generally speaking, he aligned himself much more closely with the *philosophes*. Thus, Crève-coeur avoided the word for "God" (*Dieu*), which, for the *philo-sophes* smacked far too much of Romish superstition. Like them, he preferred to speak of "l'Être Suprême" (the Supreme Being) or "le Tout-Puissant" (the Almighty). The new book was indeed tailored to meet the demands of the time.

Naturally, Crèvecoeur wanted to return to the United States as soon as possible to find out what had become of his wife and children. He had had no news of them since his departure from his farm. His tireless activity in Paris may well have been an attempt to keep them off his mind. So it was a great relief to him when peace between the Thirteen Colonies and Great Britain was at last in sight. He followed with great impatience the protracted negotiations which were going on in Paris.

He has himself told how he unexpectedly became involved in them as an expert on America.

At last the news spread in Paris of the arrival of the English and American commissioners. From then on in all circles nothing counted any more except this great and important thing. Much to my surprise, my good Countess, whom I had never heard talking politics, suddenly started arguing as skilfully as the most clever. But what surprised me still more, were the frequent trips to Versailles that she was making, trips whose purpose the Count and his family seemed to be quite ignorant of. She probably goes there, I thought to myself, to press for the promotion of her husband, who was not yet at that date lieutenant-general of the King's Armies. [Crèvecoeur, who wrote this memoir some thirty years later, was in error, for Count d'Houdetot had been lieutenant general since 1780.] Such were my suppositions when, on her return from her fifth trip, she ordered Girard to invite me to call on her as soon as I came back [. . .]. The face of the good Countess, which was more vivacious than usual, seemed to announce something fortunate. "Rejoice, my friend," she told me, "I bring you a package of good news. The Minister of the Navy [Marshal de Castries] has a pressing need to borrow part of the vast knowledge you have acquired during your long sojourn in the English colonies [. . .]. Here is what

he wants: You must answer in writing the numerous questions he will ask you about the population, agriculture,
industry, etc. [. . .] Do you feel in a position to carry out
this task?"—"Yes, my angel of kindness and friendship,"
I answered with eyes full of tears and kissing her tenderly.
"I can flatter myself I am capable of satisfying the Minister's demands from A to Z."—"Since it is so, (I was sure
of it in advance,) you will go to Versailles to-morrow,
you'll settle in my husband's apartment [. . .]. You'll dine
as often as you wish at Duke d'Harcourt's, for I have seen
him about it knowing that he thinks very highly of you. I
have been asked to extend the same invitation on behalf
of Baron de Breteuil [minister of the king's household], an
old friend of your father's. Marquis de Tilly and several
other officers of the City of Caen will also see you with
pleasure."[9]

Crèvecoeur left for Versailles without delay and set to
work immediately. With the help of two secretaries, he prepared a report which, at the end of seven weeks, he handed
to Marshal de Castries. The minister was enthusiastic, Crèvecoeur recalled:

"The geographical part of your answers, based on your
fine English maps of whose publication I did not know, has
greatly pleased the King, who is quite versed in this science. All that you have brought to my notice about the
activity and industry of the Americans, the forms of colonial government so little known here before the present
war, has interested me so vividly that I have ordered your
notes to be bound in order to preserve them. As soon as
the number and location of the consulates and vice-consu-
lates which we will open in that country are decided, I'll
have your name as consul put at the head of the list which
I will present to His Majesty. To what town of the new
continent would you prefer to be appointed?"
More deeply moved perhaps than I should have
shown: "New York, my Lord!" I answered him, daring to

take his hand, "it is the town in which I spent many years
as well as in the State of which it is the capital!" [Albany
was not yet the capital.][10]

The minister kept his promise. Crèvecoeur's appointment
to the New York (as well as New Jersey and Connecticut)
consulship was signed on June 22, 1783, though there were
seventeen candidates for the position. All his friends flocked
to Versailles to congratulate him. Cadet de Vaux, a well-
known chemist and friend of Parmentier's, who had founded
the *Journal de Paris* a few years before, inserted a flattering note
in his paper. Buffon wrote to congratulate him. And, on top
of it all, he was elected correspondent of the Academy of
Sciences for his work as an agronomist. In short, honors were
showered upon him. He was overjoyed, not only because it
flattered his vanity, but also because he hoped at last to be
reunited with his family.

He left Caen as soon as he could to say good-bye to his
father and his elder son Alexandre and sailed for New York
on a French packet, the *Courier de l'Europe,* after taking the
precaution of having a lightning rod erected upon it. The ship
belonged to a line of regular packets plying between Lorient
and New York which he had tried to organize before leaving
France. It was an idea of his own and it received the blessing
and financial support of the Duke de Castries. But even in
those days much red tape was involved and there were times
when Crèvecoeur cursed the whole undertaking, all the more
as he had failed to receive the advance of three thousand
French pounds which he had been promised on his salary as
consul. He once felt so discouraged that he confided to the
Duke de La Rochefoucauld: "Ah, if I only had a two-hundred-
pound income, I would go back to cultivate my land and my
friends and would leave the consulship to whoever'd want
it."[11] There was definitely a thwarted Candide dormant in
him.

M. de Castries was impatient to have him go. "It is advisable," he wrote to one of his agents on August 10, 1783, "that he should embark on the first ship that will set sail from Lorient on the 15th of next month." Crèvecoeur was equally impatient to return to America, but he had difficulties which he very humbly and candidly set forth in a letter to the minister dated Caen, August 27:

> I have received your order to leave from L'Orient [sic] on the first packet-boat that is to sail from there. Will you take it amiss if a man whom you have deigned to honor with your kindnesses takes the liberty of informing you of the difficulties in which he finds himself on account of the cost of the voyage.
>
> With the little money that the war has left me, I have to pay for the education and upkeep of a dear child whom I leave here. I take with me a secretary, and this necessarily will double the expense. I will land in a half destroyed city which will be almost deserted, when all the Royalists have left. I will find my plantation burnt to the ground. Shall I dare, owing to all these circumstances, to beg you to grant me free passage on the packet-boat and give the necessary orders to pay me in advance as much of my salary as you think fit?
>
> It required no less than the extraordinary difficulties in which I find myself to decide me to make a request of this kind.[12]

Marshal de Castries decided two days later to grant free passage to Crèvecoeur and his secretary and give him the advance of £3,000. Crèvecoeur could thus take passage on the very first ship of the new line to sail for America, but it sailed later than originally planned and the crossing was long and uncomfortable, lasting fifty-four days. This is how the *Pennsylvania Packet* of December 6 described the voyage: "We hear that the Packet from L'Orient [sic] lately arrived in New York, met with extremely bad weather on the passage, and after being eight days at sea was obliged to put back to the port whence she came, by which means the Definitive Treaty, which had just arrived, was put on board her. When she arrived on the American coast, she was several times driven off by contrary winds. The last time, not having for many days had an observation, they were at a loss how to proceed. When they came in sight of several ships, among which was an English man of war, whose captain sent his boat [*sic*] on board with a lieutenant and his compliments, requesting that they would take on board and carry back a Pilot they had on board, and by reason of bad weather had been obliged to carry on with them. The Captain of the Packet gladly complied, and a few days later got into the Hook" [i.e., Sandy Hook, New Jersey].[13]

VII

Consul in New York

CRÈVECOEUR RETURNED to New York on November 19, 1783,[1] at one of the most exciting times in American history.[2] After Britain and America had tried for two years to negotiate a peace treaty in Paris, they finally succeeded. With the arrival of the *Courier de l'Europe,* carrying the final draft of the treaty as well as Crèvecoeur, the British army would evacuate the city in six days, after eight months of preparation. While General Washington waited with his troops two miles away on Harlem Heights, General Guy Carleton was working feverishly to meet the promised deadline for withdrawing British troops. Although Crèvecoeur was keenly interested in every detail of these historical events, at the time of his landing and for days afterward he could think of little except his own worries and fears. For three years he had not been able to get any information about his wife and the two children he had left at Pine Hill.

His heart pounding and his nerves tingling, he stumbled onto the dock. William Seton, his New York merchant friend, was not in sight, but he spotted a man he knew and asked him if he had heard anything about his wife and children. Yes, the man said, he had; Mrs. Crèvecoeur was dead, the house had burned to the ground, and someone had taken the children, but he didn't know where. At this news Crèvecoeur staggered and would have fallen had not Mr. Seton rushed up at that moment and caught him. Seton had doubted that Crèvecoeur would be on the *Courier de l'Europe,* and only at the last moment had decided to meet it anyway. He tried to comfort his friend with reassuring words and invited him to his home to stay as long as he wished.[3] He said he had tried to locate the children and would continue to do so.

Pale and still trembling, Crèvecoeur managed with Seton's help to climb into a carriage. He said he had had a very difficult crossing. The weather had been stormy all the way; the ship had several times been blown off course, and the trip had taken fifty-four days, instead of the usual four or five weeks. He had been ill most of that time, and the epileptic symptoms he had first experienced in New York after being released from prison had returned. Mr. Seton could see that he was a very sick man.

The whole town was in a feverish state of excitement over the impending departure of the British troops, which would bring great changes. A civilian government would take charge again, most Loyalists would leave, and the Patriots would return—several thousand of them. The Loyalists, still called Tories, were the big problem. Many of those remaining loyal to the king had seen their property confiscated by the American rebels. After the surrender of Lord Cornwallis at Yorktown on October 19, 1781, the British government had promised to protect their rights, but eventually Parliament, in its anxiety to obtain a peace treaty, had abandoned them to the jurisdiction of the state governments. Even the Loyalists whose homes had been occupied by British officers had great difficulty collecting the compensation they had been promised. All that Great Britain was willing to do was to provide transportation to some place of their choice; and if they were willing to emigrate to Canada, especially Nova Scotia, which was thinly settled, they might receive free grants of land.[4]

The exact number who accepted this offer is not known, but they numbered in the thousands. For example, on April 26, 1774, ten ships carried three thousand to St. John in New Brunswick, and during the summer twenty thousand more sailed to Canada. Historians agree that General Carleton, who had assumed command in May 1782, was competent, honest, and as humane as he could possibly be, but he was faced with the almost impossible task of providing ships for the emigration of the Loyalists while at the same time trying to assemble enough ships to carry British troops and military equipment back to England.

The exact number of troops who returned to England is also difficult to estimate, because many had deserted, and others had decided (as Crèvecoeur had done in Canada) to stay rather than return home. Ironically, many Hessian soldiers, whom the Americans had hated even more than the British at the beginning of the Revolution, were now warmly encouraged to settle. But even with these subtractions from the number of people leaving New York, the transportation problem was enormous. About fifteen hundred persons was the limit for the largest sailing vessels. The limited shipping space did not permit the transportation of livestock and household goods which most of the civilians wished to take with them. And with so many trying to sell their possessions at the same time, the market was glutted; if they were sold at all, the price was discouragingly low.

The scene that greeted Crèvecoeur when his ship dropped anchor in the New York harbor was hundreds of ships tied up at the docks or anchored in the East or Hudson river waiting for a berth. The city itself was a sorry sight, even shabbier than when he had left it three years earlier; the streets were littered, and looked bare without their former attractive shade trees and ornamental shrubs. Sidewalks had been torn up, and in many places where houses had stood there was now a black-ened pile of debris. Churches and hospitals had been used as barracks for soldiers.

The second day after Crèvecoeur's arrival a terrific wind-storm caused further damage, and that night a fire broke out in midtown, creating near-panic. A rumor spread that some disgruntled Loyalists had set the fire. Crèvecoeur described the situation later in the 1787 edition of *Lettres*:

> The Continental troops encamped on Harlem Heights, in full view of the flames, had the same suspicion; a great many of the soldiers, convinced that the city was to be burned, left camp to aid in putting out the fire; but fortu-nately they were stopped on the way. The authority of General Washington prevented an outbreak which would have completed the general disaster, and finished the de-struction of the unlucky city.[5]

Crèvecoeur believed that if the American soldiers had tried to force their way into the city, British soldiers would have re-sisted, and a riot would probably have broken out. Later it was learned that the fire had started by accident in a brewery.

In spite of the windstorm and the fire, General Carleton's preparations went on, and he notified General Washington that at noon on November 25 he would depart with the last of the British troops. On that day he put his plan into opera-tion according to schedule. Crèvecoeur described these events as if he had been an eyewitness, but, though close to them, he was almost certainly too ill to stand in the crowd that lined the streets to watch the spectacle; two days later he was too ill to accept an invitation from "The Citizens of New York Returned from Exile" to a dinner to be held at Cape's Tavern on the following day.[6]

November 25 was a bright, clear day, though cold. Specta-tors took up positions all the way from McGowan's Pass, where the British had set up barricades, to the Battery, at the tip of Manhattan Island. At the barrier the American and British officers chatted in friendly banter. Many citizens on horseback rode out the Bowery Road to escort General Washington and Governor Clinton to Bull's Tavern in the Bowery. When the procession started at one o'clock, General Washington and Governor Clinton rode at the head of the American troops, and behind them Lieutenant Governor Pierre Van Cortlandt, members of the council, and high-ranking officers followed by the citizens on horseback. In front of them the British officers and troops marched along the Bowery to Chatham Street, and on to Pearl until they turned off to the river to embark. In Abbott's description, "The Americans marched along Wall Street to Broadway and so to Cape's Tavern, where the main body halted, while a detachment of infantry and artillery proceeded to Fort George, accompanied by a curious crowd, eager to see the final act."[7]

This act, however, turned into comedy. The very last ceremony was to be the lowering of the British flag at the Battery and the raising of the newly created Stars and Stripes. But when the American standard-bearers reached the flagpole, they found that the British had carried away the halyard and blocks which raised the flag. Not only that, some prankster had greased the pole, so that it could not be climbed. Finally, with the aid of a ladder, hammer, cleats, and nails, the British flag was removed and the American run up. Then, as Abbott tells the story, "the remaining British, who had rested on their oars, to watch the by-play, rowed in silence to their ships." Crèvecoeur did not describe this farce, but no doubt he heard about it.

What he did describe with great enthusiasm was the simplicity and dignity of General Washington. By this time he was as great an admirer of the hero-general as the most patriotic Americans. Writing for his European audience, he begged, "Cease, I pray you, for a moment, to be European, and put yourself in the place of these courageous citizens, who, in 1776, abandoned their houses, their fortunes . . . to oppose the powerful nation which tried to make them submit to unjust laws and tyranny. . . . How beautiful and sublime human nature appears in this epoch!"[8] It is hardly necessary to remark on the change he had undergone since leaving Pine Hill.

At the end of the day, when the Americans repossessed their city, Governor Clinton gave a dinner at Fraunces Tavern for General Washington, his officers, and invited guests. Presumably Crèvecoeur was still too ill to be one of the guests, but he took a lively interest in the toasts and speeches reported in the newspapers, which he translated for French readers. Next evening at a dinner in Fraunces Tavern, General Washington bade farewell to his officers with these words: "With a heart full of love and gratitude I now take leave of you; I most devoutly wish that your latter days may be as prosperous and happy as your former ones have been glorious and honorable."[9] Perhaps Crèvecoeur was able to leave the Seton home on the night of December 3 to watch the fireworks, which he called "the most beautiful fire-works ever seen in this country."[10]

Though as a French consul Crèvecoeur had been required to give up his American citizenship, he nevertheless identified with these people celebrating their independence, and shared their pride in the new nation. The bitter years of his persecution seemed forgotten. Yet he was not happy because he worried day and night about his missing children. Where could they be? Were they even alive? Yet all this time a letter was lying in the New York post office containing the answer. Captain Gustavus Fellowes had written it on December 11, 1781; it had gone to London and been returned to New York.[11] The postmaster finally discovered it in a great pile of unsorted letters left by the departing British.

Lieutenant George Little, one of the five American naval officers who had landed on the Normandy coast two years earlier, had delivered Crèvecoeur's letters to Captain Fellowes in Boston a few months after leaving France, and in December the captain had promptly decided to go in a sleigh to Orange County to search for the children. The snow was already very deep, for this was the worst winter on record—even worse than the terrible winter of 1779–80, when Crèvecoeur and Ally had nearly frozen in New York. But other travelers had packed the snow, and the captain made fairly good time, though he was on the road seven days before he reached Fishkill, east of the Hudson River. Colonel James Woodhull, Crèvecoeur's former neighbor and friend, was stationed there with a regiment of Continental soldiers. In his letter to Fellowes, Crèvecoeur had enclosed a message to Woodhull, which the captain delivered as soon as he learned the officer's identity. Woodhull said that he did indeed know where his old friend's children were. After the burning of Crèvecoeur's house, a kindhearted couple had taken them to their home, but they had other children and could not properly care for them. No one ever mentioned how Mrs. Crèvecoeur died, whether she perished in the burning house or died later of disease, shock, or perhaps both. Crèvecoeur himself did not give even a hint in any of his published writings.

The captain resolved immediately to rescue the children and take them back to Boston, though he had seven children of his own. Colonel Woodhull crossed the river with him and guided him to the home in Chester where the children were. They found them hungry, poorly clothed, without shoes and stockings, and looking emaciated. Yet the poor mother resisted giving them up to a stranger, and her husband protested too. The captain had brought warm clothing for them, which won eleven-year-old Fanny's trust immediately. She liked this kind man and was ready to go with him, pointing out to the mother that she could not even afford to feed and clothe her own children. Louis, seven, cried and wanted to stay, but Captain Fellowes snatched him out of the mother's arms and carried him from the house. He tucked the children into the sleigh, wrapped bearskin rugs around them, and placed a charcoal stove at their feet. When they started to cross the frozen Hudson, Fanny was terrified, but Captain Fellowes diverted her attention from the clear ice by telling her stories about this region. At Hartford someone asked the captain what he had there in the sleigh. He responded, "They are two lost children whom I have found; I take them to Boston, where my wife will make them forget all they have suffered—we already have seven and these two little refound ones will make nine."[12]

Two days after finally receiving Captain Fellowes's letter, Crèvecoeur received another letter from Boston written by M. de Létombe, the French consul stationed there. He had learned that Crèvecoeur's children were with Mr. and Mrs. Fellowes and had visited them. He wanted Crèvecoeur to know that they were in good health and well cared for.[13]

Though vastly relieved that his children were safe, and had been for two years, Crèvecoeur was now almost overcome by the desire to go immediately to Boston to see them. But he knew that in his weakened condition he could not stand the exposure and fatigue of so long a trip in an open sleigh, the only vehicle able to get through the deep snow. The cause of this unusually severe winter his friend Benjamin Franklin, now American ambassador in Paris, believed to be a terrific volcanic explosion in Iceland a few months earlier. Franklin reasoned that the explosion had propelled dust and gas into the upper atmosphere, where it blocked out much of the sunlight, thus causing storms and severe cold in Europe and North America.[14] Franklin seems to have been the first to advance this theory. It was the kind of theory that interested Crèvecoeur, but it would not have consoled him for the delay in seeing his children.

However, his mind was now clear enough for him to turn his attention to his consular duties. In addition to acting as consul for New York, New Jersey, and Connecticut, he was also agent for the new line of packet ships.[15] Crèvecoeur had encouraged his government to start the line because he thought one of the best ways to promote cultural relations between France and the United States was to inaugurate trade and travel between them—there had been only a little before the Revolution. Even while France was furnishing troops and generals to fight for the Continentals, trade had been almost nonexistent. In fact, because of England's superior navy, it would have been hazardous. But now with peace and, presumably, American gratitude for France's assistance, Marshal de Castries, minister of the navy, under whom Crèvecoeur served, thought the time was right for France to capture much of the trade England had carried on with her colonies. The *Courier de l'Europe,* which had brought Crèvecoeur from Lorient to New York, was intended to inaugurate the schedule of packet ships to the United States.

Crèvecoeur had hoped to publish the French version of his *Lettres d'un cultivateur américain* before leaving France, but M. de Castries had been eager for him to begin his work before the British had time to woo back their former customers. So Crèvecoeur had departed hurriedly, leaving several friends, especially Lacretelle and Target, to oversee the printing of the book. The first step he took was to set up an office for the packet ships at 215 Water Street, and appoint William Seton as his deputy agent. The French government had provided him with a secretary, but he was unfamiliar with American ways. Mr. Seton was ideal because he spoke and wrote French, and was experienced in international trade. Crèvecoeur himself received no extra salary for representing the packet line; whether Mr. Seton did is not known. He had made sacrifices for Crèvecoeur before, and may have again in assuming these duties. In *St. John de Crèvecoeur,* Julia Post Mitchell surmised that the packet office may have been in a corner of Mr. Seton's store, for he was still in the mercantile business. In fact, Crèvecoeur may have had his office there, too, for no other address is known for the consular office at this time. What is known is that Mr. Seton began immediately to insert advertisements in the newspapers to inform the public of the packet-line services. In a few weeks Crèvecoeur took over the agency himself.

It is surprising that William Seton, who had served as a justice of the peace for the British government, and had been on friendly terms with the officers who controlled the city during the occupation, was not resented or even hated by the Americans who took over the city after the British left. Crèvecoeur's explanation was that "although a sincere Royalist, he prefers his own country to the fogs and sterile soil of New Scotland [Nova Scotia]. And what I had foreseen has since happened. His political opinions are forgotten; he enjoys the public esteem he deserves, and today he is at the head of the National Bank, an important position to which the subscribers unanimously elected him."[16]

This report, however, is incorrect in one detail: Mr. Seton helped found the National Bank and was elected one of the directors. The president was Alexander MacDougall,[17] the major general who had treated Crèvecoeur and Ally to a broiled beef dinner on their way from Chester to New York City in 1779. Perhaps Mr. Seton's former association with the British did prevent him from being made president of the bank, as his grandson would state in a history of the family.[18] But President MacDougall gave him the important position of first cashier. A year later he was also a member of the mercantile firm of Seton, Maitland, and Co. He was evidently a very energetic and successful businessman.

Crèvecoeur may also have been indebted to William Seton for getting him started on *Letters from an American Farmer*. In 1785 he stated in a letter to Thomas Jefferson that a friend had encouraged him to begin writing the *Letters*,[19] and in the first English edition he pretended to be writing to a friend in Europe who wanted to know about American life and customs. Seton may have returned to England in 1770 for a three-year stay, though the evidence is questionable.[20] Crèvecoeur's first biographer, Robert de Crèvecoeur, said that the pretense of writing the essays for a friend was a literary device.[21] However, the title page of the French edition of *Lettres d'un cultivateur américain* has as its subtitle "adressées à Wm S...on Esqr," and this is repeated on the first page of the text, except "esquire" is spelled out: "Écuyer." Perhaps the essays were never part of a private correspondence, but undoubtedly William Seton encouraged Crèvecoeur to write them, and the experiment enabled Crèvecoeur to discover a real talent for writing.

Volume 3 of the 1787 edition of *Lettres* begins with Crèvecoeur's account of his arrival in New York and proceeds quickly to his trip to Boston, which he dated "le 28 Mars 1784." "As soon as the roads were passable," he wrote, "I set out in a sleigh to see again the members of my family whom I had not seen since the year 1779."[22] He probably arrived in Boston the first week in April.

Whether Crèvecoeur himself drove or hired a driver he does not say, nor does he give any details of the days spent on the road or the taverns where he slept at night. What he remembered most vividly when he wrote about the experience some time later was his increased anxiety and agitation as he approached Boston. He had received clear instructions on the location of the Fellowes residence, and had no difficulty finding it on the corner of Harvard and Washington streets.

I knocked on the door and asked with trembling lips if this were not the house of Gustavus Fellowes, and if the children of . . . were not here. . . .
"Yes," was the response, "they are here"; and my agitation made it easy to guess that I was their father. I entered a spacious room and instantly recognized my

daughter doing housework beside the mistress of the house. The moment she saw me, she turned pale, closed her eyes, and bowed her head.—"My dear Fanny!" I said as I embraced her.—"Here is your father, whom Providence has permitted to see you again after four years of separation, and who has the happiness of finding you again under the roof of these humane and generous people!"[23]

Soon little Louis came in, and was kissed and hugged like his sister. Then, seated beside Fanny with Louis on his knee, father and children began to feel the great joy of being together again. Fanny said that several months before she had seen her father's name in a copy of a London newspaper which had happened to fall into Mr. Fellowes's hands. The article said "that someone bearing your name, formerly a farmer in Orange County, had been named French consul in New York." She showed the newspaper account to Mr. Fellowes and asked if it really referred to her father. He answered that it did, and she was wild with joy to know that he was still alive. She had clipped the article and placed it in her purse: "here it is, and today I have seen and embraced you again, thank God."

In his happy reunion with his thirteen-year-old daughter and ten-year-old son, Crèvecoeur did not forget to thank Mr. and Mrs. Fellowes for all they had done for the children. He said he could not understand why the captain had gone to such extraordinary efforts to help a man he had never heard of before and to rescue two children nearly two hundred miles away. Captain Fellowes said it had all begun not with his but with Crèvecoeur's own kindness to five Americans, men very dear to him, who couldn't speak French and were helpless when he came to their aid on the Normandy coast. He wanted to repay that debt by finding the kind Frenchman's children. Crèvecoeur insisted that what he had done did not compare with Captain Fellowes's heroic effort, but the latter maintained that there was no difference.

Fanny told her father how Mr. and Mrs. Fellowes had immediately made them part of their family, even at first favoring them over their own children. But as soon as she had recovered her strength, she had insisted on sharing all the household duties and responsibilities with the other children. Later, when Mrs. Fellowes gave birth to her eighth child, whom they named for her, Fanny voluntarily assumed responsibility for caring for her namesake. She called Mrs. Fellowes "mother" and Mr. Fellowes "father," and their children brothers and sisters. Of these children, Abigail was near Fanny's age, and Gustavus, Jr., near Louis's. Fanny's description of the harmony in the family and their devotion to each other sounds almost too good to be true—certainly an ideal family, living in almost utopian happiness.

But the things that Captain Fellowes and his wife actually did for the Crèvecoeur children lend credence to Fanny's account. Gustavus Fellowes was at this time, as might be guessed, a man of considerable wealth, though he had two brothers wealthier than he.[24] Besides his large house on Harvard Street he owned other real estate, a distillery, a whaling ship, and partnership in an auction house. During the Revolution he had loaned money to his state, which was never repaid, and a few years later he suffered business losses and had to sell the Harvard house and move into a smaller one on Hollis Street, which he also owned.

Both Fanny and her father marveled at the fortuitous chain of circumstances which had finally brought them together again. He told her that it was impossible for the human mind to know "first causes," but he did suspect that Divine Providence had been at work. His meeting the five marines on the coast near his home had set in motion the rescue of Fanny and Louis and heaped up the blessing by giving them these loving foster parents. And just think, Crèvecoeur mused, if these marines had happened to land a mile or so farther up or down the coast, he might never have met them. Yes, it did seem providential, and together they gave thanks to God for His kindness.

The first Sunday Crèvecoeur spent in Boston he went to church with the Fellowes family. The denomination was probably Congregationalist, once practically the state religion of New England. As a Patriot, Captain Fellowes would scarcely have attended an Anglican church. In his letter which had been delayed two years, he had asked if Crèvecoeur had any preferences in the religious instruction of his children. He said that until he received an answer, he would take them to church with his family; they also attended school with his children.

What most impressed Crèvecoeur in attending church with the Fellowes family was the friendliness of the congregation to him and his children. He heard people saying, "There's Fanny's father," and at the end of the service they flocked around him to shake his hand and congratulate him. But the biggest surprise was that the five naval officers who had brought back his letter from Normandy had heard he would attend church that day and had come especially to see him again. Captain Fellowes invited them to dinner at his house, and there, with some neighbors who had also been invited, they rejoiced over the circumstances which had linked the rescue of five Americans and Crèvecoeur's two children.

Crèvecoeur remained a guest of the Fellowes family for two months. He had not intended to stay that long, but Fanny became ill and he could not leave her until she recovered. In the interval he explored Boston and wrote descriptions to friends in Paris and sent information to the minister of the navy. He wished France would send over a good artist to sketch or paint the architecture and the scenery. He was also greatly impressed by the mechanical skill and ingenuity of these Americans. They had built a huge furnace to melt down old cannons so the iron could be reused to make useful implements. But he was impressed most of all by American ship builders.

He met John Peck,[25] who during the Revolution had built three frigates for the United States navy; the *Belisarius*, the *Hazard*, and the *Rattlesnake*. In 1781, the *Rattlesnake* had been captured by the British Royal Navy which described her as having a displacement of 221.3 long tons, and a quarterdeck of 76 feet. She had three masts. The Americans had used this fast ship as a privateer to raid British shipping. He had designed and built the fastest frigate in the world, and Crèvecoeur urged his government to employ him to build a ship for the packet line. In a letter to the Duke de La Rochefoucauld dated May 1, 1784, he declared, "In point of swiftness these new vessels are the Birds of the sea, from 16 to 25 days is the common Length of their Passage from here to Europe." Peck's vessels were so sturdy and well balanced that "they cannot be overset,"[26] though carrying more sail than any other ship, and four times as much freight.

John Peck had indeed discovered (or invented) new principles of ship construction, and the "clipper," as this type of sailing ship later came to be called, was the fastest ship afloat for more than half a century—in fact, until steamships were perfected nearly three-quarters of a century later. And France did employ Peck to build a packet ship, which was named *Maréchal de Castries*. But the French government could not be persuaded to buy American wood for ship construction. Crèvecoeur pointed out that white pine trees in Maine made better masts than those France bought from Russia, and the transportation would be less expensive. He also recommended live-oak from Georgia for certain parts of ships, but French builders were prejudiced against American wood, partly because they had received some inferior lumber during the war. Crèvecoeur also tried without success to get France to employ Mr. Peck to build two large frigates in Nantes, and if possible buy his design. During the autumn he would make another trip to Boston to gather more information and samples of wood for shipbuilding, but he could not overcome the French prejudices.

Finally, in mid-June Crèvecoeur said good-bye to the Fellowes family and returned to New York with Louis, and possibly with Fanny and Abigail.[27] However, if the girls did come, Fanny returned to Boston with Abigail when Crèvecoeur made his second trip there, and remained with the Fellowes family for two more years. Crèvecoeur brought Louis because he had decided to send him to France to join Alexandre in Caen, where his father thought the boy would receive better schooling. But he may also have had a secret motive. He thought Louis resembled his grandfather, and if the grandfather liked him it might help in getting the children accepted as legitimate. On July 15, 1784, Crèvecoeur wrote to La Rochefoucauld: "My Lord Duke: Louis, Ally's brother, is going to France; the same vessel which will carry this letter to you, will take him to Lorient. Everything is so expensive here, and the schools have been so turned upside down, that I think I am doing wisely in sending him to join his brother in Caen."[28]

By the end of 1784, the long-delayed edition of *Lettres d'un cultivateur américain* had finally been published in Paris in two volumes and immediately won literary fame for Crèvecoeur in his own country—or, perhaps more accurately, more fame, for the English edition had been warmly praised in intellectual circles. Mme. d'Houdetot wrote Ally, "Your father's book is on sale, and has the most flattering success. . . . Men of letters and men of the world are equally delighted with it."[29]

The Duke de La Rochefoucauld praised it highly in letters to Crèvecoeur, but the author seemed to take little pleasure in his triumph. The edition contained many typographical errors, something that can easily dampen an author's enthusiasm. Furthermore, he felt that his work as consul, in which he hoped to be a cultural liaison between France and the United States, was far more important than his literary productions. By this time he may also have begun to doubt the accuracy of some of his interpretations of life in North America, for in writing the French edition he had supplemented his experiences with secondary sources. In the second edition printed in Paris the following year, most of the errors were corrected, but he still took greater pride in his consulship.

Indeed, his efforts to promote cooperation between the two countries had met with some success. Medical societies had been formed in Cambridge, Massachusetts, and New Haven, Connecticut, with his encouragement, and were being considered at other places. Crèvecoeur thought the exchange of medical information, in which France at that time excelled, would help to bind the two nations to each other. During his first months in office he had announced in the *New York Gazette* that he would send free copies of the *Journal de médecine, chirurgie et pharmacie militaire* to anyone who requested it. He received so many requests, for France was famous for her advances in medicine, that he contracted to have this prized *journal* reprinted.[30] Crèvecoeur also corresponded extensively with officials in Cambridge, New Haven, Hartford, Trenton, and Philadelphia about starting botanical gardens with assistance from France. He wrote letters to Louis XVI and others begging them to send books to American colleges and scientific societies, and the king made some donations.

But Crèvecoeur's American correspondence was minor compared with the letters and official reports he sent to France. He sent detailed information to the Marshal de Castries on ways to promote trade between the United States and France, and wrote frequently to the Duke de La Rochefoucauld. One of Crèvecoeur's greatest handicaps was that France and the United States had been trying to agree on a treaty defining the duties of consuls.[31] Both agreed that the purpose of having consuls was to promote trade and the exchange of political information, and that no consul should himself engage in trade—that is, personally profit from it. But beyond this, there was wide disagreement, which was not settled until 1788, and then only because Benjamin Franklin had made certain promises to France which Congress did not have the will to break, though it preferred no treaty at all. One fear on both sides was increased emigration, though few Americans were interested in going to France; but in spite of the French government's disapproval, some French adventurers were coming to the United States. Crèvecoeur's *Lettres d'un cultivateur américain* encouraged many Europeans to think that it would be easy to make a fortune there, ignoring the author's cautions. When Crèvecoeur received his appointment as consul for New York, Connecticut, and New Jersey, France also had in the United States a consul general and consuls in Boston, Philadelphia, and Baltimore, and vice-consuls in Portsmouth, New Hampshire, Providence, Rhode Island, Richmond, Virginia, and Wilmington, North Carolina.[32] Crèvecoeur frequently complained that he needed a vice-consul in New York to share his duties. One may wonder, if these duties were so ambiguous, why were they so burdensome? His correspondence shows that he was not idle. In addition to the letters mentioned above about scientific societies and botanical gardens, he wrote lengthy reports to the secretary of the navy, suggesting goods to send to the United States and American goods that could be imported by France. He pointed out that America could not be expected to buy from France unless France also bought something from them.

In January 1784, both Crèvecoeur and William Seton wrote long letters to the Duke de La Rochefoucauld about sending the choicest French wines to New York for sale.[33] Mr. Seton said he had imported some wines for eighteen years, but he thought he could sell more if the right kind were shipped, properly packed and stored. Before the Revolution Americans preferred white wine, but they were beginning to like red. The wine should be of sufficient body to stand the long ocean voyage, and be reasonably priced. He supposed there was little chance of getting Rochefort or Charente, but he would be glad to try selling "a few Three dozen cases of each Sort, well corked and packed, and shipped so as to arrive in the Spring or Summer. . . ."

Both Crèvecoeur and he suggested establishing a "National Cellar," presumably in New York, to preserve and provide a sufficient quantity for the American market. In a letter to the duke written about the same time as Seton's letter, Crèvecoeur endorsed all his ideas on shipping wine to the United States, and added that he had bought forty-eight bottles of brandy from Captain Dabonville of the *Courier de l'Amérique* and distributed them to his friends, "& all of them wanted to get some of the same, so that your grace may see that I am like to succeed in this first Trial.[34]

Though Crèvecoeur may have succeeded in selling a few bottles of brandy, his attempt to promote the sale of wine in the United States had only a very limited success. Part of the trouble was the lack of a trade treaty between the two countries, causing much confusion and irritation over custom duties. France was reluctant to admit any American goods free, and the various ports in the United States (New York, Boston, Philadelphia, Baltimore, Charleston) had different schedules of fees; there was no semblance of a uniform system.

Then, Crèvecoeur complained, the packet boats were not being run efficiently, or even sensibly. He praised highly the captain of the *Courier de l'Amérique,* and hoped the minister of the navy would point him out as a model for other captains. The port of Lorient was careless in preparing the ships for the long voyage across the Atlantic. One ship arrived so poorly painted that he had it properly painted at his own expense. He wrote the duke that he thought the management in Lorient were "des Pillar[d]s et des Ignorants" (pilferers and ignoramuses).[35]

By the spring of 1785 Crèvecoeur was becoming discouraged, though he still tried desperately to get France to
send what Americans needed and wanted, not jewelry, silks,
laces, ribbons, and other trifles. They needed glass, nails,
paper, cutlery, porcelain, and medical supplies. In exchange
they could supply excellent wool (which France could weave
into cloth and return), furs, leather, excellent cheese (far superior to the cheese supplied to the French navy), whale oil,
and vegetable oil; he mentioned again wood for ships. He
wrote what could be called a treatise for the minister of the
navy describing these products and indicating some of their
uses. In letters to the duke he repeated his recommendations,
and urged him to use his influence in the government to have
his report considered seriously.

But he was waging a losing battle. On March 25, 1784, he
wrote the duke, "Generally speaking, there is a marked inferiority in everything which comes here from France; goods are
carelessly consigned, badly made, and of poor quality."[36] British goods, on the other hand, were usually of excellent quality.
And, of course, the British knew what Americans liked and
would buy. But another reason for the difficulty in selling
French products in the United States was the bad reputations
of the French merchants who came over to engage in commerce. Distrust of these persons led to distrust of everything
made in France.

In a letter to the Duke de La Rochefoucauld dated July 15,
1784, Crèvecoeur was already, after one year as consul, disillusioned by some of his countrymen. "Here the French whom
I see are for me a new race of men—liars, back-biters, destroy-
ers of each other ... without good faith and without manners.
They think that outside of France there is no longer law or
restraint for them; they mock American promises. Such are
the French, with perhaps a dozen exceptions. Consuls are
their pet abominations, and calumny is their ordinary weapon.
If I oblige them, they say I am stupid and a fop. If I am firm,

they accuse me of being more American than French. That I am haughty and proud—I haughty and proud, as if I could be."[37]

This sounds like a petulant outburst from a person with bad nerves. Perhaps he was irritable because of poor health, but his opinion is supported by an official dispatch (unknown to him) written two months earlier from Philadelphia by the French minister to the United States, Anne-César de la Luzerne. To the minister of foreign affairs he wrote in his dispatch of May 17, 1784: ". . . French adventurers are here in greater number than in any other city of this continent: they are a plague on the honest French established here and they conduct themselves in the most licentious manner. Their insolence spares no one and it is painful for me to associate with them."[38]

Besides the ill-mannered French, Crèvecoeur had other annoyances during his first year as consul. Among the respectable traveling French in America at this time, gathering material for a book, was Jacques-Pierre Brissot de Warville (who would lead the Girondist party during the French Revolution and lose his life). Brissot stated in his *Mémoires* that some Americans were astonished that the French government had chosen for a consul a man who had once opposed American independence.[39] Crèvecoeur surely knew of this criticism behind his back, but was too sensitive to mention it in his writings. For a man given to worrying, having his qualifications questioned again placed further strain on his nerves.

In the summer of 1784 Crèvecoeur began to worry again about his health.[40] Extremely cold winters are often, it seems, followed by abnormally hot summers, and the summer of 1784 was both hot and humid. In the same letter to the duke in which he announced he was sending Louis to join his brother in Caen, Crèvecoeur complained that his health was so very uncertain that it was difficult for him to discharge his official duties. He asked his friend, therefore, if he would kindly use his influence to secure the permission of Marshal de Castries for him to return to France for six months to rest and consult French physicians, "who are more skilled than those which are to be found here." The duke did not encourage the idea, and Crèvecoeur would not be able to secure the furlough until the following spring, after the Princess de Beauvau had used her influence.

Fortunately, Crèvecoeur was given an emotional boost by the arrival of Marquis de Lafayette in New York on August 4 for a six-month visit to the new nation[41] he had helped win its independence. This twenty-seven-year-old aristocrat was a great American hero for his distinguished military leadership as a major general in the Continental Army. He had borne the hardships of General Washington and his troops in Pennsylvania, been present at the capture and execution of Major André, and helped defeat General Cornwallis at Yorktown. George Washington thought highly of him, and in gratitude Lafayette had named his son George Washington. He had volunteered his services in the American Revolution because he passionately believed in freedom, and advocated reform in his own country.[42]

Though Lafayette was not an intimate friend, Crèvecoeur had met him at Versailles while preparing his report on North America for Louis XVI. And he must have known he and Lafayette held similar liberal ideas on politics and religion. At any rate, he admired Lafayette, and the marquis seems to have liked him. In New York they may have seen each other frequently, since Lafayette would likely have stayed at what Crèvecoeur called an elegant boardinghouse on Maiden Lane, where generals and visiting dignitaries usually stayed. In the spring of 1785 Crèvecoeur referred to this place as "la maison voisine" where he took his meals. Whether he ate there six months earlier is not known for sure, but he lived in the neighborhood.

What is most definitely known is that Crèvecoeur took a

personal interest in Lafayette's triumphant tour of the Eastern Seaboard. He translated his speeches for Paris newspapers, and in volume 3 of *Lettres d'un cultivateur américain* he collected the speeches welcoming the marquis as well as his responses.[43] Crèvecoeur admitted that these speeches, filled with flattery for the guest, and his responses might be somewhat monotonous, but he wanted to record them for future historians. He caused Lafayette considerable embarrassment by reporting to American newspapers his address at Fort Schuyler, because as a former American officer commissioned by the Continental Congress, he was forbidden to publish anything without the permission of Congress. However, Crèvecoeur smoothed things over by explaining that he had published the speech without Lafayette's knowledge or consent.

In September James Madison accompanied Lafayette to Fort Schuyler, near present-day Utica, New York, to a council called by the "Six Nations" of the Iroquois Federation of Indian tribes to discuss their relations to the new American government.[44] (The Six Nations comprised the Mohawks, Senecas, Cayugas, Oneidas, Onondagas, and Tuscaroras, all belonging to the linguistic group called Iroquois.) All except the Oneida tribe had allied with the British in the American Revolution. Now, in an assembly lasting several days, both they and the United States government met to reassess and redefine their relations.

The tribal chiefs invited Lafayette, whom they had known in 1777 and given the name Kayewla, to address them, and he did so on September 26, in the style of Indian orators. Calling them "my children," he said: "If you recognize the voice of *Kayewla*, recall also the council and the beads which he sent you by messengers." They all knew, of course, that except for the Oneidas, they had not followed his advice. He reminded them that they should at least have remained neutral in the war between the British and the Americans. But they had believed the British when they said that in the north they would take Boston and in the south Virginia, and drive General Washington out of the country.

The American cause was just, Lafayette told them, and they should have helped their brothers win their freedom. But now that the war was over and the white birds of peace had descended on the shores, the new American government wanted to deal justly and mercifully with them. "Grasp the outstretched hand," he urged them. Besides, the alliance between France and America was strong and durable, and this was cause for them to trust the Americans. Then, to assist Crèvecoeur in his efforts to promote trade, Lafayette advised the Indians to buy articles of French manufacture, as they had once done.

A frequent cause of friction between the Indians and the white settlers had been that, in the absence of private ownership of land, individual Indians had often been induced to sign agreements of sale without the consent of the whole tribe. Therefore, Lafayette advised them: "In selling your land do not consult a barrel of whiskey before signing it away, but only the chiefs among your brothers and your *Sachems*: unite around the fire, and make reasonable bargains. . . . If you have opened your ears, and listened carefully to my words, I have said enough to you. —Repeat my words to each other, so that on the other side of the great lake I will receive news of you with pleasure, and at this moment when we smoke together, when we sleep under the same bark, I wish you good health, happy hunting, union, abundance, and the success of all your dreams which promise you prosperity.—I have spoken."

From Fort Schuyler Lafayette went to Albany, and then on to Hartford. Hearing that he was coming, citizens rode out on horseback to meet him and escort him ceremoniously into the city. The Connecticut Legislature voted honorary citizenship to Lafayette and his son, George Washington. In Boston he was also received with wild acclamation. He visited, perhaps at Crèvecoeur's suggestion, Mr. and Mrs. Fellowes and Fanny Crèvecoeur. Fanny's father wrote the Duke de La Rochefoucauld that for this kindness he would be grateful to the marquis all his life.

When Lafayette traveled southward, he met similar receptions. Everywhere there were parades and banquets in his honor. The state legislature in session in Philadelphia named a county for him. Thomas Jefferson, United States Minister to France, wrote him that the state of Virginia had resolved to place a bust of him beside a statue of George Washington in the capitol at Richmond. The United States Congress voted to commission an equestrian statue of him to stand in the national capitol. (In 1785 New York would become the temporary capital; then the capital would move to Philadelphia in 1790, and permanently to Washington, D.C., in 1800.)

By the time Lafayette left the United States, a day or so after Christmas 1784, cities, states, and the United States had heaped upon him every honor they could think of. He told Madison that his three greatest desires were the continuation of friendship and cooperation between France and the new nation, the union of the Thirteen States, and the abolition of slavery—he urged George Washington to free his slaves. When he left New York to return home on the *Courier de l'Europe,* he was escorted to the pier by Governor Clinton on one side and Crèvecoeur on the other.[45] He had made a glorious visit to the new nation, and no one had enjoyed it more than his friend Crèvecoeur. Their political philosophy was almost identical, but Lafayette was an activist, whose deeds exemplified his thoughts, and he would have a role to play in the approaching French Revolution.

Meanwhile, Crèvecoeur had been receiving some honors of his own, though mild compared with Lafayette's. New Haven made him an honorary citizen at the same time it extended that honor to Lafayette and other distinguished Frenchmen, and so did Hartford. Ethan Allen, the Revolutionary hero and principal founder of the state of Vermont, had citizenship conferred not only on Crèvecoeur but also on his three children.[46] His letter conveying this information especially pleased Crèvecoeur because he could offer these citizenship papers in France as proof of his children's legitimacy. He was now gathering every scrap of evidence he could find to prove that his marriage had been proper, even though it had not been performed by a Catholic priest. As a further gesture of gratitude to the consul who had done so much good for the nation, Allen also proposed that a new town in Vermont be named for him. Crèvecoeur wrote back that since several towns in the nation already bore the name St. John, he suggested St. Johnsbury, which was accepted, and the town still bears this name, though probably few people know it refers to St. John de Crèvecoeur.[47]

The furlough which Crèvecoeur had been longing for since the previous summer was finally granted him in the spring of 1785, not through the efforts of his friend the duke, who tried to discourage the idea, but through the influence of Princess de Beauvau. In December Baron Marbé de Marbois had arrived in New York with the title of consul general, and he would be able to take over in Crèvecoeur's absence.

In preparation for his departure, Crèvecoeur sold his farm in Orange County in May for £500. The purchaser was his former neighbor Hezekiah Moffatt. Whether Crèvecoeur visited Pine Hill again before selling it is not recorded. Possibly his memories of the place where he had been so happy and later so miserable, and worst of all, where his wife had died, were too painful for him to look upon the scene once more.

Because of his health problems and close application to his consular duties, Crèvecoeur did very little traveling during these two years in New York. His letters indicate only the two trips to Boston, but he may have visited Niagara Falls a few weeks after selling his farm. Robert Crèvecoeur mentions a manuscript, dated 1789, which describes an excursion to Niagara Falls in July 1785, "which is evidently an error because by this time he had already returned to France."[48] As we have seen several times, Crèvecoeur was notoriously un-reliable about dates.

This particular instance is also indicative of the problem of the dates he assigned "sketches." For example, his account of George Washington entering New York on November 25, 1783, on the heels of the British evacuation, is dated "New York, 16 Juillet 1784."[49] Presumably Crèvecoeur wrote the narrative in New York on the sixteenth of July the following summer. And "Relation of some circumstances relative to the voyage of Monsieur the Marquis de Lafayette made to us," is dated "New York, 30 Juin 1785,"[50] about six months after Lafayette had returned to France. Presumably Crèvecoeur wrote these "sketches" from memory, and perhaps some notes. Evidently he found time during his consular work to write a considerable part of the third volume of the 1787 edition of *Lettres d'un cultivateur américain.* He had not lost the habits of scribbling which he had acquired as a student at the *collège* in France and developed as an actual farmer in Orange County before the Revolution.

One other thing Crèvecoeur did before going on his first leave was to help about a dozen Catholics in New York City raise funds to build a church.[51] Before the Revolution Catholi-cism had been outlawed in most of the colonies, but in 1784 the New York Legislature had passed a law permitting free-dom of worship for all sects. (In 1787 the United States Con-stitution would give the same guarantee, but New York State did not wait for the adoption of the Constitution.) Crèvecoeur had not been a Catholic communicant at least since leaving Canada in 1759, and possibly earlier; he had not been sympa-thetic with the Catholic monopoly of religion in Canada. It is not known whether he even attended a church of any kind in the colonies, though, as we have seen, a Huguenot Protestant minister in Westchester had married him and baptized his children.

In theology Crèvecoeur could be called a Deist, along with

his friends Thomas Jefferson, Benjamin Franklin, and Ethan Allen, who wrote a deistic book called *Reason the Only Oracle of Man.* Perhaps now that he was returning to France to join his sons and his father in Caen (Fanny would remain in Boston for two more years), he felt it was time to return to the church of his youth. Of course, it was also true that the reassertion of his Catholicism might help him gain recognition in France of the legitimacy of his children.

Whatever his secret motive, on June 10, 1785, Crèvecoeur, José Roiz Silva, James Stewart, and Henry Duffin were registered as "trustees of the Catholic Church in the City of New York." Father Charles Whelan held services in a carpenter's shop, the only space he could find, while funds were being collected to build a church. They were still insufficient when Crèvecoeur's leave began, but during the summer Father Whelan was able to buy five lots from Trinity Church (lots Crèvecoeur had surveyed five years earlier) at Barclay and Church streets. A short time later construction of the church was begun, and on November 4 the following year, while Crèvecoeur was still in France, St. Peter's was dedicated. The present St. Peter's Church, however, was built in 1838, at the same location.

For all his hectic activity, now that he was cut off from his family and all the friends he had made in Paris, Crèvecoeur often felt depressed and homesick. If we are to believe Brissot de Warville, one of the reasons for his fits of depression may have been that he felt uncomfortable in his official position.[52] He feared lest his past as a Tory, if it became known, should make him *persona non grata* with the republican government of the United States—despite the declaration of neutrality he diplomatically made in the last chapter of his *Letters.* In the spring of 1785, he must have become tired of the false position in which he found himself. Though he liked his work, he applied for a six-month leave of absence, which he obtained. It was to last two years.

VIII

❧❧❧❧❧

On Leave in France

CRÈVECOEUR LEFT New York late in June 1785 on the *Courier de l'Europe* and arrived at Lorient on July 9. He had originally planned to proceed immediately to Paris, but he was probably too tired to do so. Besides, he may have found it difficult to wrench himself from his father and his sons after such a long absence. One month later, on August 15, he wrote to Thomas Jefferson, the American ambassador to Paris: "Had my health Permitted me, I should long since have enjoyed the Pleasure of Seeing you at Paris—but I feel that I shall not be able to Perform that Journey until the Middle of ye Fall—I have the Minister's Leave to stay here during that time."[1] Two weeks later, after communicating with Mme. d'Houdetot, he was in a position to set a date for his visit. This time he told Jefferson: "I hope to have the pleasure of seeing you Some time in Oct.re. I shall go, I believe, with my two boys to spend some Time with ye good Countess."[2]

True to his word, he left Caen toward the end of September, but his first visit was to the Duke de La Rochefoucauld, with whom he had corresponded so assiduously from New York and with whom he shared so many interests. He spent several days with him on his estate at La Roche-Guyon before going to Sannois and seeing the countess. Much to his regret, he was not accompanied by his sons, and he missed them. To make up for his failure to bring them along, he wrote to them as often as he could and so did Mme. d'Houdetot. She thus wrote to Ally on October 2: "I found him [Crèvecoeur] in fairly good condition; he is less serious than when he arrived, and I owe to his friendship and presence the first comfort I have really felt since the misfortune I experienced." (She had recently lost her brother.[3])

Crèvecoeur probably spent a restful month with Mme. d'Houdetot at Sannois. Owing to an illness of Marshal de Castries, to whom he had to report, he had no official business to transact. In November, when the marshal resumed his activities, Crèvecoeur divided his time between Sannois (or sometimes nearby Eaubonne) and Paris. It was a busy time for him, for he was both trying to settle with the minister the question of the transatlantic packet ships and working on a new edition of his *Lettres d'un cultivateur américain*. Too few shippers were using the packets, and they were sailing with greater and greater irregularity, much to the despair of Jefferson. Both he and Crèvecoeur regarded as vital to the United States and France the existence of a permanent ship line ensuring regular commercial and cultural exchanges between the two countries. They hoped the packets would continue to cross the Atlantic between New York and Havre at least once a month, but a government subsidy was needed, for the line lost money. It was this problem that Crèvecoeur was trying to solve with the minister. Fortunately, Marshal de Castries was very well disposed toward him. On November 1, Crèvecoeur wrote: "I had enemies who wanted to blacken the good opinions he had of me, but they have not succeeded. We work together at the improvement of the packets, which I think will berth at Havre."[4] As to the second edition of his book, he did not want simply to revise and correct the text of the first one.

He intended to expand it. "I will insert several useful things," he wrote to Ally on November 13, "and I am bent on telling the unhappy adventures of your sister and your brother Louis, and the marvelous help they received from Mr. Fellowes." So, eventually, a third volume was necessary. But, in order to carry out his project, Crèvecoeur had to live a spartan life. When he was by himself in Mme. d'Houdetot's Paris mansion, the Swiss valet in charge of the place prepared soup and plain boiled beef ("pot-au-feu") for his lunch, and, in the evening, Crèvecoeur said, "I eat an egg and roll, drink a glass of water and go to bed. I am always at home by four P.M. and never go out at night."[5]

He did not live all the time as a recluse, though, for, when winter came, Mme. d'Houdetot returned to Paris and he had to accompany her to the opera. They saw both French and Italian operas. It was a gay life—too gay for him, as he wrote to Ally. He also had to dine with Mme. d'Houdetot's friends, the Duke de La Rochefoucauld and the Duke de Liancourt, and others, but this was no waste of time, for he could talk politics with them. He visited some of his old friends, Target in particular, who had looked after the first edition of the *Lettres* with such devotion and efficiency in his absence. Target was the first friend on whom he called when he arrived in Paris.

Crèvecoeur was now famous in France. Mme. d'Houdetot gave an account of the success of his *Lettres* in a letter to Ally on January 1, 1785: "The book of your good father has the greatest and most flattering success. It makes people love its author and esteem his character. It is equally appreciated by literary and society people."[6] His notoriety naturally attracted new friends, notably Brissot de Warville, who had read Crèvecoeur's *Lettres* with such enthusiasm that he sought to make his acquaintance at the earliest opportunity. He was a fervent abolitionist and was to found in 1788 the Société des Amis des Noirs; however, later, as an influential member of the Convention, he found himself in the wrong camp and was guillotined in 1793. Even in those pre-Revolutionary years he found Crèvecoeur's political views too lukewarm and depicted him in rather dark colors in his *Mémoires*. They appeared posthumously in 1830, so Crèvecoeur fortunately did not read them.

On February 13, 1786, Crèvecoeur accompanied Mme. d'Houdetot to a great ceremony at the French Academy held in honor of a new member, Count Jacques de Guibert, a well-known general who had written on the art of war and even composed tragedies in alexandrines. Crèvecoeur was delighted, having a chance to see in the audience all kinds of important people, from his protector, Marshal de Castries, to Mme. de Staël.

He himself did not belong to such exalted circles, but had just been elected a member of the Royal Agricultural Society as an authority on potato culture, and he considered it his duty to take an active part in its sessions. In March 1786, he offered to read a paper on several utensils he had mentioned in his 1782 *Traité de la culture des pommes de terre*: a special hoe used in America to dig up potatoes, a small hand plow to harrow between rows, and a steam cooker of a special type he had also seen in America. As Parmentier, who considered himself *the* supreme authority on potatoes, was there and was known to be very touchy, Crèvecoeur was advised to speak only on the cooker, which he did. Parmentier was so pleased with his tact that he lavished praise on Crèvecoeur and his expertise in the huge and definitive treatise he wrote on potato culture in 1789, *Traité sur la culture et les usages de la pomme de terre*.

Crèvecoeur had another specialty: the common locust tree, or false acacia. On March 30, 1786, he read a paper on this topic, which was printed in the *acta* of the Royal Agricultural Society under the title *Mémoire sur la culture et les usages du faux acacia (Robinia pseudoacacia) dans les États-Unis de l'Amérique septentrionale*. His paper was well received and became influential in France and Germany, contributing to the increased planting of this tree in Europe. It has since become a pest in some regions, for, once acclimatized, it is almost impossible to get rid of.

When spring came, Crèvecoeur became restless. He needed time to work at the new edition of his *Lettres* and he also wanted to see his sons. At last, in April, he obtained an extension of his leave of absence and the permission to quit Paris. He made a round of visits to take leave of his friends and wrote to Ally on April 1: "Yesterday I went to Eaubonne at M. de Saint-Lambert's where I found the good Countess and they bade me a most affectionate farewell. This morning, I spent an hour at Princess de Beauvau's, who is always good and kind. Today, the good old Count [Mme. d'Houdetot's husband] and I are to dine at M. Target's, my good friend Target, the best of men."[7]

Crèvecoeur was at Pierrepont in the latter half of April, but he had been preceded there by some gifts of his: portraits of friends and relatives brought by his father, who, as usual, had spent part of the winter in Paris. Crèvecoeur announced these gifts in a letter to Ally dated April 3: "My father leaves to-morrow [for Normandy]. . . . He will stop at Malliot [?], from where he will send Porée [his servant] to Pierrepont. The latter, when going through Caen will see you and kiss you on my behalf. He will give you a box wrapped in paper which contains a portrait of the good Countess, those of Fanny, Mr. Fellowes and your own father. . . ." (These portraits, drawn in pencil and heightened with gouache, still exist.[8]) Mme. d'Houdetot, for her part, sent Ally some books (the two-volume *History of England* by Lord Littleton): "they are meant to show you," she wrote to him on April 8, "that you are not forgotten by your good mother from Paris. . . ."

Once settled at Pierrepont, Crèvecoeur worked hard at his book and probably read every night to his relatives and friends what he had been writing during the day. Such had been his custom at Mme. d'Houdetot's in Paris, if we are to believe

Target, who wrote to him: "I do not doubt that the third volume will make me cry like the others, as it already began to do at Mme. d'Houdetot's."[9] His reaction may surprise one, but, for all their cult of reason, people in the eighteenth century cried on the least provocation.

The book was finished and printed before Crèvecoeur's return to America. He distributed copies of it to his friends toward the end of March 1787, and it was on sale in April. The reviews appeared only after his departure.

All his energies, however, were not absorbed by his literary labors. At Jefferson's instigation, he pulled strings to obtain the enfranchising of the port of Honfleur (at the mouth of the Seine, opposite Havre). If he had succeeded, it would have enabled the Americans to divert a good part of the trade between America and Europe from Great Britain to France. As Jefferson pointed out to John Jay, the secretary of foreign affairs, this would be "peculiarly advantageous for our rice and whale oil. . . . Being free, they can be re-exported when the market here [in France] shall happen to be overstocked." On February 3, 1787, Crèvecoeur wrote to the governor of Massachusetts, James Bowdoin, with whom Crèvecoeur was on very good terms: "Yesterday we had a great meeting at the Duke de Harcourt's about obtaining the freedom of Honfleur. . . . I have been encouraged to apply to that Duke on account of his great kindness to me and of the power and influence he has at Court."[10] After this meeting, Jefferson thought that the affair would be "speedily concluded," but it dragged on and on after Crèvecoeur's departure and was never settled.

Crèvecoeur was also busy with another pet project of his, which he had entertained for several years and mentioned in his correspondence with the Duke de La Rochefoucauld. He described it in a note he wrote twenty years later, in 1807: "As I enjoyed the friendship and esteem of the Baron de Breteuil, who was head of the Ministry of the Interior, I pressed him to induce M. de Vergennes [the influential and efficient foreign minister] to order all ministers, ambassadors and diplomatic agents to send him reports, drawings and models of machines, factories and inventions unknown in France, which would be placed on exhibition and shown to the public. This simple, useful and inexpensive project was not carried out."[11]

Private initiative tried to supply the deficiency of the government. To replace "the enlightenment bureau" ("le bureau des lumières") of which Crèvecoeur had been dreaming, Brissot undertook to found a Société Gallo-Américaine, which he described in a letter to Jefferson:

"France, by her arms, has contributed to confirm the independence of free America. A treaty of commerce founded on the interest of the two countries would unite them more and more closely. The object and principal result of such a commercial bond ought to be the moral and political good of both nations. This cannot be attained unless the two countries are put into position to know each other better, until the individual Frenchman is enabled to know the individual American. Nothing, therefore, is more necessary than to establish a center to which reports on everything of consequence that is done in either country may be brought. Our society will form this center."[12]

Crèvecoeur, of course, was a member of this society. Brissot, at the last meeting Crèvecoeur attended before his return to America, paid tribute to him: "To him chiefly," he declared, "we owe the idea and the formation of our Society." After his departure, it was not heard of anymore. It either disappeared or merged into the Société des Amis des Noirs, which disbanded in 1793 following the death of Brissot and the society's co-founder Étienne Clavière, a Swiss merchant who had become involved in French politics.

Crèvecoeur also had to attend to the education of his sons. He attached great importance to this duty, exchanged views about it with Target, and was ready to make great financial sacrifices if necessary to secure good teachers for them. He first placed them in the charge of a M. de Longpré and later sent them to one of the best schools in Paris, kept by a M. Lemoyne. A nephew of Mme. d'Houdetot's was a pupil there, and she promised to look after them: ". . . until your return I shall adopt them," she assured him. "I hope that they will love me and look upon me as their mother, and that they will call me so [which they did, addressing her as "maman d'Houdetot"]. Every Thursday I shall take them to dine at Mr. Jefferson's, every Sunday he and your children will dine with me. On occasion I shall take them to the theater. Their vacations will be spent with me at Sannois or in Le Marais or at Méréville."[13] William Short, who was the chargé d'affaires in Paris after Jefferson's departure, also promised to see them frequently and to take charge of their letters to him. Thus Crèvecoeur could be fully reassured about their welfare and happiness during his absence. In May he spent a few days at Sannois with Mme. d'Houdetot to take leave of her. His long vacation, if one can call it so, was over. He went to Caen to say good-bye to his father and then to Havre, from where he sailed on January 10.

IX

~~~~~~~~~~

Last Years as Consul

AFTER his two-year absence, Crèvecoeur was astonished on his return to New York at the end of June 1787 to see the physical improvements which had taken place in his absence. Remnants of the burned-out buildings had been removed, houses had been repaired, young trees had been planted along many streets, and the city pulsed with new vitality.[1] Of course, hogs still roamed the streets devouring garbage, and shallow wells still supplied unsafe water for the citizens. In these deficiencies, however, New York was no worse than Paris. Perhaps it was no worse either in street crime, though crime had increased during Crèvecoeur's furlough in France. New York newspapers claimed that the footpads came from Philadelphia.

Crèvecoeur had arrived on the *Courier de l'Europe,* the same ship that had brought him to his post in 1783 and carried him back to France two years later.[2] It was one of the two packet ships with good accommodations for about twenty passengers. Newspaper reports reveal that on this trip the *Courier de l'Europe* carried ten. Besides several businessmen from Philadelphia and Virginia, the passengers included the great

American naval hero John Paul Jones; Mlle. Beaumanoir, daughter of the governor of the Hôtel des Invalides, the great military hospital in Paris; and the Marquis de Lotbinière of Canada. Mlle. Beaumanoir was being escorted to New York by Crèvecoeur to marry a M. de Laforest, who had been performing Crèvecoeur's consular duties during his absence.

The Marquis de Lotbinière may have caused Crèvecoeur some uneasiness during the stormy, forty-five-day crossing of the Atlantic. He had also served in Canada in the regiment of the Sarre, employed in engineering, as Lieutenant Crèvecoeur had. The marquis could reveal his having fought in Canada against England and her American colonies, details which might be harmful to Crèvecoeur in his present position.[3] This, however, is speculation. Lotbinière himself had had a rather erratic career, having gone to England after France lost Canada and rendered some ambiguous service to the British government, then volunteered his services to France after the Americans won their Revolution. The main object of his returning to America in 1787, according to Robert de Crèvecoeur, was to reclaim land he owned in Canada which after the adjustment of the Canadian-American border was now in United States territory. The biographer thinks he was not successful.[4]

On the whole, however, Crèvecoeur had good reasons for feeling confident on his return to his consular office. He now had many friends in the United States, some with great political influence, such as Thomas Jefferson, Benjamin Franklin, and the eccentric but influential Ethan Allen. He wanted to meet the statesman and political theorist James Madison, and Jefferson's secretary, William Short, had written a very flattering letter of introduction which Crèvecoeur brought with him from France. Short said Crèvecoeur had intended to ask Jefferson for this favor, but "in his absence addresses himself to me— You may well suppose Sir that my pride would not permit me to let M. de Crèvecoeur or anybody here believe that I was not well enough acquainted with you to give a letter of recommendation." Mr. Short would hardly have used such language if he had not indeed been well acquainted with Mr. Madison. He continued:

> There is no body whom I would introduce to you more readily Sir than M. de Crèvecoeur, because there is no body more capable of explaining to you the present ideas of France with respect to America—because there is no body who understands more perfectly the interests of the two countries as they relate to each other, and none more zealous to produce them mutually, as he has uniformly manifested during his residence in Paris. . . . Such a man cannot fail being useful to you, at New York, whether considered as a member of the federal head or a private philosopher.[5]

Crèvecoeur would not be able to present this letter of introduction to Madison until some months later, because during the summer of 1787 he was still in Philadelphia attending the Federal Convention, called to persuade the thirteen states to agree upon a constitution. The Articles of Confederation, ratified by nine states in 1778, had failed to provide for raising revenue, to give Congress legal power to regulate commerce, and to conduct foreign affairs. In fact, there was as yet no real federal government; the states were united in name only, and some of them were quarreling with each other.

On July 25 Crèvecoeur wrote the Duke de La Rochefoucauld:

> The confederation can be compared to a bundle of sticks bound by a straw. The good citizens here are divided into two parties: the first one is composed of those who despair and fear that everything will collapse, if not into anarchy, at least into a state of disunion. The other one is composed of those who flatter themselves that things are not

so bad yet and there is a strong probability that Congress
will at last have enough power to become a more respectable Congress.[6]

Yet in spite of these formidable difficulties in forming a
strong federal government, "local laws are still in force, Agriculture begins to prosper, a large number of families daily
leave towns to go settle on their own lands. . . ." He thought
these families were superior to some of the people he had met
on the frontier before the Revolution, and if they were industrious they could be "as happy as it is possible to be." He said
that for the present he would reserve his opinion on the future
of the American experiment, but he was nevertheless hopeful.
"I want to wait and have a closer look at things. However bad
I find them, I feel better disposed to find them good than
otherwise, because I come from Europe where I have seen the
despotism of governors . . . , the perpetual war waged by the
tax-collectors, the inequality of fortunes, the extraordinary
destitution of the countryside where man is degraded by
the most profound ignorance and the crushing weight of
poverty."

He was depressed, however, "on seeing the luxury which
developed here in the last two years, owing to the presence of
Congress, which attracts several ambassadors and a large
number of foreigners." Some Americans had also been to
Europe and acquired a taste for fine clothes and expensive
foods. He did not blame native Americans so much as their
foreign corrupters. Three years earlier Congress had begun
considering building a capital "far from our large seaside
towns, in a rural and more central location, [where] they can
enjoy the pleasure of meeting without any danger of dissipa-
tion. . . ." But now Congress had no funds to build a capital
anywhere, and eventually they would build it on the Potomac
River, which was rural enough, but not far from Baltimore, a
seaside town.

Crèvecoeur's complaints about the increase of luxurious living in New York were not entirely the ideological reactions of a radical democrat. Two contemporary historians, John and Mary Mason, in *Fourteen Miles Round* (the circumference of Manhattan) described "a dame of high degree" wearing "a pierrot of Gray Indian taffeta with dark gray stripes; two collars (one white and one yellow) both trimmed with blue silk; a pale yellow corset (called 'shapes') with large blue stripes and a satin hat with a large wreath of artificial roses."[7]

And men of fashion dressed just as extravagantly:

> A well-known man was clad in a scarlet coat, white silk waistcoat embroidered with colored flowers, black satin breeches with paste knee-buckles, white silk stockings, low shoes with large silver buckles, and a small cocked hat on the upper part of his powdered hair, leaving the curls at his ears displayed. He carried a gold-headed cane and gold snuff-box, and is rather an agreeable bit of color against the gray background of New York in 1789.[8]

Crèvecoeur, however, did not spend much of the summer of 1787 in New York. As usual, he found the heat and humidity oppressive, and he also wanted to see his daughter in Boston. In April a fire had broken out in a malt house on Beech Street and spread to Hollis. Only a shift in the wind saved the Fellowes house. Fanny, with delicate nerves like her father, was so terrified that she became ill, and did not recover until weeks later.

At the time he was greatly worried about the American political situation, and he devoted to this subject most of his letter of July 25 to La Rochefoucauld. The country was threatened, he said, not only by the inability of the states to form a viable federal government, but it also seemed powerless before the threats of Spain to close the Mississippi River to American navigation. Spain claimed all land west of the Mississippi except the Oregon territory (which England claimed), and a strip of land along the Gulf Coast from Louisiana to Florida, including all of Florida.

Exactly when Crèvecoeur left New York for Boston is not certain. Although this letter to the Duke de La Rochefoucauld was dated July 25, it was not in his handwriting. He probably wrote it earlier, leaving a draft for his secretary to copy and mail. The holograph contains several misspellings, as if copied carelessly. He was in Boston when he wrote "Monsieur le Duc" again on July 27 in his own neat script.

His anxiety over the American political situation had increased. Adding to the dangers enumerated in his previous letter, he now mentioned that England was building up her military forces in Canada. He did not say why, but perhaps it was because of the dispute with the United States over the Oregon territory. However, he believed that the Federal Convention in Philadelphia, presided over by General Washington, was attended by the most capable men of the continent. He no doubt had in mind such men as James Madison, John Jay, and Alexander Hamilton, who would publish *The Federalist* papers a few months later, a masterpiece of argument for a strong federal constitution which would justify Crèvecoeur's high opinion of these men.

These and others had convinced General Washington that unless the problem of a constitution was solved promptly there was great danger to the nation, not only from abroad but also from within, and Washington wanted above all else to avoid a civil war. Consequently, he agreed to use his influence and prestige, which were still as high as they had ever been, to persuade the states to agree upon a constitution. "I fear, however," Crèvecoeur wrote, "that this will not happen without some compromises."[9]

One other great danger was the dissatisfaction of the American soldiers of the Revolution. During the war they had been paid in certificates promising future payment. But Congress still had no means to redeem them in real money because it had no power to collect taxes from the individual states. Disaffected veterans were assembling in Boston, New York, and Philadelphia loudly demanding financial help. To mollify them, Congress promised to accept the certificates in exchange for large tracts of land northwest of the Ohio River, which had been surveyed and subdivided the previous year. The war veterans were to receive a large portion of these tracts, and others were to be sold to support churches and schools in the region. It was also hoped that the sale of this land would help reduce the national debt. Crèvecoeur was skeptical of the whole scheme, because "such is the fate of man, that he is destined everywhere to be unfortunate, either by injustice, or by the ponderous operation of laws, or by their inadequacy and weakness."

He also shrewdly analyzed the American situation:

At the beginning of the Revolution, the Americans regarded their federal government (then more a dream than a reality) as the only means which could act to unite them and conciliate their different interests, as the only center of power by which they could attain safety and protection . . . but later they transferred their allegiance and affections to the idol of individual sovereignty. . . . They seemed to think that only this idol would bring them safety and true independence, but instead it brought them confusion and loss of national dignity.[10]

His skepticism regarding the distribution of the Ohio land did not mean that he opposed settling the region. In fact, ever since he had visited it while a map maker for the French Colonial Army he had thought it held great opportunities for future farmers. There is no proof, however, that he had any part in the settling of a French colony on the Scioto River sponsored by a group of French speculators who called themselves the Ohio Company.[11] In July they circulated a pamphlet called *Articles of the Association by the Name of the Ohio Company,* which quoted Crèvecoeur's praise of the region.[12] In the third volume of his *Lettres,* recently published in Paris, he had declared of the place at which the Cuyahoga River empties into Lake Erie (where the city of Cleveland would later stand): "This place seems to be designed for a city; and many persons of my knowledge think so;—all the travelers and hunters have spoken with admiration of the fertility of the plains and the hills watered by the Muskinghum, also of the excellent springs, as well as the salt mines, coal mines, game, and fuller's clay is found everywhere."[13]

There is no evidence that Crèvecoeur himself was a stockholder in the Ohio Company, or had anything directly to do with the bungled French settlement on the Scioto River. But after its failure a few years later he would be blamed for having exaggerated the opportunities for settlers of this region. Two former friends, Marquis de Lézay-Marnésia and Count Constantin François Volney would blame him bitterly for his "too rosy" descriptions. They would even accuse him of having "destroyed" five hundred French families. Both Robert Crèvecoeur and Julia Mitchell believe these accusations unfair. Mitchell says, "The miserable fate of the settlers on the Scioto was due to false representations on the part of unscrupulous speculators in France, and consequent false hopes on the part of the emigrants who went there."[14]

However, there are some passages in Crèvecoeur's descriptions in which his enthusiasm ran very high, and they lose nothing in the Ohio Company's translation. For example:

. . . My imagination involuntarily leaped into futurity! The absence of which was not afflicting, because it appeared to me nigh——I saw those beautiful shores [of the Muskingum] ornamented with decent houses, covered with harvests and well cultivated fields; on the hills exposed to the north, I saw orchards regularly laid out in squares; on the others vine-yard plats, plantations of mulberry trees, *acacias*, &c.—I saw there also, in the inferior lands, the cotton tree, and the sugar maple, the sap of which had become an object of commerce. I agree, however, that all those banks did not appear to me equally proper for culture; but as they will probably remain covered by their native forests, it must add to the beauty, to the variety of this future spectacle. What an immense chain of plantations! What a long succession of activity, industry, culture and commerce is offered to the Americans! I consider then the settling of the lands which are watered by this river, as one of the finest conquests that could ever be presented to man; it will be so much the more glorious as it will be legally acquired of the ancient proprietors and will not exact a single drop of blood. It is destined to become the source of force, riches, and the future glory of the United States.[15]

Crèvecoeur had always insisted that success on the frontier demanded good judgment in selecting the land, and then wise and industrious use of it. A previous passage in this same "Sketch of the Ohio River and the Country of Kentucky" contains an anecdote which was probably intended as a fable, not autobiography. The author tells of meeting a Frenchman who had come to Kentucky to make his fortune, though he did not know a word of English; and as the son of a noble family he thought it dishonorable to work with his hands.[16] (It seems highly improbable that a person so ignorant of the language and the country could have reached Kentucky.)

The author says he took pity on this misguided young man, with whom he could communicate only in bad Latin (pretending that he could not communicate in French marks this narrative as fiction), and taught him that he must learn English, take up a trade, and begin working with his hands. Being young, strong, and willing to take advice, the man discarded his aristocratic illusions and began adapting himself to American life.

Yet sometimes he would still say, "What would my parents say if they knew that I operate a sawmill on the shores of the Ohio, and that I help you cut down trees to be converted into planks?" However, he was learning that in America only idleness and not physical labor is dishonorable.

Crèvecoeur did not return from Boston until sometime in mid-autumn, and his daughter may have returned with him. By this time she was an attractive, sociable young lady with many friends in Boston, Hartford, and New York—her own and her father's.

Mitchell says "there is a tradition that upon his return from New England, Crèvecoeur accompanied Benjamin Franklin to Lancaster [Pennsylvania], when the cornerstone of Franklin College was laid."[17]

This tradition stemmed from the beginning of Chapter II in *Voyage dans la haute Pensylvanie,* which begins: "In 1787 I accompanied the venerable Franklin, then governor of Pennsylvania, on a trip to Lancaster where he had been invited to lay a cornerstone for the college he had founded for the Pennsylvania Dutch." (Now Franklin and Marshall College; Franklin was not really the founder, though he had made a large contribution.) Mitchell suggests that this was fiction, and she was right. In the first place, the ceremony was held on June 6, while Crèvecoeur was still on the Atlantic Ocean; and in the second, Franklin himself did not attend. One of his biographers, Carl Van Doren, says: "The facts are that in the state of his health he could not have gone and that he did not go. He was present on the 6th at the meeting of the Executive Council in Philadelphia and had guests at dinner one of whom was Washington."[18] Franklin was afflicted with kidney stones, which made traveling painful.

This is another example of Crèvecoeur's dramatizing his narrative by writing it as personal experience. Even in his reporting the return of Dr. Franklin to Philadelphia in 1785,[19] he used his imagination: "The *London Packet* had almost reached port before it was known that it carried this great man; the news spread throughout the harbor, and all the ships of all the nations, as if by a spontaneous impulse hoisted their flags."[20] Even the English, he added, and the whole town resounded with bells, gun salutes, and cheering crowds.

Franklin did receive a very noisy and exuberant welcome home, but again, according to Van Doren: "Another ship had outsailed the London packet and brought news of Franklin nine days before him. Philadelphia awaited in hourly excitement. Cannon announced his landing at the Market Street wharf. . . ." Of course, Crèvecoeur had written his account while he was still in France, but he evidently did have some American newspapers for sources, from which he translated the speeches of welcome and Franklin's responses, as he had done for Lafayette during his American visit. At that time he excused the tediousness of this routine reporting by saying he was doing it for future historians. He also believed just as strongly in the importance of Franklin for future historians, declaring, "The names of *Washington & Franklin* will become in future centuries the pride of our country." By "our country" did he mean France or the United States? Perhaps this ambiguity reflected his own national ambivalence, though he could have replied, "Both."

By the time Crèvecoeur returned from Boston he was worried less about conditions in the United States than the increasing political turmoil in France. He also worried about pains in Ally's lungs, fearing his son might be contracting tuberculosis. Yet he continued as best he could to serve the interests of the two countries. In December he made a trip to the copper mines in New Jersey at the suggestion of Marshal de Castries, who had hoped that the ore could be carried by packet ship for use in the foundries at Romilly.[21] But unfortunately the amount of ore available was negligible. Furthermore, by the beginning of 1788 the packets were making less frequent trips. Crèvecoeur wrote a few letters to the ministry

of foreign affairs about conditions in America, but he began
to take less interest in promoting commerce between the two
countries because it was a losing battle.

A serious split had developed in the French government.
One faction loyal to the queen was led by Baron de Breteuil,
formerly friendly to Crèvecoeur. But the queen hated Americans, because she thought their revolution had incited revolt
in France; consequently, the baron became cool toward the
New York consul. The other faction included the friends of
Jacques Necker, who as finance minister 1776–1781 had tried
to promote both political and financial reform. Breteuil won
the struggle and Castries, friend of Necker, resigned. Count
de la Luzerne, brother of a former minister to the United
States, took his place. Lafayette visited him to urge the reten-
tion of Crèvecoeur as consul in New York, and Luzerne assured him that he did not intend to make any change. Lafayette asked if he might report this to Crèvecoeur, and
Luzerne replied, "Certainly."

On January 28, 1788, the Countess de Damas wrote Crèvecoeur:

> The good Marquis [Lafayette] has had many conversa-
> tions with Mme. d'Houdetot, who had desired to consult
> him in your behalf. . . . He is on good terms with the new
> minister, M. the Count de Luzerne, [is] extremely intimate
> with Count de Montmorin [who served as minister of the
> navy between Castries's resigning and Luzerne's appoint-
> ment], and the Archbishop [Brienne]. Do not fear, mon-
> sieur; his influence on all American affairs and your excel-
> lent reputation will guard the position you have used so
> well for the good of France and America.[22]

Yet in spite of these assurances, says his first biographer,
"Crèvecoeur was not fooled." His apprehension was increased by a letter from Count de Moustier, who had been
named minister to the United States, saying that he had had

"to defend the consul of New York against certain attacks coming from the minister [Luzerne]." Count de Moustier arrived in New York early in January 1788 to take up his duties. His sister, the Marquise de Bréthan, was a friend of Crèvecoeur, who would later use her portrait of Washington as a frontispiece for his *Voyage dans la haute Pensylvanie*.

Count de Moustier was not altogether unfriendly toward Crèvecoeur, but he was critical. Temperamentally and philosophically they were quite different. He did not share Crèvecoeur's democratic sympathies, and was always conscious of being a French aristocrat. In an official dispatch he objected especially to Crèvecoeur's anglophilia: "Living too long abroad and too little at home [in France], he has contracted prejudices in favor of English customs and laws, which he should prudently hide. One could recommend him not to extol a nation which is already only too admired in America and to be French in his speech and behavior."[23]

Of course, as we have seen, Crèvecoeur had admired the British since his youthful sojourn in Salisbury; and when he resigned from the French army in Canada, he had chosen to live in a British colony instead of returning to France. Furthermore, he had remained loyal to Great Britain during the Revolution, though his imprisonment by the British commander in New York had caused him to consider the cruelties of both sides.

Count de Moustier, after serving nearly a year as ambassador to the United States, residing in New York, the temporary capital, gave an official evaluation of the consul on December 25, 1788:

M. de Crèvecoeur, whom I am in a position to see frequently, seems to have improved recently, since he has applied himself to knowing better in what respect he must consider the position entrusted to him. The knowledge he has of the United States will become more useful when he has acquired the habit of carefully checking his facts, a few which a simple narrator or philosophical writer hastens to collect merely to show off. I am confident that M. de Crèvecoeur can be very usefully employed in this country, but he will require guidance.[23a]

This appears to be a case of the haughty count pulling rank on a mere knight, considering himself infinitely superior to him, though he does concede that Crèvecoeur knows the country very well indeed; but he disapproves of his enthusiasm for things American. Probably also, he disliked his attitude toward emigration from France, encouraged in the *Lettres d'un cultivateur américain.* He thought the emigration of skilled workers from France to America caused what today would be called *caeteris paribus,* "brain-drain."

Crèvecoeur was finding his relation with the new minister of the navy increasingly frustrating. Often his recommendations were not acknowledged, and he began to wonder if they were even read.[24] Nevertheless, he continued to attend to his duties conscientiously. On April 25, 1788, he reported: "The packet-boat *Maréchal de Castries* had such a long and difficult crossing that, in order to put everything in order again, I have been obliged to set her departure at the time when the February packet-boat was to leave; the latter, since her arrival here only a few days ago, will be sent back only on May 10." Thomas Jefferson had become so disgusted with the French mail service that he had begun sending his letters by way of London on British ships.[25]

Crèvecoeur also sent the minister of the navy a report on an experiment he thought would interest the French navy. Square pieces of timber coated with tar extracted from pit coal in Scotland had been immersed in the New York harbor for a year without showing signs of decay or being attacked by worms. In Holland wooden lock gates in canals had been preserved for two years by coating them with tar. "The introduction and application of this new preservative have seemed so important for our navy that I have considered it my duty to inform you of it."

Early in 1788 Crèvecoeur had an occasion to uphold the principle of "extraterritoriality."[26] One of the gunners on a French warship anchored in the New York harbor was accused of having stolen a silver watch worth six crowns. On February 19 Crèvecoeur wrote an account of this incident in an official dispatch. The owner of the watch appealed to a magistrate, who ordered a constable to board the ship and arrest the accused gunner. The captain of the frigate *L'Aigrette* refused to let the constable set foot on the ship. Crèvecoeur was indignant that "a peace officer of the State of New York should have taken the liberty of attempting to violate His Majesty's flag. . . ." Then the plaintiff turned to the mayor of New York City, who gave his permission for the constable to carry out the search. Apparently by this time the magistrate had learned the seriousness of this request and he wrote to Crèvecoeur for advice.

Crèvecoeur made a copy of his letter in translation and sent it with his reply to the minister of the navy. "I hope," he wrote, "you will approve of the principles it contains. The United States by attaining the rank of an independent power have tacitly agreed to observe the usages which decency and reciprocal respect have gradually established between sovereigns. Since the departure of the frigate I have not heard any more of this affair."

A few days later an American who did not know a word of French arrived on a packet ship under the command of a M. de Sionville. He called on Crèvecoeur to complain that "the captain had not treated him as well as he had a right to expect." After listening to his grievances, Crèvecoeur explained that the captain himself had had a difficult trip because of the storms which lengthened the time of the voyage, and, furthermore, it was not the captain's fault that the ship had been hastily prepared at Havre. The other passengers had shared the same inconveniences without complaining. He advised the man to forget it. However:

Five days later, some affairs having obliged me to go to Major Popham's, one of the barristers of the city, I was no little surprised to find there the same passenger, who, egged on by the barrister, confessed to me that he had sought for redress from the Captain and tried to obtain from him a compensation of 200 pounds.

Feeling indignant at such behavior, I left the house and called immediately on Colonel [Alexander] Hamilton, a former aide of General Washington, and one of the best barristers of this city. He promised he would see our Mr. Popham right away and show him the impropriety of his proceeding. He was quite sure that he would be ashamed and drop the affair.

My visit had the effect I expected from it. The packet-ship left, the compensation was not paid, and fortunately I have not heard of it since.

These annoyances were only minor irritations, but they show how conscientious Crèvecoeur was in representing France. He also tried that year to serve his country and the United States by attempting to help John Fitch, a New England inventor, secure financial backing for his steamship invention.[27] Transportation in the United States was still mainly by water. Few highways and bridges had been built; in winter the roads were often impassable, and the few bridges were frequently swept away by spring floods. Of course, for coastal travel or commercial shipping, sailing vessels were used. They were less useful on the inland rivers, and on the smaller streams impossible. The great difficulty was going upstream against the current. Americans had already proven themselves to be ingenious mechanics, and to encourage them to solve this problem, Congress had voted in 1784 to award thirty thousand acres of land in Ohio to the inventor of a simple and practical means of propelling boats upstream.

In the last edition of his *Lettres d'un cultivateur américain* Crèvecoeur had reported that Jacques Ramsay (actually James Rumsey) had "invented a boat carrying six tons, which can navigate against the current of a river, at the rate of five miles an hour. . . ."[28] After repeated experiments witnessed by General Wood and members of the Philadelphia Council, he had convinced them that his invention worked. George Washington read the reports, examined a model, and certified on September 7, 1789, that he believed that Rumsey "has finally discovered the art of building boats which, by means of easy manual assistance, can travel upstream against the strongest currents."[29] He was especially impressed by the fact that the boat did not require special skill or training to operate. Apparently he thought Mr. Rumsey deserved the reward of thirty thousand acres of Ohio land.

However, Washington's description of the means of propulsion is curiously vague. What did he mean by "manual assistance"? Later Rumsey is known to have experimented with a boat powered by a horse pulling a sweep around an axis mounted on the boat, which, by means of cogs, transmitted power to paddlewheels mounted on the sides. But this does not sound like "manual assistance." Possibly it was a pump, as in later experiments, which provided jet propulsion. At any rate, steam is not mentioned.

It is not certain that John Fitch, a Connecticut inventor, preceded Rumsey in experimenting with a steam-powered boat, but from 1785 to 1787 he conducted numerous experiments, and by 1787 was able to stage a successful demonstration on the Delaware River. In the summer of that year a demonstration was witnessed by members of Congress and David Rittenhouse, treasurer of Pennsylvania and an inventor himself. All certified that they were completely satisfied with

Mr. Fitch's success, and recommended that he receive the land reward. But first a committee from Congress wanted to investigate the claim, and here the inventor's troubles began.

Crèvecoeur was impressed by the reports on Fitch's steamboat and wanted France to consider buying his design. Fearing that a letter to Luzerne might not be read, he wrote to the Duke d'Harcourt and asked him to see that the minister of the navy knew about the American steamboat. Following is the gist of the letter written January 7, 1788, by Crèvecoeur:

> The usefulness of this invention, immeasurable for a country like this, is no less so for France, where the expense of towing is often so great as to decide people to transport their merchandise by land rather than by water, as I noticed between Rouen and Paris, and Havre and Rouen. . . . I cannot help wishing that a device so simple and so important [as Fitch's] might be introduced into France as soon as possible. I would suggest, to that end, that the king should authorize me to have this man make a model of the machine and install it in a boat large enough to enable one to judge of its effect, all of which could easily be sent to France by one of the packets. Further, I would propose that the king should offer several hundred louis to the inventor, by way of compensation, for Mr. Fitch does not make any charge for imparting the principles of this device, nor for showing how it is to be used.[30]

The duke received this letter in March and immediately passed it on to the minister of the navy. Luzerne was impressed and wrote promptly to Laforest, the consul general in New York, asking him to cooperate with Crèvecoeur in trying to get Mr. Fitch's invention for France. But mail sent by the packet boats was so carelessly handled that Laforest did not receive Luzerne's letter until the end of January 1789.

Meanwhile, Crèvecoeur had written to Dr. Franklin for his

opinion, hoping, of course, that his endorsement could be used to impress the French government.[31] However, Franklin wrote disappointedly that he had only heard of the invention, and had doubts about the practicality of Fitch's design. He did not doubt that steam could be used to power a boat, but he feared that Fitch's engine was too large and heavy to be economical, and there was also the added cost of having to employ a skilled mechanic to operate it.

This was an unexpected setback, but a more serious obstacle had also arisen. Rumsey had begun a pamphlet campaign to assert the priority of his invention, and to raise doubts about the feasibility of Fitch's. This caused Congress to delay its decision. By the time Laforest finally received Luzerne's letter, he had formed a strong prejudice against Fitch's claims.[32] Crèvecoeur's support of Fitch could also have influenced Laforest's opposition, for as we have seen, he was also biased against the too-Americanized New York consul. He even took the trouble to contradict Crèvecoeur on the use of coal tar to insulate ship bottoms. He offered no proof, but asserted dogmatically that experiments to use it had been total failures. Perhaps the fact that they had been pronounced successes in Scotland and New York was enough to convince him otherwise.

Robert Crèvecoeur made a thorough study of Rumsey's claims and came to the conclusion that Fitch had not only a legitimate prior claim but also that his invention was unmistakably superior to Mr. Rumsey's.[33] Had either the American or the French government supported Fitch, history would have given him rather than Robert Fulton credit for this invention. And it was not Crèvecoeur's fault but Consul General Laforest's that France did not have the first operable steamship, for the American Congress also delayed helping Fitch until he went bankrupt. Fitch became deeply depressed and Crèvecoeur did his best to cheer him up with sympathetic letters.

Crèvecoeur continued to carry on a heavy correspondence, but it was more social than official. To his friends in Paris he reported the continued debate over a United States constitution, and his relief when the required nine states ratified it in June 1788; eventually all thirteen states accepted it. But the news from France was increasingly disturbing. It is ironic that as Crèvecoeur's influence in France declined, it grew steadily in the United States. He was on friendly terms with the most influential members of the American government, and corresponded extensively with Washington, Jefferson, and Madison on agricultural subjects.

It was in the summer of 1788 that Crèvecoeur became most worried about his elder son's health. In August, Jefferson tried to calm his fears.[34] He, the Countess de Damas, and of course, Mme. d'Houdetot guarded the welfare of Ally and Louis and reported regularly to their anxious father. Jefferson wrote, "Their master speaks highly of Alexandre's disposition and industry, but speaks more favorably of Louis's disposition than of his application." Crèvecoeur replied, "I return you my thanks for the good account you are pleased to give me of my boys. . . . I intend to have the oldest one over here next spring, and am in hopes the sea and the exercise of a horse will confirm his health."

In the same letter Jefferson wrote optimistically of discussion between the French "Estates" and the king. He thought that eventually they would reach a peaceful accord and adopt a moderate constitution, but the same month the Countess de Damas wrote, "We are in a solemn and frightful crisis. It is a question with us of submitting to the most abject slavery or of obtaining a reasonable portion of liberty."[35] Even though of the nobility herself, she was as "democratic" as the agitators for political reform. In fact, most of Crèvecoeur's closest friends in France (Lafayette, Mme. d'Houdetot, Duke de La Rochefoucauld, Duke d'Harcourt) were all liberal in politics.

A friend not of the nobility was the brilliant and Revolutionary lawyer Brissot de Warville,[36] whom Crèvecoeur had first met in Paris in 1784 soon after Brissot's release from the

Bastille, where he had been imprisoned for three months for his political agitation. Brissot liked Crèvecoeur personally and was almost ecstatic over the 1784 edition of *Lettres d'un cultivateur américain.* In 1788 he went to New York to gather material for a book about America. He seems to have arrived unexpectedly at Crèvecoeur's residence—probably still 202 Queen Street—expecting a warm welcome and extended hospitality. But after giving him one night's lodging, Crèvecoeur arranged for him to stay in the house next door. Although they remained friends, Brissot later in his *Voyage dans les États-Unis* (Paris, 1791) bitterly reproached Crèvecoeur for having slighted him, and thought he had done so for fear of M. de Moustier:

> He was under the authority of Ambassador de Moustier, who hated Americans and [French] revolutionary writers; I was one of those he proscribed; without ceasing he exhibited his impotent hatred against me. I defied him, but Crèvecoeur, who feared losing his position, acted coolly toward me to fool him. What can I think of a man who degrades himself by such cowardly dissimulation.[37]

Possibly Brissot misinterpreted Crèvecoeur's actions, but he was a firebrand and probably did embarrass the consul, for whom discretion was necessary in his rather delicate situation. Brissot, of course, scorned discretion. Robert de Crèvecoeur thought that Brissot's bitter attack on his friend did not truly represent his opinion. In at least twenty places in his *Mémoires* he warmly praised Crèvecoeur. Moreover, "What is certain is that on his return to France he continued to correspond amicably with the man against whom he had pretended to have such grave reasons for complaint."[38]

In November 1788 Crèvecoeur had the pleasure of a visit from his daughter, Fanny, now a young lady almost eighteen and said by her biographer, Emily Delesdernier *(Fanny St. John,* Boston, 1874) to have been a striking beauty.[39] She had auburn hair, a high forehead like her father, and eyebrows darker than her hair, which set off her unusually dark blue eyes. To these details her biographer adds: "A fine straight nose, thin sensitive nostrils, a mouth not too small for expression; teeth even and white; a rich Norman shape; with distinguished manners, and a mind of high order, made her unusually attractive." Whatever a "Norman shape" may have been, she undoubtedly had charm, and not least for the diplomatic circles.

One of the diplomats who would play an important role in the lives of both Fanny and her father was M. Louis-Guillaume Otto, secretary of the French legation in 1788.[40] As a precocious student at the University of Strasburg he had specialized in foreign languages, and at twenty-one began serving in the French legation in Munich under Count Luzerne. In 1779 he had come to the United States as Luzerne's secretary, had returned with him to France four years later, and then come back to New York in 1785 as secretary of the French legation.

From 1785 until 1788, when Count de Moustier arrived as minister to the United States, Otto had served as chargé d'affaires. He spoke excellent English, was well liked by Americans, had been elected to membership in the American Philosophical Society, and received an honorary doctor of laws degree at Yale. In March 1787 he married Elizabeth Livingston, daughter of Peter Van Brugh Livingston, who bore one of the most distinguished names in New York City.

Apparently the French legation paid Otto very well, for he was able to live handsomely on Queen Street, as reported in the diary of Manasseh Cutler, a leading botanist and a man of considerable social and political importance. His diary entry reads:

Thursd. July 26 1787

We called first on the Sieur Otto, Chargé des Affaires from the French Court, in Queen Street. He received us very politely, and was exceedingly sociable. He speaks good English and has a truly philosophical mind. Although he is not the Minister plenipotentiary, for there is none at present from France, but he acts as such and lives in the style of a nobleman. His servants and attendants were numerous.[41]

Otto's marriage to Elizabeth Livingston, however, lasted only from March to December 17, when she died in childbirth, leaving a son. New York observed the funeral with elaborate ceremony. Crèvecoeur was one of the pallbearers, along with the ministers of Holland and Spain, the secretary of Congress, the secretary of the War Department, and the British consul general. The cortege, including the foreign ministers, the governor of New York, members of Congress, and all the clergy of the city, marched from Queen Street to Hanover Square and down Wall Street to Trinity Church, where the funeral service and burial took place. A French packet ship fired salutes and all ships in the harbor lowered their flags to half-mast. The fact that Crèvecoeur was a pallbearer suggests that already he had special personal relationship with M. Otto.

After his wife's death, Otto bought a fine house on Broadway, which he improved so much that in 1789, when the United States government was looking for a residence for President Washington, this one was thought to be the most suitable in the city. Meanwhile, Otto had moved to Cherry Street, so there was no difficulty leasing his former home on Broadway for the president. In Cherry Street he continued to live in the grand manner.

In May 1789 Count de Moustier gave a ball for President Washington, recently inaugurated in New York. Of course, all the high officials of the United States government were invited, all foreign ministers, and eminent citizens. Mitchell speculates that Fanny Crèvecoeur's engagement to the secretary of the legation may have been announced at this gala event. However, her marriage did not take place until a year and a half later, and how long she was engaged is not known.

On February 6, 1790, the anniversary of the alliance between France and the Revolutionary American government (though hardly then a government), Crèvecoeur gave a party to celebrate the date. The February 8 issue of the *Daily Advertiser* reported that the French chargé d'affaires had entertained Vice-President Adams, the speaker of the House of Representatives, the chief justice, the heads of the various federal departments, the governor of New York, and the diplomatic corps of foreign nations.

In the spring of this year Crèvecoeur obtained permission from the minister of the navy for another leave of absence. The increased unrest in France had aroused new worries about the health and safety of his sons. But he hoped to return to his position in New York. His somewhat hasty decision to leave the United States may have hastened the date of his daughter's marriage to M. Otto. The ceremony took place on April 13, 1790, in St. Peter's Church, with Father Burke, pastor of the Catholic church Crèvecoeur had helped found, officiating.

The wedding was attended by Thomas Jefferson, now secretary of state; some members of Congress—Jeremiah Wadsworth and Jonathan Trumbull among them; Richard Morris, justice of the Supreme Court of New York State; M. and Mme. Laforest; and Crèvecoeur's old friend William Seton. Both Wadsworth and Trumbull had served on General Washington's staff during the Revolution. These names are mentioned by Robert Crèvecoeur, perhaps as the most conspicuously famous.[42]

A month later Crèvecoeur embarked on the packet ship *Washington,* leaving his daughter, América-Francés, in New York with a man he trusted and loved. For his voyage he had the companionship of M. and Mme. Leray de Chaumont, friends of Benjamin Franklin. He did not suspect that he would never see the United States again.

X

Surviving the French Revolution

WHEN the Bastille fell into the hands of Parisian insurgents on July 14, 1789, it was the beginning of the end for the *ancien régime*. From then, the French Revolution followed a tumultuous course. In New York, Crèvecoeur became increasingly alarmed at the stories he read in English and American newspapers, and found it increasingly difficult to understand what was taking place on the other side of the Atlantic. Because of lack of cooperation in France, it was becoming almost impossible for him to carry out his task according to the high conception he had of his role as a consul. Crèvecoeur considered it his duty to protect all French interests in the United States against possible encroachments on the part of American authorities, and he saw to it in particular that the extraterritoriality of all French ships lying at anchor in American harbors was respected. But how could he discharge his duty if anarchy prevailed at home and he could not count on the support of the French government? He had no choice but to return to France and see for himself how matters stood. The situation seemed hopeless, and he was ready to resign his consulship, if necessary.

Jefferson, who had returned to the United States and seen him in April, wrote to Mme. d'Houdetot: "Monsr de Crève-coeur is well, but a little apprehensive that the spirit of reform-ing and economizing will reach his office. A good man will suffer if it does."[1] He was right. Crèvecoeur was so apprehen-sive that he applied for a leave of absence on account of ill health and took passage on the *Washington* bound for France on May 31.

He must have had quite a shock when he landed, for things had changed considerably since his last stay in France three years before. He may have had the same impression as Count de Ségur who returned to France about the same time. In his *Mémoires,* the count wrote:

> On my way, and before I spoke to anyone, I had a very vivid surprise, for everything put on an unexpected ap-pearance: middle-class people, peasants, laborers, even women showed in their attitudes, gestures, and on all their features something vivid, proud, independent and lively that I had never seen in them before. If I questioned members of the lower classes, they answered me with proud glances, in a loud and bold voice. I saw everywhere signs of those feelings of equality, and liberty which had then become such violent passions. In short, on leaving France, I had left peaceful people bent resignedly under the yoke of a long subjection; on my return, I found it upright, independent and probably too impatient to enjoy its freedom wisely.[2]

Crèvecoeur arrived at a time when things were almost abnormally quiet, during a lull in the storm. King Louis XVI had apparently accepted the curtailment of his powers. He had been obliged to move from his Palace at Versailles, where he lived in the middle of his Court among faithful supporters, to the Tuileries in the heart of Paris, where he was in a way the prisoner of his people. It seemed that the Revolution was over and civil peace had returned. People were either elated or relieved, and joyful preparations were being made for the Fête de la Fédération. It was to be held on the Champ de Mars on July 14, 1790, to celebrate both the storming of the Bastille the year before and the indestructible unity of the French nation. Wordsworth, who "chanced / To land at Calais on the very eve / Of that great federal day [. . .] saw [. . .] / How bright a face is worn when joy of one / Is joy for tens of millions," and on his way to Paris on foot along the elm-lined roads, he "found benevolence and blessedness / Spread like a fragrance everywhere. . . ." People danced in the open air well into the night, "though gray-haired lookers-on / Might waste their breath in chiding."[3]

Crèvecoeur was not in the least deluded by this brief spell of fair weather. He could hear claps of thunder in the distance and feel subterranean tremors anouncing the commotions to come. He did not proceed to Paris, where he could have joined his friends and conferred with General Lafayette. He had dedicated the French edition of his *Lettres d'un cultivateur américain* to him in 1784 and Lafayette was now at the height of his power and influence. He was "the hero of Liberty in two worlds" and about to preside over the Fête de la Fédération as the supreme arbiter between the king and the Constituent Assembly. Through him, Crèvecoeur could have obtained an important position among the leaders of the republican party. He would undoubtedly have been welcome as one of its theoreticians. He was also friends with Brissot de Warville, the abolitionist, who was to become one of the leaders of the Girondists, and Jean-Baptiste Target, the well-known lawyer who had seen his *Lettres* through the press in 1784, and who, as speaker of the Constituent Assembly in 1790, tried to make constitutional monarchy work in France. His friend Countess de Damas tried to reassure him. "I daresay you are probably afraid of coming to Paris," she wrote to him in October 1790, "I can give you my word that so long as our hero [Lafayette] commands here, honest people will be safe."[4] But despite her exhortations, he resisted the temptation of going to Paris.

He must have been quite bewildered by the extraordinary change that had taken place in his absence. He had left a prosperous and peaceful kingdom and on his return he discovered a country torn by civil strife and on the verge of civil war. The stratified and strongly hierarchical society he had known was replaced by one in which respect for authority had ceased to exist. The land which had roused the admiration and envy of foreign visitors was now threatened with famine in some districts. All this sounded almost incredible to most of his contemporaries. In 1788, only one year before the beginning of the Revolution, Sébastien Mercier had written in his *Tableau de Paris*: "It is unthinkable that any important revolution may occur in Europe, unless it be in some remote days."[5]

In *L'Emigré*, Gabriel Sénac de Meilhan, a shrewd observer of the manners of the time, explained the change by the irresponsible volatility of French people. The French, he pointed out, were capable of both covering with kisses the horse of the messenger who brought the good news of the recovery of King Louis XV, a king who had done nothing whatever for them, and of beheading his grandson, who had done his best to relieve their misery. This behavior seemed to him utterly incomprehensible and quite irrational.

Yet the Revolution which was taking place had been foreseeable and was easy to understand. Under the brilliant surface of French eighteenth-century society there was far too much unjust and unjustified inequality, and, too often, grinding poverty. During the reign of Louis XVI, who was a man of good will but of no will of his own, the situation had further deteriorated and social inequalities had become still worse. The nobility, as Voltaire had shown in his *Lettres philosophiques,* was an idle and parasitical class which lived exclusively on the income of the land it possessed without ever creating new wealth. A well-born French noble considered it below his condition to have anything to do with trade or industry. It would have been *déroger*.

The result of this scornful attitude was that the commoners of the middle class, the so-called bourgeois, grew rich, while the nobles became more and more impoverished. In an attempt to maintain or regain their superiority, they obtained from Louis XVI the pledge that all the financially rewarding positions in the army, the church, or the magistracy would be reserved for them to the exclusion of all commoners, whatever their talents or aptitudes. Such a measure naturally caused great resentment in the bourgeoisie. In order to increase the income which the nobles derived from their lands, feudal rights which had fallen into desuetude were revived and this roused the anger of the peasant class. This retrograde policy isolated the king and the nobility from the rest of the nation.

To illustrate the state of mind of even the most enlightened nobles, Sénac de Meilhan tells how Target, a distinguished lawyer, once deeply shocked a very open-minded duchess by helping himself uninvited to a pinch of snuff from her open snuff box. The rights of man, to her mind, did not extend quite so far! How could a commoner, a mere member of the Third Estate, presume to help himself to her snuff, as if it were "a natural consequence of the equality of all men"?[6]

Arthur Young aptly summed up the situation in 1789–1790 when he noted:

It is impossible to justify the excesses of the people or their taking up arms; they were certainly guilty of cruelties [. . .]. But is it really the people to whom we are to impute the whole; or their oppressors who have kept them so long in a state of bondage? [. . .] When such evils happen, they surely are more imputable to the tyranny of the master than to the cruelty of the servant [. . .] the murder of the *seigneur* or a *château* in flames is recorded in every newspaper [. . .] but where do we find the register of that *seigneur*'s oppressions of his peasantry, and the exactions of feudal services from those whose children are dying around them for want of bread? [. . .]. Who has dwelt sufficiently upon explaining all the ramifications of despotism, regal, aristocratical, and ecclesiastical [without counting those stemming from the provincial *parlements,* which both passed laws and enforced them and combined legislative, executive, and judiciary powers] pervading the whole mass of the people; reaching like a circulating fluid the most distant capillary tubes of poverty and wretchedness [. . .]. The true judgment to be made of the French Revolution must surely be gained from an attentive consideration of the evils of the old Government.[7]

In addition to these socio-economic causes, there were moral and intellectual ones. The higher classes had little sense of responsibility and selfishly clung to their *privilèges,* as they were called traditionally, though they had no reason for existing anymore. In exchange, they led dissolute lives. Sénac de Meilhan reported a newly married count saying to his young wife, no doubt in exchange for a similar freedom of action: "I allow you everything, except princes and footmen."[7] The higher clergy (which consisted exclusively of nobles) were just as corrupt. Arthur Young tells how the bishop of Béziers had a road cut through some mere *abbé*'s land, "at the expense of the province, to lead to the house of his mistress." And he concludes: "This is a pretty feature of a government that a man is to be forced to sell his estate [. . .] because bishops make love, I suppose, to their neighbours' wives, as no other love is fashionable in France." (As Mark Twain observed more epigrammatically one hundred years later: "A Frenchman's home is where another man's wife is."[8])

Such manners aroused the contempt—and envy—of those who did not have enough money and leisure to sin as elegantly. But worse, and more dangerous, was the undermining of all the institutions which constituted the backbone of the *régime*. This undermining had started as early as Pierre Bayle's *Dictionnaire historique et critique* in 1697 and was carried on by the Encyclopedists under the leadership of Diderot from 1752 on. These men had absolute faith in reason, science, and material progress, and slyly derided all beliefs based on custom and tradition. Religion in their eyes was mere superstition; the divine right of kings and all political systems based on the inequality of men held no legitimacy for them. Their teachings permeated all the literate classes, including the nobility, and were the rage in the Parisian *salons* where Diderot and his friends reigned supreme. For his part, Crèvecoeur had adopted them, as we have seen, even before his arrival in Paris, since he had read Abbé Raynal's *Histoire philosophique et politique* before writing his *Letters from an American Farmer,* and Raynal, as Arthur Young said, was "one of the undoubted precursors of the present revolution." Count de Ségur noted that "it was not only for its true worth that this important book [*Histoire philosophique et politique*] was admired, but for the most violent declamations it contained against priests, kings and Negro slavery."[9] Mme. de Staël (Necker's daughter) was one of his admirers and, on his return from banishment, she invited him to dine at her table.

If we are to believe Brissot, society women were just as enthusiastic about the *Lettres d'un cultivateur américain,* and, for his part, he thought that Crèvecoeur must have, besides "the most sensitive soul and the kindest humane heart, the strongest hatred of tyranny and the most profound contempt for kings and nobles."[10] In short, all French intellectuals as well as society people were seduced by the new ideas. United States ambassador Gouverneur Morris very lucidly saw the danger: "Their *Literati,*" he wrote, "whose heads are turned by romantic notions picked up in books, and who are all too lofty to look down upon the kind of man which really exists, and too wise to heed the dictates of common sense and experience, have turned the heads of their countrymen and they have run a-muck at a Don Quixotic constitution. . . ."[11]

Mme. d'Houdetot shared the general enthusiasm, but her intuitive nature made her foresee the dreadful consequences of this collective frenzy. Jefferson's secretary, William Short, reported that she ardently wished for the success of the Revolution, but her wishes were so ardent that they almost sounded like fears. Her anxiety, he added, was the necessary consequence of the kindness of her heart and the weakness of her nerves.[12] Like many of her compatriots, she wanted for France the same kind of Revolution that had resulted in the creation of a harmonious republic in America. (The American Revolution was undoubtedly the fuse which ultimately detonated the French powder keg.) But she did not want anyone to suffer and she may very well have warned Crèvecoeur against the dangers of the situation.

She did not feel at home in Paris anymore. The tolerant and liberal intellectual atmosphere which had reigned in the *salons* had gradually disappeared as the Revolution approached. The eclectic *salons* of former years were replaced and displaced by clubs *à l'anglaise* where men without women met to play cards, eat and drink together and, above all, talk politics endlessly—to the exclusion of any other topic. The softening influence of women ceased to be felt. There were instead a gradual masculinization and politicization of society, which contributed to a brutalization of manners.

Even fashions had changed and acquired a political coloring. It was considered unpatriotic and aristocratic for men to wear breeches with white or black stockings. One should wear trousers. For women, full dresses worn over an abundance of petticoats were replaced by straight skirts and short bodices, called *pierrots* because they had a short tail behind ("pierrot" is a word for *sparrow*). It was fashionable, too, to dress in three colors: white for the king, plus blue and red, which were the colors of Paris and therefore of the Revolution. One must at least sport a tricolored cockade on one's hat or breast. Many men wore red Phrygian caps, which formerly had been worn by liberated convicts. Marat was to write: "I don't think I am mistaken, but I wouldn't be surprised if in twenty years' time there won't be anyone in Paris who knows how to make a hat."[13] Arthur Young was surprised. At a dinner to which he was invited in Paris, "most of the deputies [of the National Assembly], especially the younger ones, were dressed *au polisson* [literally, like scapegraces], many of them without any powder in their hair, and some in boots; not above four or five were neatly dressed. How times have changed! When they had nothing better to attend to, the fashionable Parisians were correctness itself in all that pertained to the *toilette* and were, therefore, thought a frivolous people, but now they have something of more importance to occupy them."[14]

Language, too, reflected the change. When addressing a person in French, one can use either the second person plural, in the case of a stranger or a superior, or the second person singular, in the case of a person one is on intimate terms with. But all men being equal, there ceased to be any reason for such nice distinctions. *Tu,* the second person singular, became the rule, whatever the rank of the person addressed. Besides, you did not call your interlocutor *Monsieur* or *Madame* anymore. These words were felt to imply social superiority (*mon seigneur, mea domina*), though such forms of address were used only as a matter of courtesy. They were replaced by unceremonious but staunchly republican terms: *citoyen* and *citoyenne* (*citizen*).

Pierrepont was not Paris, however. Such changes had hardly reached Lower Normandy when Crèvecoeur came back from New York. Newspapers were rare in those days. They were all printed in Paris and they sometimes arrived in the more distant provinces weeks after the events they reported.

But what was Crèvecoeur's position in the middle of this turmoil? He belonged to the nobility, but only to the *petite noblesse.* He was neither duke nor count, nor even baron, but a plain knight, and he did not share the prejudices of his class. He did not consider it below his station to work for a living. He had been a land surveyor and a farmer in America, and he was now ready to settle in France as a farmer on his father's estate. He intended to improve the output of his land by applying the methods devised by English agronomists. He had learned in America to hate idleness, as he had said in his *Lettres.* Besides, as an enlightened *philosophe,* he believed in material progress and, like the Encyclopedists, was passionately interested, as we have seen, in new inventions and in industrial and commercial techniques. He had no real stake in the old *régime.* He should normally have looked forward to a time when the bourgeoisie would have political power and would encourage trade and industry. He had tried to do so himself almost single-handedly during his consulship in New York. But, like Gouverneur Morris, who had landed in France one year before him, he probably was so frightened by the prospect of a nation which "existed only in hopes and expectations" and in which all "existing forms [had been] shaken to the foundation" that, though theoretically in sympathy with the American republic, he "preached incessant respect for the Prince, attention to the rights of the nobility, and moderation not only in the object, but also in the pursuit of it."[15]

But the moderates were not heard. The Revolution ruthlessly resumed its course after the truce of the Fête de la Fédération. It might have been a mere revolt, as Louis XVI had at first believed, but it soon became a true revolution, as the Duke de Liancourt had rightly diagnosed as early as July 14, 1789. ("Sire, it is not a revolt, it is a revolution," he had told the king.) To begin with, in order to break the power of the Catholic Church, the National Assembly decided that it must be subordinated to the state. All priests were obliged to take an oath of allegiance. Many refused and the Church was divided into jurors, who became civil servants, and nonjurors, who were persecuted. Red caps replaced crosses on steeples and in most churches an inscription warned the visitor that "French people believe in the immortality of the soul and the existence of the Supreme Being" (in other words, in the God of Deists rather than in the God of Christians).

The king tried to escape from Paris with his family and join the army of the nobles which was gathering near Metz, but he was caught and brought back to Paris. Though he swore to respect the Constitution of 1791, which gave the legislative power to a new Assembly, he soon lost all power himself, after a mob invaded the Tuileries in August 1792. From then on, things got worse. Hundreds of political prisoners were massacred in the jails of Paris in September, nonjuror priests were banished, and thousands of suspects were arrested.

Crèvecoeur by that time was in Paris. Some differences had apparently once more arisen between him and his father, and, above all, he had to be in the capital in order to be in touch with the Ministry of the Navy, on which he depended, since he was still in principle French consul in New York. With the help of Lafayette, he had obtained successive extensions of his leave of absence until April 1792. But Lafayette had fled from France and could not obtain favors for him anymore. At the beginning of February 1792, the minister of the navy, one Bertrand de Molleville, had ordered him to return to his post. On February 10, he answered that he was still too ill to do so, but would go to New York as soon as his health permitted:

I re-read the day before yesterday the letter which I had the honor of receiving from you and which I should have answered immediately, if the fit of fever which has been plaguing me for the last three weeks had not prevented me from doing so; as soon as it has left me and I have recovered sufficient strength to undertake the crossing to New York, I will hasten to obey His Majesty's orders

and carry out your instructions. I will leave as soon as my
doctor considers me fit. . . .[16]

But Crèvecoeur must have received another letter from the
minister enjoining him to return to New York without further
delay, for, five days later, on February 15, he sent him the
following answer:

> Under the terms of a leave of absence which does not
> expire before the end of the month of April of this year,
> I was waiting for my recovery before returning to New
> York to take up again my duties as consul, when I received
> the King's orders rescinding my leave and enjoining me
> to go back without any delay.
>
> Besides the obstacle to my departure which the poor
> condition of my health raises right now, I see another
> which it is very difficult to overcome in the necessity in
> which I would be to change in specie, with a loss of three-
> fifths and a half, the paper money which has been and will
> be given to me in payment of my salary, and this, since I
> have no other source of income, would make it impossible
> for me to keep, even in the most modest and indispensably
> necessary condition, the house of a consul in New York,
> not to mention the fact that the cost of the passage alone
> would absorb a considerable portion of my salary.
>
> Under these circumstances, I find myself obliged—
> however reluctantly—to apply to you, Sir, for my retire-
> ment with a pension proportioned to the number of years
> during which I served and to the zeal I showed in the
> discharge of the duties the King had entrusted to me.
>
> As to the duration of my services, I can date their
> beginning from the beginning of the month of September
> 1782, when Marshal de Castries obtained my appointment
> as consul, for, if my commission bears only the date of July
> 1783, it is because, as the English were not to evacuate the
> city before November 1783, it was not considered fitting
> that I should arrive there before this date.
>
> I am sixty, I have three children and no patrimony, I

hope therefore that thanks to the King's kindness and thanks to you, Sir, I will obtain after my resignation a retirement pension proportioned to the duration of my services and the zeal with which I discharged my duties.

On the same day, probably thinking he had not given sufficient proof of his zeal to a minister who did not know him, Crèvecoeur sent another letter on the heels of the first, listing some of the high points of his career:

You will forgive me, Sir, if I recall the nature of my services and the zeal with which I discharged my duties.

As soon as I took my post, I proposed and had the Minister accept the assignment of six packet boats between Lorient and New York, an assignment which resulted in the first regular commercial links between the two countries; I supervised them in the capacity of manager without any salary.

As I was the first French consul in New York, I may well say that I overcame the difficulties which beset all beginnings and they were considerable.

I had the luck of contributing personally to save the Frigate called *The Nymph,* of 40 cannon, stranded on the western banks six leagues from New York in November 1784, which won me a letter recognizing, on behalf of Marshal de Castries, the services I rendered on that occasion.

By the King's order, towards the end of 1784, I had built in New Hampshire a corvette of 26 cannon in conformity with the new principles of naval architecture of [illegible] Pech. The beauty and speed of this ship (the *Marshal de Castries*), which were duly recognized by the inspection ordered by the Minister on her arrival in France, are well known.

I constantly took an interest in all the useful things which the Northern Continent of America might supply to the Kingdom. I sent a carefully assembled collection of woods suitable for building and other purposes, which by the Minister's order, was submitted to a survey by the Academy of Sciences and won its approval.

I was the first to propose—and I used all my influence with the members of Congress and some of my own money for the purpose—the foundation of the first Catholic church in New York, taking advantage of the wise toleration which the Government had just enforced there. . . .

These letters remained unanswered and Crèvecoeur retained the title of consul until December 19, 1792, when all French agents in the United States were removed from office. Crèvecoeur applied again for a pension on March 10, 1793, and, when he heard that the recent decree of February 16 had transferred the administration of the consular service from the Ministry of the Navy to the Ministry for Foreign Affairs, he applied once more, this time to the minister for foreign affairs, a certain Lebrun-Tondu. Once more his application remained unanswered, and he was left without any income. He found it difficult to make ends meet. Those were trying times. All his friends and protectors had either disappeared or were in hiding—in particular, Marshal de Beauvau. The Duke de Castries had emigrated. The Duke de La Rochefoucauld had been stoned to death by a mob in 1792, and the Duke de Liancourt, his cousin, inherited his title. Liancourt was a liberal and progressive aristocrat who believed in the abolition of privileges and was a great friend of Arthur Young. He emigrated to England and later went to the United States. Lafayette had been obliged to expatriate himself. As to Target, after playing an important role in the Constituent Assembly and very nearly becoming minister of justice in 1789, he had faded out.

Most members of the diplomatic corps had left Paris and even the ambassador of a friendly nation, like Gouverneur Morris, who had remained, did not feel safe. Once his residence was searched. He protested violently and received a rather insolent answer from the foreign minister by way of apology. He nevertheless decided to stay, because, as he wrote to Jefferson, "I do not indeed feel offended by what is done by the people, because they cannot be supposed to understand the law of nations, and because they are in a state of fury which is inconceivable [. . .] and renders them capable of all excesses."[17] It was even rumored for a time in London that he had been guillotined. He was very closely watched and his mail regularly opened by the police. When he went to his country place at Sainport (Morris's mispelling of Seine-port, on the Seine between Corbeil and Melun), he experienced, like everyone else, "as much difficulty [. . .] as [he] would have been exposed to in going to the territory of a power at war." "Such [was] the distracted condition of the times. . . ." He warned one of his correspondents: "Pray tell your French friends [in America] not to name anyone in their letters, for they will bring their friends to the guillotine."

Crèvecoeur had no choice but to remain as inconspicuous and invisible as possible, especially after the Convention succeeded the Legislative Assembly and held unchecked both the legislative and the executive powers. Royalty was then quickly abolished and Louis XVI guillotined. A Revolutionary Tribunal and a Committee of Public Safety were set up in order to concentrate all powers in a few hands. The extremists (called Montagnards) soon eliminated the moderates (called Girondists), notably Brissot, and, for over a year, France was under the Reign of Terror. Thousands of political suspects were sent to the guillotine after a summary judgment. No one was safe. Even Lavoisier, the founder of modern chemistry (but also a former *fermier-général,* i.e., tax farmer) was condemned to death by Fouquier-Tinville, the public prosecutor, who stupidly declared: "The Republic has no need of scientists." André Chénier, the poet, was guillotined, too, and Condorcet, the mathematician, preferred to commit suicide in jail. The Republic apparently did not need mathematicians or poets either. Impelled by a passionate sense of social justice and a fanatical faith in the rightness of their cause, the Revolutionary leaders provided a perfect illustration of the often forgotten truth that the enforcement of equality is incompatible with the enjoyment of liberty. Long before these excesses, Abbé Raynal had written to the president of the National Assembly, regretting to have been "one of those who, by expressing a generous indignation against arbitrary power, may have given arms to licence and anarchy."[18]

Crèvecoeur was very prudent in those days and neglected no precaution. He even scratched out such taboo words as *count* and *marquis* in the few letters from his friends that he dared to keep. If his house had been searched and his correspondence examined, these naïve precautions would undoubtedly have proved quite useless.

It may seem strange that he did not claim immunity as an American citizen. Thanks to his friend Ethan Allen, he and his three children had obtained American naturalization in the state of Vermont in 1787, though he then had diplomatic status and represented a foreign power. He had applied for it, because, he said to Allen, he thought his children would benefit from it. It would be not only "highly honorable to them but also highly conducive to the completion of their Bill of naturalization in France which I am now soliciting in order that they may inherit my father's succession which will be pretty considerable." He was essentially moved, he protested, by "an honest intention of establishing his children in the full possession of the rights of Frenchmen born."[19] As soon as he had this document in hand, he had his children's legal existence recognized by French authorities, and he probably renounced his American citizenship in order to remain eligible for his consulship in New York in the eyes of the French naval ministry, which could not employ a foreigner in this capacity.

In the middle of all these disorders, Crèvecoeur thought above all of assuring the safety of his children. This may be the reason why he left the relative safety of Pierrepont for the dangers of Paris. He had found a position for Ally, his elder son, in an important British bank in Paris—Boyd, Ker & Co. But, when the Convention decreed in September and October 1793 that all British subjects residing in France would be imprisoned and their possessions confiscated, Walter Boyd, the bank's manager, returned hurriedly to England. Crèvecoeur, fearing for the safety of Ally, who not only worked for enemy aliens but bore the English-sounding name St. John, sent him to Havre with his younger brother, Louis. They worked there for an American importer and they obtained from the local authorities papers certifying they were born in the United States and had arrived from America five weeks before. This way, they would not be mistaken for French aristocrats waiting for a chance to emigrate. Crèvecoeur would have liked to send them to America, but the seas were then infested with Algerian pirates.

Toward the end of October, however, Ally found passage on a ship bound for Hamburg and there, by a stroke of luck, happened on a merchant named Barbazan, who had been born in Bordeaux, but was a naturalized American citizen. This man welcomed him, as if Ally had been his own son, helped him to settle down, and launched him into business. Thus Ally was soon in a position to provide for himself and even to send money to his family in France. In the neighboring city of Lübeck, he met admirers of the *Letters from an American Farmer*. Crèvecoeur was quite flattered, when he heard of it, for Ally kept up a frequent correspondence with him through an American merchant in Paris, J. Swan, who belonged to a firm specializing in maritime transport which frequently worked for the French government. They corresponded in English. Crèvecoeur addressed his letters either to William-Alexander Saint-John or to William Hastings. The better to deceive the censor in case the letters should be opened, he dated them from Orange County, Pine Hill, or New Haven,

Newport, Providence, or Oswego. He also used Indian names: Cahio-Harro, to refer to himself, Téwénissa and Mataxen, to designate Ally and Otto; the Old Sachem was his father; Potowmack, the Elbe.

Louis, who had remained at Havre after his brother's departure, was supposed to follow him to Hamburg at the first opportunity, but the opportunity never came and he was eventually obliged to return to Paris. However, in April 1794, Crèvecoeur sent him to Bordeaux with a passport delivered by Gouverneur Morris in the name of Philip-Lewis Saint-John, citizen of the United States, on his way to Philadelphia. It was hoped that from Bordeaux he could at last sail to Hamburg. In May, he found passage on a Danish ship bound for America. He was to disembark in Lisbon and go from there to Germany. Such was not his intention, though. He had always dreamt of returning to America, where his father had been so happy as a farmer. So he proceeded from Lisbon to Boston instead of Hamburg—unknown to his father, who heard of his arrival in the United States only in August, several months later, and much to his relief. Once in America, Louis bought a tract of land of two hundred acres in New Jersey, near Navesink. Some of the people there still remembered his father, who had surveyed their land, and they gave him a hearty welcome. He led the life of a pioneer for two years and roughed it very courageously, clearing the land, setting up a sawmill near a waterfall, living in a log house with a tree trunk cut near the root for a table, and subsisting on the flesh of frozen pigs in winter. He held out until 1796, when his father thought the experiment had lasted long enough and asked him to come back home now that there was no danger.

Crèvecoeur's son-in-law, Count Otto, chargé d'affaires in the United States, had returned to France on leave in 1792 with Fanny, who thus came to France for the first time.[20] When Otto arrived, he was told that he had been dismissed, but he applied for a new job and was appointed head of the

Premier Bureau (First Bureau) of the Ministry for Foreign Affairs. This position brought him in touch with François Deforgues, a former clerk of Danton's, who had been named commissioner for foreign affairs. Unlike most of the other revolutionaries, Deforgues believed in good manners and respected the traditions of the diplomatic service. So Otto did not feel too unhappy in his new position.

He sometimes even had the privilege of being present at the dinners given by Deforgues to Danton, Fabre d'Églantine, and other important Montagnards. But when Danton fell, Deforgues's turn soon came. He was arrested on April 1, 1794, and replaced two weeks later by a vulgar and ignorant demagogue named Buchot, an elementary school teacher who had never left his native village in Jura before the Revolution and so was not particularly qualified to deal with foreign affairs. He spent most of his time in cafés and, naturally, resented the good manners of the heads of the various services of his department and could not forgive them their superiority and their competence. He had them all arrested, including Otto, on July 7, 1794. Fortunately, three weeks later on 9 Thermidor (July 27) Robespierre was overthrown by a coalition of all the politicians who felt threatened by him. Deforgues was immediately released and without delay sought to obtain the liberation of his former subordinates. They were all freed, but Otto was soon arrested a second time, on an anonymous denunciation, and kept in jail incommunicado in the Palais du Luxembourg. Deforgues had once more to pull strings to obtain his release, but Otto fully justified himself in a memoir sent to the Committee of Public Safety in which he refuted all the charges brought against him. His innocence was so patent that he was reinstated in his job and retained his position until the reorganization of the department in 1795, when the Directoire succeeded the Convention.[21] Thermidor 9 had practically brought the Terror to an end. The Revolution was over. Crèvecoeur had weathered the storm and managed to survive.

He had survived, but the years 1790 to 1794 had nonetheless been years of constant fear and anxiety for himself and his two sons, and, after his sons had left French soil, for his son-in-law and his daughter. During all that time, like most French people, they were permanently under the threat of a denunciation or a house search, with possibly the guillotine at the end. They were years of penury and discomfort, too, when the family had to live in cramped quarters. Even though Otto had an important position in the foreign service, he and his wife had to content themselves with a very small apartment, which housed, besides them, a boarder and Crèvecoeur himself. Poor Crèvecoeur kept complaining that that nuisance of a boarder would read aloud at night, occupy the best seat next to the fireplace, and leave no room for his books and papers, so that he could not do any writing anymore. But they had to put up with him. He paid a good rent and, being a vegetarian, did not cost much to feed.

Even during the Revolution, Crèvecoeur kept working. Whenever he could and the weather was favorable, he escaped from Paris and went to Target's house at Montmorency, which he called Cherry Valley, because the place was famous for the cherries that were grown there. The house was hardly visible from the road. He felt quite safe, and he told Ally he sometimes wrote for eight hours a day with the eagerness of a young man. He had no possibility of publishing anything, but he was still passionately interested in all his old projects. When his friend and successor in New York, de Lafont, returned to France briefly in 1793, before being once more appointed to the New York consulship, with Otto's support, Crèvecoeur had a chance to have long conversations with him. They spoke of the packet-boat line between France and New York which he set so much store by, but, as he wrote to Ally: "Laf. [Lafont] and Pet. [Petry, the French consul in Philadelphia] have gone back. I have not pushed my project concerning the P.B., [packet boats], for fear of attracting attention; I prefer to remain in obscurity."[22]

For all his prudence, he remained in touch not only with

a number of people who were connected with or interested in the United States, but also with old friends. He occasionally saw Abbé Grégoire, the juror bishop and member of the Convention, because of their common interest in the abolition of slavery. Abbé Grégoire mentions their encounters in his *Mémoires*. He also supplied materials to Abbé Raynal, who was preparing a new edition of his *Histoire philosophique et historique des deux Indes*. The d'Houdetots and Saint-Lambert, perhaps because of their age and former connection with Rousseau, went on living very much as before. They divided their life between Paris, Sannois, and Eaubonne. They were short of money, but still sometimes gave receptions. Crèvecoeur did not dare to see them, but he often met Mme. d'Houdetot's faithful factotum, Girard, who intrepidly ran errands for his mistress and even for Crèvecoeur. In particular, he visited in jail a prisoner to whom Crèvecoeur referred as Thomas, and who may have been Thomas Paine. Though an important member of the Convention and an American citizen, Paine had been arrested as an Englishman by birth. Crèvecoeur had known him and now, through Girard, generously sent him clothes, sheets, blankets, and even money despite his own reduced circumstances.

Crèvecoeur still had contacts with some Americans. He several times met James Leray, with whom he had returned from New York on board the *Washington*. James Leray was actually M. Leray de Chaumont, a Frenchman by birth, the son of the former governor of the Invalides, who had been Franklin's host at Passy. He was a wealthy landowner on both sides of the Atlantic and, besides, had the luck to be an American citizen by naturalization and to enjoy semidiplomatic status under the protection of the American ambassador. He tried to recruit settlers and sell them land in small lots in America. The time was favorable for such a business venture, since so many people were trying to leave France. Crèvecoeur envied less his fortune than his immunity, and must have more than once regretted that his own naturalization was no longer valid.

He also knew Joel Barlow, who was then in his mid-thirties and, like Leray, involved in land speculations. He represented La Compagnie de Scioto, which sold land in Ohio in a region which Crèvecoeur had praised in the third volume of his *Lettres*: "If a poor man with only his hands for capital asked me where shall I settle down to live comfortably without the help of oxen or horses? I would tell him, go to the banks of one of the creeks in the plains of Scioto."[23]

Unfortunately the Compagnie de Scioto had no title to the land it sold, only an option. It thus rested on very shaky foundations and it soon foundered in spite of Barlow's efforts. Barlow had also business connections with some maritime companies and found himself in a position to help Crèvecoeur exchange letters with Ally. It is mainly for this reason that Crèvecoeur came to know him, but they may have shared literary interests, too.

As a former American citizen, Crèvecoeur should have had the support and protection of the American ambassador, Gouverneur Morris, who had succeeded Jefferson, but Morris, unlike his predecessor, was a cold-hearted realist. He despised French politicians, whom he regarded as bloodthirsty bawlers and brawlers, and had no sympathy whatever for a naïve idealist like Crèvecoeur. Besides, this undiplomatic diplomat was well known in Paris as a staunch conservative and even rabid reactionary. He was unable to help those who needed his protection. He let down—or could not do anything for—Countess de Damas, who had taken refuge in his country house at Sainport and was arrested there. She escaped the guillotine through no credit to him. On this occasion, Crèvecoeur passed along severe comments on Morris in some of his letters; he wrote, for instance: "The CCD [Countess Charles de Damas] is severely treated in jail, and, what is worse, because she was under the protection of G.M. [Gouverneur Morris], who in this affair never behaved sensibly. It has made him still more unpopular and given rise to a hundred rumors."[24]

Crèvecoeur was quite relieved when the French government demanded Morris's recall in exchange for the recall of Genêt demanded by Washington. He was replaced by James Monroe. The fall of Robespierre, followed by Monroe's arrival in Paris, seemed to mark the end of a long nightmare and to announce better days at last. Both Crèvecoeur and Otto had known Monroe in the United States. Fanny was even an intimate friend of Mrs. Monroe. Crèvecoeur thought they would all work fruitfully together for the improvement of Franco-American relations, and when Monroe arrived in August 1794, Crèvecoeur and his son-in-law did everything they could to help him settle down and inform him about the political situation. Their help was all the more needed as neither the new ambassador nor his secretary knew a word of French. Crèvecoeur rendered various personal services to Monroe, found a pleasant country house for him, and supervised the making of American flags for the legation and for his carriage, as well as for the Convention. For it had been decided that the American flag would float there side by side with the French one to symbolize the friendship of the two nations.

As a reward, Crèvecoeur hoped that he would be entrusted with a diplomatic mission to the United States and thus have a chance to return to America. He wanted to see all his old friends again and breathe more freely after being confined for several years in the oppressive atmosphere of Revolutionary France. When he suggested this to Monroe as tactfully as possible, Monroe was very evasive and discouraged him— probably even gave him a flat refusal. Crèvecoeur announced the sad news to Ally in a letter he sent him on September 19. A few days later, he left for Caen, where Fanny had preceded him. After all the trials, anxieties, and disappointments of those terrible years, he needed some comfort and relaxation, and he found them at Pierrepont. His father, too, had managed to survive the Revolution and to save the family estate, which was as dear to him as his own life.[25] Their old disagreements were forgotten. The main thing, after all, was to maintain the unity and continuity of the Crèvecoeur family against wind and tide.

XI

❧❧❧❧❧

In the Wake of Napoleon

AFTER THE COUP of 9 Thermidor (July 27, 1794) and the fall of Robespierre and his supporters (who were all immediately guillotined), the Revolution followed a downward course. What remained of the Convention after so many bloody purges tried henceforward to steer between the extreme left and the Royalists. The Jacobins were systematically eliminated and replaced by the surviving Girondists who had gone into hiding. People were tired of politics and things gradually calmed down, but the country, which was still at war, was in a sorry plight.[1]

On this point we have the testimony of Jacques-Henri Meister, a Swiss friend of Grimm, who succeeded him as editor of the *Correspondance littéraire, philosophique et critique*. He was obliged to leave France in 1792, but he hastened to return after Thermidor. Though he belonged to the camp of the *philosophes* and had written in French *The Origin of Religious Principles,* a book which had made him unacceptable in Switzerland, he had become thoroughly disillusioned with revolutions. At the beginning, he could notice no appreciable improvement in the condition of the poor. The sale of the so-called *biens nationaux* (the land confiscated from the *émigrés,* the victims of the guillotine, and the church) profited only those who already had money at their disposal—or speculators. So, on the whole, small landowners had become richer and the poor poorer. Besides, many people now starved in what had been before the Revolution the richest country in Europe. Bread, the staple of most French people's diet, was so scarce that it had to be rationed and distributed to the poor at a price far inferior to its cost (three *sous,* while it cost five or six), and it was not white bread as before, but a black, coarse, and doughy substance in which flour was, to a large extent, replaced by boiled potatoes, chick-peas, Indian corn, and millet. It was not even correctly baked, since bakers derived no profit from it. Moreover, it could be obtained only after waiting in line for hours. Meat, rice, oil, sugar, candles, and coal were similarly rationed and very hard to get.

The scarcity of vital commodities was caused by inflation. The *assignats,* the paper money created by the Convention, had become devalued as the government printed more of it in a desperate effort to pay all its expenses. So prices went up and soon exceeded the means of the poorer classes. What made the situation still more scandalous and unbearable was that there had appeared a class of profiteers and new rich who lacked nothing. They frequented well-appointed restaurants, went to the theater or dancing halls at night, and drove through Paris in their private coaches, splashing the populace with mud and the revolting display of their dishonestly acquired luxury. Parodying the phrase used to designate noblemen in Revolutionary parlance, Meister contemptuously called them "les ci-devant pouilleux" (the former lousy poor). According to Johann Georg Heinzmann, another observer from Switzerland, "in Paris, you find morality only among the laboring classes, among people with mediocre means and the poor, those who earn their living in the sweat of their brows," and he stigmatized "the arrogant insolence of people who from nothing had managed to become something."[2]

What struck Meister most was that, though "the impetuous torrent of the Revolution," as he called it, had ravaged whole regions, others seemed to have been spared and had hardly changed at all. This was the case in particular of Lower Normandy, where Crèvecoeur's father lived. The region was inhabited mostly by small landowners. The Revolution had not affected them too much and the Terror never really reached Pierrepont. In this rich agricultural district, each farmer was self-sufficient, so everyone had enough to eat, though white bread was scarce and expensive, and no wine could be found. Crèvecoeur's father kept complaining of it in his letters,[3] but this was inevitable, since Normandy produced no corn and no wine—only excellent cider.

Crèvecoeur returned to Normandy after Thermidor, in September 1794, when he realized that Ambassador Monroe would never help him to return to America. By that time, it had become much easier to travel from one province to another, and, Otto having been released from jail, Crèvecoeur no longer had to worry about the fate of his son-in-law. The opportunity was too good to be missed. He left Paris as soon as he could. It must have been a great joy for him to find his father unchanged and the family estate intact, just as it undoubtedly was a great relief for his father to see his elder son again, the heir to the name, safe and sound after so many trials and dangers. Under such circumstances, it was easy for them to let bygones be bygones and to be reconciled.

They could not stay together very long, though, for Otto was arrested a second time in November. Crèvecoeur returned to Paris in haste to help secure his liberation. As it was soon obtained, he did not linger in Paris. As early as May 1795, he was with Ally at Altona, near Hamburg. From that time, the American farmer was to be essentially a European traveler. But this first experience was rather distasteful to him. Ally was obliged to go to Paris and London on business and to leave Crèvecoeur alone in Altona in the middle of people whose language he did not understand. He had to meet the merchants with whom his son usually transacted business, and they bored him to death. He hated the dinners to which he was invited and the weekends he had to spend with his son's business relations. He thus wrote in a letter: "All this country bears the stamp of strangeness. Every single door is not only locked, but barred and chained, and you must ring for a whole day to be admitted. The inhabitants are pale and small; nowhere else would you see so many cripples; out of ten persons, there are bound to be a dwarf and an invalid. They have no books, no conversation."[4]

The only documents we have about his stay in Altona are the letters he exchanged with Ally, and the image we can conjure through them is necessarily partial and imperfect. Crèvecoeur, for instance, did not dare mention the French *émigrés* whom he no doubt met. There were quite a few in the Hamburg area. It is known that he saw Mme. de Lafayette, who was on her way to Olmütz, where her husband was detained.[5] He must have seen others, too. Mary Wollstonecraft, who would marry William Godwin and be the mother-in-law of Shelley, was in Altona at the time. She had intrepidly seen the Revolution through in Paris out of curiosity despite the dangers she incurred. It is unlikely Crèvecoeur met her then, but he made her acquaintance in Altona. She wrote to her friend Gilbert Imlay that they often dined together. He enjoyed her company, for he shared her hatred of conversation "forever flowing in the muddy channels of business," as he said.

Ally returned to Altona in September and Crèvecoeur remained with him until the following spring. He went back to France by sea in April 1796 and headed immediately for Paris. The political situation had changed considerably in his absence. In application of the Constitution of Year III of the Republic (1795), a new *régime* called the Directoire had succeeded the Convention. France was now governed by five *directeurs* and two chambers: a higher one called the Conseil des Anciens and a lower one called the Cinq Cents, both elected not by universal suffrage but according to a system of limited suffrage based on property qualification. This new government was confronted with the same insoluble problems as the Convention in the last months of its existence. It was faced with a galloping inflation; and though its coffers were empty, it was obliged to maintain large armies to wage war against England, Austria, and Italy. Politically it was threatened both on the left and the right, and had to steer a middle course by striking alternately at the last *chouans* and at what remained of the Jacobins and other levelers of French persuasion. It was bound sooner or later to founder, for the country was in a state of anarchy. Strong measures were taken at the top, but there were no nerves to transmit the orders to the limbs. Thus all French citizens had to pay a progressive tax on their property, chastely called, rather than *impôt, contribution* (to the expenses of the state), but in many parts of the country tax collectors could not collect any money for lack of paper on which to correspond with the taxpayers. Another legacy of the Revolution was conscription, the compulsory military service of all French males between the ages of twenty and twenty-five, but there were thousands of deserters and defaulters who never reported for service. The government reacted as it could. To restore order it no longer resorted to the guillotine proper, but to the "dry guillotine" (*la guillotine sèche*): illegally returned *émigrés,* nonjuror priests, and political opponents of all persuasions were deported—in principle to French Guiana, where they died like flies owing to the climate, but more often, because of the English blockade, to the island of Ré, off the coast of Vendée.

The new top classes were corrupt and immoral, especially the political class, which consisted mostly of scheming politicians who had weathered all the storms because they knew all the tricks and of former members of the Convention, like Paul-François Barras, who had survived because they were more clever than honest. All had dirty hands. These so-called *élite* thought of nothing but having a good time in order to forget the horrors of the recent past and the tragic uncertainty of the near future. *Carpe diem* was their motto.

Crèvecoeur, of course, had no truck with such people. They did not belong to his world. He was a sexagenarian, a writer, a scholar. Only his family and his intellectual pursuits counted for him. His only care on arriving in Paris was to see his daughter and her husband, from whom he had been cut off for several months. Shortly afterward, he had the joy of being reunited with his younger son, Louis, who had recently returned from America via Hamburg, where he had arrived a few months after his father and Ally had left.

Crèvecoeur also had the pleasure of taking part in the activities of the section of moral and political sciences of the French Institut, to which he had been elected as corresponding member in February 1796. The Institut was a creation of the Convention. For all its savage fanaticism, the Convention had done excellent work in the domains of administration and culture. It had reorganized the administration of the country rationally and created a number of institutions which still exist. In particular, it had added to the French Academy, founded by Cardinal Richelieu in the seventeenth century, new academies corresponding to the new branches of knowledge which had developed since. As the author of *Lettres d'un cultivateur américain,* it was natural that Crèvecoeur become a member of the Academy of Moral and Political Sciences, and he enjoyed meeting there writers and scholars with the same interests as his own.

However, he could not stay in Paris indefinitely. His father was nearly ninety and no longer able to look after his estate. He needed the help of his elder son. So Crèvecoeur returned to Pierrepont and, for a change, became a French farmer, some seventeen years after abandoning his American farm. He remained at Pierrepont for nearly four years, until the death of his father in 1799—a stay interrupted only by the visits he paid to Otto and Fanny. For Otto, having lost his position in the foreign service, had decided, like many other impoverished and unemployed nobles, to buy a farm at Lesches, near Meaux, in 1796, in order to make a living for his family. Crèvecoeur helped him financially, by paying half the price of the farm, and technically, for Otto had no experience of farming and, though Louis had joined him, badly needed his father-in-law's advice.

Consequently, Crèvecoeur went to Lesches to give him a start and, afterward, from Pierrepont, kept up an active correspondence with him, supplying him with precious information about such subjects as the rotation of crops, lumbering, and the cultivation of useful vegetables. In December 1796, before embarking on this venture, Otto had humbly told him: "Your advice will guide me and you must consider me from now on as merely your steward." Later, he half jocularly addressed Crèvecoeur as his "cher patron" (dear boss).[6]

Crèvecoeur loved managing Otto's farm from Normandy. It gave him a chance to write long letters, and he loved writing more than anything else. He could not live without it. Ever since the beginning of his stay in America (and probably before), he accumulated notes on everything he saw or did. He continued making notes when he became a farmer in New York State and never stopped, even during the darkest hours of the Revolution, as we have seen. While at Pierrepont with his family he occasionally wrote short pieces, like his "Pensées sur le départ des hirondelles" ("Thoughts Occasioned by the Departure of Swallows"), whose manuscript has survived, and he was busy preparing the final version of the book he was to publish under the title *Voyage dans la haute Pensylvanie et dans l'état de New-York*.[7]

During Crèvecoeur's stay at Pierrepont, on June 26, 1798,

Ally married a young Norman aristocrat, Gabrielle-Narcisse Mesnage de Cagny. This occasion prompted an affectionate letter of congratulations from Mme. d'Houdetot.[8] The young couple joined Louis and Fanny at Lesches and Crèvecoeur himself moved there after the death of his father. Lesches thus became the new family seat. Otto's period of unemployment at last came to an end. The Directoire, wishing to get rid of Abbé Siéyès, had appointed him ambassador to Prussia, and in May 1798 Siéyès, who realized he needed the collaboration of a professional diplomat, invited Otto in the most flattering terms to join him in Berlin as first secretary. If we are to believe Fanny, he told Otto that "he would have more confidence in the success of his mission if Otto consented to share it with him."[9] Naturally, Otto was overjoyed, and accepted immediately. One year later, Siéyès was called back to Paris to become one of the five *directeurs* and Otto remained in Berlin as chargé d'affaires. He excelled in this role, which was the first step in a brilliant career, for, after the coup of 18 Brumaire (November 9, 1799), which had the support of Siéyès, he was appointed French commissioner in London, officially to negotiate an exchange of prisoners with the British government, but actually with a much more important mission.

While in Berlin, Otto, knowing his father-in-law's insatiable curiosity, sent him much information about Germany. He insisted in his letters on the inferiority of German agriculture: Prussian peasants could not raise good crops of rye on their sandy soil and even in fertile Saxony farmers were not so well-off as their French counterparts. He sang the praises of Frederick the Great, whose innumerable achievements he admired, and was enthusiastic over Berlin Jews (he knew that Crèvecoeur had conceived a strong distaste for the Jews he had met in Hamburg): "You must know," he told him, "that the Jewish colony, which has produced Mendelssohn, is the richest, the most learned and the most sociable in Berlin, and it includes women whom you'd love to hear call me *mein lieber.*" (This was a term which Crèvecoeur seems to have particularly hated in Hamburg, when applied to himself.) But like his father-in-law, Otto did not think much of the Berlin equivalents of French *salons*: "the men smoke majestically in one corner of the room and women knit silently in another [. . .]. It's quite different from what we have at home."[10]

Crèvecoeur must have been delighted to receive these reports. In the meantime, at Lesches, he was putting the finishing touches on his *Voyage dans la haute Pensylvanie et dans l'état de New-York.* He read chapters of it to whoever was at hand and enclosed fragments in letters to his friends, asking for their advice and candid opinion. He even asked an acquaintance of his, a Mme. Esmangard, who was his neighbor at Lesches, to write on his behalf to Jacques-Alexandre Charles, the distinguished physicist. He wanted to know how to explain the rainbows he had observed at Niagara Falls. Later, he worried terribly when he heard that Count de Volney, the popular author of *Ruines,* was coming back from the United States after spending three years there. He asked a friend, a M. de Joguet, to try to find out if he intended to write a book on his travels in America, for he thought Volney would be a dangerous rival and might publish before him. Volney was indeed to write *Tableau du sol et du climat des États-Unis,* but it did not appear until 1803, after Crèvecoeur's own book had been published.

Crèvecoeur entertained high hopes for his new volume of travels in America. He expected it to have the same success as his *Lettres d'un cultivateur américain,* since it exploited the same subject and was in a way its sequel. So, while the Ottos were in London, he entrusted them with the mission of finding a publisher for an English version of his *Voyage.* But Fanny was obliged to report on October 6, 1800: "Several publishers showed great readiness to undertake it [the publication of the book], some after merely reading the title and the author's name, others after reading the various fragments we had lent them. But I am sorry to say that they soon changed their minds as soon as they realized it was not really a travel story, but a purely philosophical work, which, though very well written, was not of a kind likely to succeed in this country."[11]

In France, *Voyage dans la haute Pensylvanie et dans l'état de New-York* appeared in 1801, in three volumes, published by Maradan. But its reception was disappointing despite favorable reviews in such influential papers as the quasi-official *Moniteur* (in which the reviewer was Baron Trouvé, a member of the Tribunat, Napoleon's lower chamber) and in *La décade philosophique, littéraire et politique.* [12] Trouvé, very generously, offered to act as a go-between and give a copy of Crèvecoeur's book directly to Napoleon, with whom he dined regularly: "As a member of the *Institut,* it is your right to offer him your book; a covering letter of just one or two lines would suffice [. . .] in which you might drop the name of Washington."[13] Following Trouvé's advice, Crèvecoeur also gave a copy to the Institut itself on the occasion of a meeting of its three sections, but it caused no great stir. Napoleon was apparently too busy even to acknowledge receipt of the gift—though he entertained the highest regard for Otto and his family. Otto had recently been kind enough to send a collection of English trees for Empress Joséphine's park after she had expressed the desire of acquiring some. But Bonaparte's failure to respond was natural. He was exclusively preoccupied with the European situation and was not in the least interested in America—even in French possessions there—which he was later to sell to the government of the United States at a bargain price. The general public shared his indifference—all the more as the English blockade almost cut off France from America. It is not surprising, therefore, that for all its merits Crèvecoeur's book fell flat. The times were not favorable. People preferred Chateaubriand's *Atala,* which appeared the same year. It was a touching romance taking place in a mythical America exclusively inhabited by noble savages. People preferred romantic fiction to hard facts.

Crèvecoeur was quite disappointed, but he had the comfort of seeing his book translated into German by a professor at the University of Marburg, Dietrich Tiedemann, under the title *Reise in Ober-Pensylvanien und im Staate New York* (published in Berlin in 1802). It was a condensed version of Crèvecoeur's book in which the translator had kept only the essentials—that is, the passages in which readers could feel that they dealt with the candid report of an eyewitness; he dropped all the idealistic embellishments.

Another compensation came with Crèvecoeur's election to the Society of Agriculture, Sciences, and Arts at Meaux. It was a minor honor, but flattering just the same. He had also been reelected to the Society of Agriculture of Caen after its reorganization the year before.

He now lived at Lesches permanently, but, in the summer of 1802, at the age of sixty-seven, he paid a visit to the Ottos in London. His son-in-law's mission had taken on an unexpected importance. After protracted negotiations with the British government, he had succeeded in drafting the preliminaries of the Treaty of Amiens, which was to be signed on March 25, 1802. It was a considerable event which seemed to bring peace to Europe after ten years of uninterrupted warfare—though the truce proved to be short-lived. The signing of the preliminary treaty on October 1, 1801, and that of the treaty itself were widely acclaimed on both sides of the Channel. In London, the overjoyed crowd, to show its gratitude, unhitched the horses of Otto's coach and dragged it to his residence.

Despite several interesting excursions, notably to Greenwich, and the pleasure it gave him to find himself once more in England, where he had not been since 1781, Crèvecoeur's sojourn in London was to a large extent spoiled by the disappointment he shared with Otto that the brilliant services of the young diplomat were not better rewarded. Though he had the honor of signing the preliminary treaty, Otto was not invited to sign the definitive treaty at Amiens, and, contrary to his expectation, he was not offered the post of ambassador at the Court of St. James's, because he did not have the required seniority. True, he had been offered the ambassadorship to the United States, but he had declined it on account of his wife's health.

So Crèvecoeur, after his brief visit, returned to the family farm at Lesches, where he spent four years with his two sons, surrounded by congenial friends and neighbors like the Bonfils. Mr. Bonfils had even drawn some of the illustrations for the *Voyage en Pensylvanie* and contributed notes to it, those marked "Note sent to the editor by Citizen B . . ." But this peaceful happiness did not last. On July 13, 1806, the untimely death of Ally, his favorite son, broke his heart and obliged him to seek comfort with the Ottos at Munich, in the kingdom of Bavaria, where his son-in-law had been appointed ambassador.

By then the French Republic had become the French Empire and General Bonaparte, after a transitional stage as first consul, had in 1804 proclaimed himself emperor of the French. The pope had crowned him, not in Rome, but in Paris —at home, as it were—and Napoleon even had the audacity to crown himself during the ceremony, without the intervention of the pope. The Republic, which had proved a failure and had become but a name, was buried without regret and even mocked at. People sang:

> *"The Republic—that indivisible citizen*
> *That was never to be abolished*
> *Has recently perished,*
> *The victim of a caesarean."*

Under Napoleon's command French armies had in quick succession defeated two powerful coalitions and reduced a large part of Europe to a state of vassalage. He had become extraordinarily popular, not only because of his military victories, but because, after years of anarchy, he had restored order at home and brought civil strife to an end. His decision to become emperor was sanctioned by a triumphant plebiscite. Over three and a half million Frenchmen voted aye and only two thousand and five hundred nay. It was a spectacular success and the emperors of Austria and Russia, feeling threatened by this upstart, formed a third coalition with England, but Napoleon forestalled them by suddenly moving to Austria the huge army he had mustered at Boulogne with a view to invading England, his implacable and invincible enemy. After a masterly campaign of less than four months, he inflicted a terrible defeat on the Austro-Russian armies at Austerlitz. He was then at the height of his power. He appointed his elder brother king of Naples, one of his younger brothers king of Holland, and elevated to king the Elector of Bavaria, who had been loyal to him. Thus it was that Otto, as a consequence of the victorious progress of Napoleon's troops, found himself French ambassador in Munich, and Crèvecoeur visited him there to share his joy.

In fact, Otto had been appointed to Munich as early as 1802, for the capital of the Duchy of Bavaria occupied a key position in the diplomatic war waged by Napoleon. Its neutrality was vital to give French forces easy access to Austria, and Otto managed to counter the intrigues of the British ambassador, though the latter was backed by St. George's cavalry. When the Austrian troops occupied Munich in 1805, he even persuaded Maximilian-Joseph, the Elector of Bavaria, not to side with them, but to withdraw and conclude an alliance with France. So, after Austerlitz, he occupied an influential position in Munich, and Crèvecoeur basked in his glory.

He soon met the king in his castle at Nymphenburg, for the king, who had read the *Letters of an American Farmer* in English as well as in French, wanted to make his acquaintance and asked a friend to bring Crèvecoeur to Nymphenburg under the pretext of showing him the castle. Once there, Crèvecoeur was directly taken to the top floor, where he was received by a man who he thought was a caretaker, but who, he soon found out, was none other than the king himself, "a tall and handsome man, with a fresh complexion, blue eyes, a smiling and graceful face, somewhat brusque in his gestures, always walking at a brisk pace," and expressing himself fluently in incorrect French (he had been colonel of an Alsatian regiment in Paris before the Revolution). On this occasion, the king received him with great cordiality, showed him his collection of paintings, and later invited him to dinner and to concerts and insisted on receiving him twice a month in his private study. Crèvecoeur appreciated this honor and felt quite flattered, but did not particularly care for the king, whom he considered poorly educated and appallingly ignorant. "If this kind and affable king had received a better education," he wrote to Ally's widow, of whom he was extremely fond, "I'd love to see him more often—which is not difficult in this country," he added, "for the King lives very simply and mixes with his subjects in Munich without any protocol or ceremony."[14]

Crèvecoeur felt at home in Bavaria, where the élite spoke French. At a dinner at Court, he noted, "you don't hear a single word of German among the guests, [though] the servants don't know a single word of French." He liked the élite, but not the aristocracy, who were all Francophobes, and, in his eyes, haughty and sullen barbarians, who, at receptions, spent their time playing ombre or whist and stopped only to stuff themselves with food and wine, completely ignoring the women who accompanied them. He consorted only with the scholars and artists, whom the aristocracy despised. He was a great friend of Friedrich Heinrich Jacobi, the philosopher and novelist who was president of the Munich Academy. He described him as "the most amiable, intelligent and clearest of the Munich metaphysicians" (and so rather an exception among German philosophers!). Crèvecoeur often invited him to the dinners he gave at the French embassy in honor of the local intelligentsia. Another of the guests was Manlich, the Bavarian Audubon, who specialized in birds, but who also unfortunately painted conventional allegories. He equally enjoyed the company of Franz Kobell, the Court painter, whose forte was battlepieces; of Seyfer, the king's astronomer; and of the Baader brothers, physicists, who were authorities on hydrostatics and galvanism in Munich. One of his favorites was a Mr. Utzschneider, a man of many talents, who headed an astonishing variety of concerns in Bavaria, from salt mines to a tannery, from a stock farm to a flint-glass factory where he applied a process of his own invention. Crèvecoeur, with his insatiable curiosity for technology, was fascinated by this many-faceted man as well as by Reichenbach, the maker of precision mathematical and optical instruments. These people delighted him, and he did as he used to do when he was French consul in New York: he sent plans and descriptions of all the new inventions to correspondents in Paris. These included lithography, which had been invented by the Bavarian Aloys Senefelder. Conversely, he tried to introduce new inventions, and with the help and cooperation of his friend Cadet de Vaux, who had recently published *Traité de blanchissage domestique à la vapeur* (*Treatise upon Steam-Laundering at Home*), he had some of the new washing boilers installed in Munich. "I work wonders with washing boilers," he wrote triumphantly in a letter, "within one month, there will be more than thirty of them in this town."[15] The humblest practical problems never left him indifferent. He even taught the Bavarians how to make bread with potatoes and tried to convert them to the use of lightning rods. A long article he wrote praising Franklin's invention appeared in the *Gazette de Munich* on September 7, 1808.

In short, Crèvecoeur's sojourn in Bavaria was a rich and stimulating experience. He bloomed again after his years of rustication at Pierrepont and Lesches. Life in Munich was for him an endless succession of intellectual and artistic pleasures of all kinds. As he wrote after visiting the salt mines at Reichenhall in the company of the finance minister, Baron Hompesch, "the sight of so many novel objects has revived my torpid old imagination." At Reichenhall he enjoyed the spectacle of hydraulic machines pumping "the precious salted waters of twenty-eight springs" and "the long and numerous galleries of the underground city, magnificently vaulted and carved in the rock" with "innumerable batteries of pumps, pistons and pipes. There is nothing more beautiful," he exclaimed, "than the sight of those underground galleries everywhere lit up, and of the underground canals along which you can walk as easily as you would in the streets of a city." In the course of his visit, he eventually discovered the torrent which revolved "the large wheel from which came the power that set all the pumps in motion and gave them their regular and silent oscillation." And he admired all the other technical feats accomplished by the Bavarian engineers who, for instance, succeeded in raising a column of water three inches in diameter to a height of two hundred and nineteen feet.[16]

What appealed most to him, or moved him most, was the music he so often had an opportunity to listen to in Munich. He found it a source of sweet emotions which he tried to describe in a long letter to his daughter-in-law. It was less a letter than a little treatise on the power and effects of aerial harmony. He titled it "Réflexions sur la puissance et les effets de l'harmonie aérienne adressées à Mme Narcisse de Saint-John." He praised the natural aptitude of the Germans for singing and playing wind instruments, and he quoted the king as saying that, while in the French army, he had never once heard a trumpeter who played in tune. He loved, above all, the open-air concerts he heard in the countryside around Munich. "Never shall I forget," he wrote, "how often these symphonies, these pleasant and gratifying songs entrusted without art or study to the uncertain oscillations of the wind and to the delicious illusions of remoteness have moistened my old eyes. What a prodigious distance there is between this aerial, touching, and yet so active and penetrating music and what I felt while listening to the grand operas in Paris! To my ignorant and timid ears, long accustomed to the majestic silence of American forests, those noisy orchestras merely sounded like storms over the ocean: a grandiose and imposing spectacle, the image of some unknown power. The small concerts of [. . .] on the contrary, whose loudness was tempered, and whose sounds were softened by distance, have always reminded me of the melodious warblings of the first birds awakening at the approach of the dawn of a sonorous and serene morning in the month of May."[17]

Unfortunately, this feast of the intellect and sensibility did not last. Napoleon's empire was constantly submitted to new onslaughts. He had hardly defeated one coalition when another was formed. He defeated a fourth one in 1807 and in six days completely crushed Prussia, which this time had joined the fray, but Russia and Great Britain remained unvanquished and in 1809 formed a fifth coalition with a revitalized Austria. "Here we are again," wrote Crèvecoeur to one of his lady friends, Mme. de Martroy, "on the eve of a fourth war. Everyone is up in arms among our neighbors [the Austrians], everything is being requisitioned. This town [Munich] is not even forty miles from that formidable war-machine [. . .]. To speak the truth, I can't help wishing I were a little farther away from it. All this infernal tumult darkens my mind. It was dark enough already before this lifting up of shields."[18] His fears were only too well founded. When hostilities broke out, the Austrian army invaded Bavaria and was soon close to Munich.

On April 12, Otto sent back to France his wife, his daughter Sophie, and his father in order to spare them the horrors of war. Crèvecoeur wrote to Louis, who was now with the French army in Italy as administrative officer on the quartermaster's staff, and for his services had recently been decorated with the Legion of Honor: "Otto is about to go to Augsburg and from there to Sellingue on the Danube, two days after the King and his family left Munich. The Emperor, to whom Otto has sent the Austrian declaration of war, is on his way to Strasburg, from where he is to proceed to Donauwörth. There Otto will see him and give him what information he has as well as the maps and itineraries he has managed to find in Bavaria and elsewhere."[19]

Though tolls had been abolished and road transportation, which Napoleon had denationalized, functioned much more efficiently than during the Revolution, Crèvecoeur's return journey lasted eleven days and was exhausting for a man of seventy-four. So he went to Lesches to take a rest.

He could have stayed in Bavaria, or at least close to it, for the Austrians, who thought they would take Napoleon by surprise were themselves surprised by the speed of his reaction. He rushed from Paris to Donauwörth in less than five days, took command of his troops, and, in a campaign which lasted only another five days, expelled the Austrians from Bavaria. He entered Vienna three weeks later, in May, and won the decisive battle of Wagram early in July. Though this time the Austrian forces were not destroyed, but retired in good order, the emperor of Austria preferred to ask for peace immediately. He had, among other losses, to surrender Salzburg and the Engadine to Bavaria. Bavaria had won again, which delighted Crèvecoeur. Though he never returned there, he had at least the pleasure of keeping up an active correspondence with the friends he had made during his stay in Munich, notably with Manlich, who put him in touch with a M. Heurtier, a French architect whom he had known in Rome, where they studied together. This made Crèvecoeur wonder: "It is quite unusual [in our time] that two persons who knew and liked each other in Rome some forty years ago should meet again with their heads still on their shoulders."[20]

In August 1809, Crèvecoeur moved from Lesches to Sarcelles, near Paris. Otto had just bought a house there with extensive grounds, and he invited his father-in-law to fit them up to his own taste. Crèvecoeur was overjoyed. This gave him a chance to apply his talents to a task he was particularly fond of. Besides, he now found himself close to Paris and also close to the cherry valley of Montmorency, where he had spent such happy days before the Revolution with Mme. d'Houdetot and her friends. He soon met old acquaintances. Thus he wrote to Otto: "Yesterday, I caught sight, in the middle of the yard, of a little old man, slightly bent, with a flat face and an austere expression, who had come in without speaking to anyone. Yet, on seeing his red ribbon [of the Legion of Honor] and the coat of fine cloth which he was wearing, I looked at him attentively and approached him slowly without being able to remember where I had seen him before. But presently [. . .] I recognized the grave and cold Senator Volney, whom in my happy days I had introduced to Mme. d'Houdetot and the academicians d'Alembert, Morellet and Marmontel, the man whom in the most terrible period of the Revolution I had dared to recommend to the President of the United States, General Washington."21

Though the coldness of the author of *Ruines* discouraged him, Crèvecoeur enjoyed his company on that day, for they shared the same tastes and were both passionately fond of gardening and agronomy. They exchanged seeds and plants and Volney gave to Crèvecoeur some young acacias, a plant whose praises he had sung shortly after his return to France. They should have become fast friends, but Volney did not even inquire after Fanny, whom he had met, and Crèvecoeur did not forgive him this oversight. He did not care for a man who was obviously more interested in trees than in human beings. Strangely enough, though they had both written books about the United States, they do not seem to have talked about that country.

Another of his neighbors was the famous Abbé Grégoire,

who had had a long political career as a member of the Estates-General and later of the Convention. He had been one of the initiators of the alliance of the low clergy and the Third Estate and of the suppression of the law of primogeniture (to the prejudice of Crèvecoeur). He was a defender of Jews and blacks and was intrumental in the abolition of slavery voted by the Convention in 1794 as well as in the creation of the Institut, of which Crèvecoeur was a corresponding member. In 1809, he was a member of the Senate, but belonged to the opposition. He and Crèvecoeur had been friends during the Revolution, as they both belonged to the Society of the Friends of the Blacks founded by Brissot in 1788. The Abbé had a warm personality. Crèvecoeur, who liked him, was delighted and felt quite flattered when Grégoire, on returning from a long and tiring trip to Alsace and Lorraine (where he was born), came to Sarcelles specially to see him, accompanied by his "hostess" in Paris, Mme. Dubois. There were rumors about her relations with the Abbé, but to Crèvecoeur, "all that people [said] about Mme. Dubois [was] sheer slander," a statement which smacks of innocence and charity rather than of lucidity. But Crèvecoeur's eighteenth-century mind could not believe in evil even when confronted with it (if evil there was in this particular case) and was also prone to be overwhelmed by sentiment. Describing his encounter with the Abbé in a letter, he exclaimed: "I am still all shaken! How I wish I could repeat everything he told me and how he said it! His voice, his accents, his eyes and his heart! [. . .] How he embraced, how he repeatedly shook my hands!"[22]

But what Crèvecoeur appreciated most about his new location was its proximity to his old friend Mme. d'Houdetot. He had not seen her for a long time and reproached himself for his negligence: "I have at last tried to repair my wrongs towards the good Countess," he wrote, "wrongs which certainly did not come from my heart, but exclusively from the indefinable laziness and lack of activity of a septuagenarian [. . .]. I decided to go and dine with the oldest and most respectable of my friends, my support, my protectress, the one to whom I owe so many prosperous days, so many precious acquaintances, a life, in short, which seemed to me all the more pleasant as I had just left the New York jails and been rid of the dark thoughts I was a prey to during my stay in Dublin and London."[23] She generously forgave him his negligence, and they made peace. But, much to his disappointment, he discovered that the good countess, who apparently, like Nature, abhorred a vacuum, had replaced Saint-Lambert after his death by a new favorite, a M.—or rather Signor—de Somma-Riva. Other things being equal, he would readily have said, like Hamlet: Saint-Lambert to this was "Hyperion to a satyr." Not given to overstatement, he merely complained: "Such is the hero of the day, the successor to Saint-Lambert and Jean-Jacques [Rousseau]! What use are the lights of reason and the experience of old age?"[24] He was obviously jealous of the newcomer and yet he could not have filled his place. He could never have spent all his time dancing attendance upon Mme. d'Houdetot. Though a septuagenarian, as he was fond of repeating, he was still too active and had too many other things to do.

He had been absent from Paris for over three years—even longer, if one counts the years spent at Lesches. After such a long absence, he felt the need to renew his acquaintance with many old friends besides Mme. d'Houdetot. So he did not remain confined to Sarcelles and the Montmorency valley, but went to Paris frequently. The capital had changed considerably since Napoleon had seized power. Arriving in Paris in 1811, after a still longer absence, Count Miot de Mélito found it much "embellished" since his departure. Most buildings had been cleaned and repaired. "Magnificent quays" had been built along the Seine as well as several bridges over it. There were everywhere new fountains, and new squares decorated with the trophies of Napoleon's victories. A wing was being added to the Louvre to connect it with the Tuileries

Palace. De Mélito concluded this lyrical catalogue with a declamatory tribute to the emperor: "Everywhere marble and bronze remind the passer-by of the man who has created so many things in such a short time and who knows how to add to the glory of the nation by the arts of peace as well as of war."[25] He complained of the lack of taste of some of the embellishments, however, and all visitors did not share his enthusiasm. Stendhal, for instance, protested in his *Journal* because Paris in winter was as muddy and dirty as ever for lack of proper sidewalks and stank in summer for lack of underground sewers. But, for all its shortcomings, Paris was regarded by foreigners and provincials alike as a wonderful place with beautiful gardens, excellent restaurants in the Palais Royal, splendid shops in rue St.-Honoré, good theaters, and entertainments of all kinds. Stendhal himself had to acknowledge that life stagnated in the provinces. For his part, he would never have lived elsewhere of his own free will, though he repeatedly had to.

Crèvecoeur was too old to enjoy all the pleasures of Paris. What interested him most was, as in Munich, his encounters with artists, scientists, and inventors like the prodigiously active Gillet de Laumont, a distinguished mineralogist and inspector of mines;[26] a certain Donavy, now forgotten, who thought for a time that he had discovered the secret of perpetual motion; and Reichenbach, his Bavarian acquaintance, who had a chance to come to Paris during this period with a supply of flint glass for the observatory. In 1811, Crèvecoeur had the great joy of welcoming to Paris his old friend Joel Barlow, who had been appointed minister to France, and they had long talks about America and all the new inventions, notably about the progress made by Fulton since he made his first experiments with a submarine in the Seine in 1802 and 1803. He had recently finished building a large steamer, the *Clermont*, whose dimensions and qualities filled Crèvecoeur with wonder. Here was one of his dreams come true. He must once more have bitterly regretted the inertia and shortsightedness of the French government, which had ignored the new invention contrary to the advice he gave during his consulship in New York.

After the defeat of Austria in 1809, Count Otto had been appointed to the French embassy in Vienna to keep watch on the intrigues of the Austrian government, but Fanny and Sophie frequently came to France on vacation. Sophie, who had by now become a young woman, was the comfort and joy of Crèvecoeur's old age. She apparently had the charm of her mother and the earnestness and intelligence of her father. When she was still a little girl in Bavaria, Crèvecoeur had composed for her, in English, a sort of Oriental tale entitled "The Three Sultanas," of which there seems to remain only an incomplete manuscript version. Later, when she was older, he took her as his confidante and loved to exchange ideas with her. He wrote to her long letters, some of which have survived.[27] Both her parents being Protestants, she had been brought up a Protestant herself and was very pious. Crèvecoeur, at best a Deist à la Rousseau, if not à la Voltaire, respected her piety and never discussed religion with her. It was one of the great joys of his life when she got married in 1812 to Baron Palet de Lozère, a serious and intelligent young man, a devout Protestant who already had a good position in the French civil service as a junior member (*auditeur*) of the Conseil d'État.

Unfortunately the last months of Crèvecoeur's life were darkened by the defeat of Napoleon's Grand Army in Russia. It was vanquished by "General Winter," as people said, and obliged to beat a painful retreat during which thousands of soldiers died of cold and privations, though it had reached and occupied Moscow a few months before, in 1812. It was the beginning of the end for Napoleon, the ebbing of his power, and a personal tragedy for Crèvecoeur, whose son Louis had been transferred to Russia and had taken part in the campaign and the retreat. For three months, his family was without news of him, until at last they received a letter dated Leipzig, March 10, 1813.[28] On the way back from Russia, he had been attacked by Cossacks, near Wilno in Poland, stripped of all his belongings, and obliged to walk from there to the border, without any gloves to protect his hands and hardly anything to eat, sleeping in the snow at night. Fortunately, his pioneering experience in America had toughened him and he survived. He managed to reach the bridge over the Beresina before it had to be blown up. As he crossed it, a cannonball decapitated a general who was walking by his side, and he was splashed with his blood. When he arrived in Germany, he hardly looked like a human being at all, he said, but at least he was saved. This good news reinvigorated Crèvecoeur—or so he thought: "The resurrection of Louis," he wrote, "has made me feel ten years younger."[29]

He did have to bear the blow of Mme. d'Houdetot's death during the same period. She died on January 28, 1813, at the age of eighty-three. It caused him a great sorrow. That "dear and kind Countess" had been as a "sister" to him, and a "second mother" to his children. By way of farewell to her, he wrote a longish memoir about her life and death which he sent to his daughter-in-law, Narcisse.[30] Almost to the end, she remained in good health and intellectually active, fond of talking and reading. She suffered only from a tendency to forget the recent past. She fell ill on January 24, felt feverish, but very sensibly refused to have cauteries applied to her legs, as the doctor recommended. She did not want to be burnt alive, she said, just as she was about to die without pain. She felt weaker and weaker, but never lost her lucidity. On January 28, after receiving the last sacraments, she complained of a contraction of the throat, sent for de Somma-Riva, exchanged a few words with him, bade adieu to the relatives and friends who had collected at her bedside, fell asleep holding de Somma-Riva's hand, and a little later peacefully breathed her last.

"The sleep of a tired traveler would not have been quieter," Crèvecoeur concluded. She had had, in his eyes, a happy life, since, as he recalled, she had been able to celebrate the fiftieth anniversary of her marriage to Count d'Houdetot as well as, later, the forty-first anniversary of her "liaison d'amitié" with Saint-Lambert.

The sorrow he experienced after this death, which marked the end of an era, and the terrible anxiety he felt for Louis during the retreat of the Grand Army made him seek refuge in the family of his daughter-in-law in Normandy. Until news of Louis's return reached him, he spent a few weeks at the castle of Argeronnes, living there in what he called "the happiness of not hearing anything about what is happening or is about to happen." "This kind of deafness," he added, "has for me an inexpressible charm and envelops my body, my heart and my mind with a quietude whose good effects I am now experiencing."[31]

Crèvecoeur returned to Paris in April, fully reassured. He found there the Ottos, who had come back from Vienna, and together they went to Lesches. There he enjoyed what seemed to him "the most magnificent spring he could remember ever having seen." All his family was safe, and the emperor had won new victories. His fears for the future dissipated. He felt happy and returned to Sarcelles in the fall. There he died suddenly at the age of seventy-eight on November 12, 1813, of what was diagnosed as a heart-attack regarded—rightly or wrongly—as a delayed consequence of his ordeals in the English jails of New York.

His death passed almost unnoticed. By then America had become remote in space and time, and no member of the new generation had read his *Letters from an American Farmer,* whether in French or English. Yet an unsigned obituary appeared in the official *Journal de l'Empire* on November 21, 1813, and paid a just tribute to him:

"No one probably has combined to a higher degree an

exquisite sensibility, a vigorous mind, an ardent imagination, considerable attainments, the love of good and the perseverance to ensure its triumph.

Having held himself aloof from public responsibilities for over twenty years, M. de Crèvecoeur spent all his spare time spreading over France a taste for an improved agriculture and recommending, in numerous publications, most of them anonymous, the introduction of many useful plants and the tools best fitted to cultivate them." The obituarist also praised his modesty, "a modesty carried to the verge of humility," and concluded: "Such men honor both their country and mankind; their memory should live forever in all hearts."[32]

Only one thing was left out, the main one, the role Crèvecoeur played as shaper of the American dream. In his *Letters,* he painted an ideal and idyllic America in which it was given him for a time to participate, but from which he was finally expelled forever for lack of faith, because he failed to cast off his allegiance to Europe. Despite all his sympathy for America, he was too much of a divided man ever to become a complete American.

AFTERWORD

WRITING to Thomas Jefferson on July 15, 1794, Crèvecoeur aptly described his situation: "I am at once an American by adoption and law, and a Frenchman by birth." He had indeed adopted America, since he had an American wife and had settled down on an American farm, and America in turn had adopted him, since he had received American citizenship; but he was a Frenchman by birth and remained one to the end. He was even obliged to give up his American citizenship when he was appointed French consul in New York, his American citizenship being incompatible with his official functions as representative and defender of French interests. His children, too, ultimately remained French, though born on American soil of an American mother and though one of his sons had valiantly tried to become an American farmer like his father. Unlike Stephen Girard, the man from Bordeaux, who immediately became a complete Philadelphian, he was too deeply rooted in French soil to become a complete American. Though a landowner in America, he never forgot that he was also his father's heir apparent and consequently a man of property in France. He was not entirely free to become a new man in

America, as he had originally dreamt of being. He was thus condemned to be a Janus, looking toward the future and America when in France, and turned toward the past and France when in America. He was torn between the ideal, which he first identified with America, as his idyllic picture of life on an American farm shows, and the real, which he thought he had left behind in France. But one cannot escape reality. Wherever Crèvecoeur went, sooner or later war broke out—in Canada, in the United States, in Europe—and his dream was shattered. He was rudely brought back to earth. Despite adverse circumstances, he was essentially a man of peace, who, like Candide (and Voltaire himself), wanted above all to cultivate his garden quietly and live in an updated version of the earthly paradise; but he had hardly found a haven when he was driven from it. The American war for independence obliged him to give up his farm, the French Revolution prevented him from living on the family estate and the Napoleonic wars from looking after his son-in-law's farm at Lesches.

However, he was a more complex man than he may seem at first sight. His idealism was a form of materialism. He thought of nothing but peacefully enjoying the fruit of the earth and making it still more enjoyable (to more and more people as well as to himself) thanks to the progress of science and the development of new technologies. In this respect, he morally remained an American, a new man, for, after his return to Europe and until the end of his life, he was passionately interested in new inventions, international trade, and material progress. Thus, though the accidents of history prevented him from becoming for good an American by law, and though he never cut his French roots, he was at heart a true American by adoption. After living in Jefferson's America as an American farmer, he kept, until his death, a foothold in Hamilton's America. In the last analysis, though he had ceased to live in America, by remaining unconquered and forever faithful to his dream, he proved himself an American in spirit.

APPENDIX

❧❧❧❧❧❧

The Cherokee Tradition*

[This Indian legend, found in volume II, chapter 1, of *Journey into Northern Pennsylvania and the State of New York*, Crève-coeur attributes to an Indian chief, translated by Adrien O'Harrah, but the attribution is fictitious. Percy G. Adams, who tried to trace Crèvecoeur's sources for the *Journey* ("Crèvecoeur's *Voyage dans la haute Pensylvanie et dans L'État de New-York*," University of Texas thesis, 1945), says Crève-coeur may have known James O'Hara, an Indian agent, who is said to have known several Indian languages. (See *Dictionary of American Biography*.) Crèvecoeur could have talked with him and received some ideas for this sketch, but it was almost certainly written by Crèvecoeur himself. Adams points out that he composed four Indian orations in *Voyage*, using the language and form of real Indian orations. The satire and moralizing, which are deftly handled in this legend, sound like Crèvecoeur. He greatly admired the beaver, to which he attributed human emotions. He said he once saw

*This account of an ancient tradition was translated in 1774 by order of the mighty war chief Attacul-Culla (the little carpenter), to be sent to the Governor of South Carolina, William Campbell, whose secretary, M. Atkins, permitted me to copy it several years later.

a beaver shed tears when its house was destroyed by an un-feeling man.

The translation is by Clarissa S. Bostelmann.]

From generation to generation this tale has been passed on by our ancestors.

From the earliest days Agan-Kitchee-Manitou, the Great Anima-tor of Matter, was known to have magic powers. One day he decided to come to earth to see how things were getting along.

He turned himself into a wolf and joined the first pack he met. Surprised at the arrival of a stranger, the chiefs surrounded and questioned him, took him in only after ascertaining that he was of ancient stock.

"I note with pleasure," he mused while hunting with them, "that they always use the same weapons I gave them; that they are just as crafty and nimble in mind and body as of yore. In dire need they are clever enough to unite under chiefs when it is a question of attacking or defending. Each is satisfied with his share of the spoils. It is true that misfortune and famine occasionally shrink their number, but then, somehow, a more favorable turn of events retrieves their losses. The fate of the individual is of little importance to me. I am interested only in the species. For the latter will not be held in check until the time when destiny brings to this land a race of farming men. That time is still far off."

Satisfied with his findings, Manitou left them five days later while they were pursuing a stag, and this time turned into a bear.

"What are you doing in my den?" said the first bear he met. "I dug it out myself, as you can see; there's room only for me, my wife, and my little ones."

"Don't your friends ever come to visit you?"

"I don't know whom you mean. Get out or I'll show you who's master here!"

"You are just like your ancestors: wild and unsociable, but I am not the least bit annoyed with you."

Whereupon, he left, this time to become a fox:

"Aha!" said the first fox he met. "You have a foreign and suspi-cious look. It seems to me you smell like a bear. Who are you, and where do you come from? Start talking!"

"I am a fox of good stock. I have come from the Cheryhum country; I'm hungry."

"You've got a lot of nerve: begging from people who live only by dint of scheming and craftiness. Why don't you hunt as we do? Where were you brought up anyway?"

"In the Noyawanda country which is rich in big game."

"Nothing like that here," replied the fox. "You should see how far we have to travel to trap any prey! What a miserable lot is ours! Racked by fear and famine, risks and gnawing need, forever surrounded by trap or ambush. Judge for yourself whether we have any food to give you! Get out of here! Back to your Cheryhum country among your Noyawandas!"

"Gladly," Manitou replied, "but come with me. You will fare sumptuously."

"What is this! You think you can betray us, then?"

"How can you conceive of one fox wanting to betray another! One would think that you had lived among men."

"True, we have, but unbeknownst to them. They are our best providers."

"How does that happen?"

"When they are at war with one another—and that happens often —we devour the carcasses of those whom the conquerors do not want to eat."

"What! Is it possible that man eats man?"

"Does he! Alas, yes, to our great regret. Were it not for that, we would be fat and sleek all year long. Why aren't men more numerous on earth! What a good time we would have!"

"Perhaps that will happen some day," concluded Manitou. And suddenly he transformed himself into a buffalo beyond the Alleghanies.

"Ah, what a fine rich country," he said to the first buffalo he met. "Wide open prairies, always lush with tender, sweet rush. What superb pasture land!"

"All very true," replied the trans-Alleghanian. "Yet we are an unhappy people."

"Why? Don't you get along with each other?"

"Yes, we live in peace and harmony among ourselves but this Mammoth who swoops down from the mountains onto the plains uprooting the trees, forever pursuing and devouring us! Why did Agan-Kitchee-Manitou give life to such a monster?"

"Because, your people would have multiplied so in this fair land that they would have died of hunger. He has done what he could to please everyone, but that was impossible. Some day Manitou will strike his forked thunder between the horns of this Mammoth, and pfft!—his bones will then be but a source of astonishment to posterity. Why don't you urge your friends to cross the Mississippi? They would find on the west bank of that beautiful river, meadows that would take more than a week to cross."

"Everyone loves his own land," replied the buffalo. "To persuade one to leave his country, things must be very bad, or else the power of the Mammoth destructive and horrible. And perhaps the Mammoth would follow beyond this river. That isn't all: we still have another enemy to combat: none the less cruel, and threatening our entire breed with total extinction."

"What could this second enemy be?"

"A puny, hairless animal that has only two feet. After taking his fill of our flesh, he sleeps in the shade of a great tree. All his strength and will comes from his knowledge of lighting a fire. Where could such extraordinary knowledge come from?"

"He has to have this knowledge to compensate for his nudity and feebleness. Otherwise what would he do on earth? Besides, he's not much happier than you. But how does he use this fire to destroy you?"

"He lights the cane and the dry reeds of the prairies in the heat of the summer and traps us in the midst of the big conflagration that follows."

"Well, why don't you flee? You have four good legs and your enemy has but two."

"Fright seizes us and checks us."

"Perhaps things had to be so. . . ." And suddenly Manitou vanished, to reappear as a dog.

"Ah, my friend," he said to the first dog he met, "give me something to eat. I'm hungry."

"Ask my master, sleeping yonder in the sun," the dog replied. "As for me, I have nothing, for instead of being his friend, I am his slave. Often he hasn't enough for himself. Then I suffer, I fast. The man with whom I live is ungrateful, brutal even. Though unfailingly busy in trying to please him, my efforts are mostly futile. But why should I complain? He has no more respect for his wife than for me. I don't think I'd enjoy changing places with her. Why must a free man have two slaves? I want to leave this tyrant and live on my own, for even though I don't express myself as easily as he does, I think nevertheless and my ideas are more just than his. I have accomplished and predicted a thousand times what he could neither have accomplished nor predicted. I should like to become a wolf; they say we are descended from the same stock. Then I would be dependent on no one. I would have a wife and children who will help me in my old age and—for the first time in my life—I would enjoy freedom."

"See that you don't carry out this plan; the wolves would scorn you because you have been a slave; they would put you through a terrible apprenticeship. Believe what I tell you, for I have just been among them. Just as calm is preferable to tempest, repose to work, sleep to nerve-wracking insomnia, a mild and fair servitude is far better than limitless liberty. Man cannot do without your service any more than you can do without his help. All men are not like your master."

And Manitou changed into an otter.

"Look how you are fitted out, wretched creature! You seem to me to be perishing with cold," he said to the first otter he met. "You are trembling despite your fine fur coat."

"Yes," she answered, "the season is severe; the ice covers the water; but I must live."

"Are you alone?"

"Yes, almost always: that is my fate; quite sad, too, I admit, but I am used to it; and as long as I can catch some fish, I am happy."

"And your little ones?"

"I hide them as best I can, for I have so many enemies and among these enemies there is always one who begrudges me my fine coat."

Just as she was saying that, an arrow shot from afar, pierced her side. Manitou, in order to talk with the hunter, suddenly changed into a man.

"What do you plan to do with this otter?" he asked him.

"I shall cover my bare shoulders with her skin and cook her flesh in my kettle."

"Is your kettle big?"

"Yes, for I have five mouths to feed. Follow me if you are hungry, and I will feast you."

Manitou followed him, and on entering his wigwam great was his surprise to see five persons busy cutting a human body to pieces.

"Is that the flesh you promised me?"

"Yes, it's the best I can offer you."

"Why do you eat this man?"

"Because he was my enemy."

"But why was that?"

"Because he and his people live on the other shore of the We-nowee River and for years we have hated and fought one another. They eat us, too, when they catch us."

"Then there is neither game in the forests, nor fish in the river?"

"Sometimes they are hard to find."

"But why do you eat your fellow-man?"

"Because his flesh is tastier than buffalo meat or venison, and because it would be absurd to abandon the carcass of one's enemy to the wolves. Otherwise, what would be the use of killing him? And would I deserve to have another victory? Then, too, how proud and happy one is to think of eating one's fill of someone he hates, to satisfy thus hunger and revenge. How proud our war chant shouts! How our women, children, and neighbors admire us! And after all, hunting is not always lucky."

"What do you do when luck is at a low ebb?"

"Oh, I starve and suffer. Everyone in my wigwam suffers. Then when need exerts its irresistible force upon me, I go away, far from here, and sate it. I kill the first man or woman I meet. Ah, I can readily see that you are not a warrior; you don't know even what it is to be hungry. Let me tell you, if ever hunger pursues you and ensnares you, you will find out."

Horror-stricken, Manitou left this cannibal, not without regretting that he had created such a man. As he made his way slowly, musing over what he had just seen and heard, he changed himself into an opossum to banish his ugly impressions.

"Well, Gossip, how is it with you?"

"Fairly well. I am able to hide easily because I am small. I have more wisdom than courage because I know my weakness. Because of this, I escape the pursuit of man, my cruelest enemy. I compensate for the distresses of my life in hiding and by the care I take of my family. The longer we live together the happier we are. You see around me here three generations, all in good health. I am the great-grandmother and still loved by my family."

"But when the enemy approaches your hideout, how do you manage to escape with all your brood?"

"We have a bag under our bellies, in which the young ones take refuge as soon as danger approaches. Only observe. . . ." She gives the alarm and immediately the little ones respond. Their sacks full, each mother takes flight and disappears.

Impressed with his happy expedient, Manitou smilingly approved his work.

Changing into a man again in order to travel more conveniently, Manitou was suddenly caught in a frightful storm. The echoes of the forest could scarcely keep up with the thunderclaps. Lightning flashed. The rain which fell in torrents began to inundate the land. Not knowing what to do, Manitou leaned against a great tree on which he had seen some squirrels. Shortly after, he turned into one and climbed among them.

"May health, happiness, and swiftness be yours!" he said to the first squirrel he saw. "Although I am a stranger, I seek shelter among you."

"Make yourself snug in this branch and curl your fine tail above your back!"

"How is the living in this region?"

"Wonderful: we have an abundance of nuts, especially beech-nuts. During the summer we play, we frolic, we make love. We are happy and content. As soon as winter comes, we retire to the hollow of big trees, where we have stored our provisions. There, united with our families, we await the return of spring 'mid the most perfect peace and harmony."

"Don't you have any enemies?"

"Some. Man is the cruelest of all and especially his accursed children. It is on us that they learn to let fly their first arrow. But our legs are so nimble, our eyes so quick, and our judgment so sure, that rarely do they reach us. We are happy with our lot and wouldn't change it for that of the buffalo, giant though he appears to us."

"Some day your people will have great dangers to encounter."

"What kind?"

"These magnificent trees will be uprooted. These fine forests will disappear."

"Who could ever uproot these mighty trees?"

"Bearded men, coming from beyond the rising sun, will invade this continent, sharp tools in their hands. They will multiply like fish in the waters. Then, everything will change in this land. They will replace these forests with harvests, these marshes with meadows. Strength, wisdom, and good luck will be theirs. As their number increases, yours will decrease. The bow and arrow will be replaced by deadly firearms."

"Is this day far off?"

"Oh, yes, quite far. You will not live to see it, for from now till then there are still more than a thousand solar revolutions."

"Well, then, let's live as we have, for too much foresight is folly."

"You reason well for a squirrel. You are the first happy creature I have met on my journey."

"Who are you, my friend? And where did you come from?"

"You would die this very hour if I were to answer your question. Suffice it for you to know that the universe and all its wonder are the work of my supple hands, the overflowing of my lifegiving bounty, the pouring forth of my creative power."

"What! You, a squirrel like me! What are you talking about anyway! Well, if you did make the world, why don't you stop the bearded men of the East from coming some day to destroy these beautiful forests which are rightfully ours?"

"There is a power which exceeds mine."

"Who is that power, then?"

"Tibarimaw (destiny). She often does strange things."

"Why don't you reason with her?"

"She is unalterable and unrelenting."

Manitou, once again a man, after the storm had ceased, resumed his journey and was still thinking of the squirrel's contentment, when inadvertently he fell into a hole which had been lightly covered over with underbrush and moss. At the bottom he found a panther, two wolves, a fox, and Wabémat.*

"You seem to be quite chilled," Manitou said to him. "Are you suffering?"

"Do I suffer! Suffering is all I know, for my life has been a perpetual maze of misfortunes. Why was breath given me, since I breathe only to suffer? Every day I feel the sting of need. And as for my family . . . their plight breaks my heart. Ah, if only I were a wolf or an eagle! How well I would fare! When I hunt, either my arrow does not pierce my prey, or a wild cat makes off with what I manage to shoot. When I fish, the fish knowing the fishhook of the unhappy Wabémat, nibbles at the hook only to carry it off. The other day I was sleeping under a tree. What do you think? A branch, snapped off by the wind, fell and broke my leg. Four times fire has destroyed my wigwam. My wife is nearly always sick. Yesterday my eldest son drowned in the river, although he could swim like a fish. In the winter, I freeze. In the summer, I suffocate. Here I am, at the bottom of this pit. A thousand times I have cursed life and all the evils it engenders. Why doesn't the mighty Manitou, who lives above the clouds, they say, come to earth occasionally? Perhaps his benevolence would be touched by the sight of man's struggle. Perhaps he is not aware of all the evil that men take such pleasure in fomenting; perhaps he does not know, either, the harshness of the elements, to which he has exposed us unclad. Why has he subjected us to gnawing hunger, and given us so many other needs, without some means of satisfying them, and with no instruments other than our wretched, helpless ten fingers? Although weak, why are we more evil than the panther, and more ferocious than the wolf who never eats his fellows? Whence comes this state of mind which arouses us unceasingly to hate, to tear in pieces our neighbor, and whence this fury that urges us ever to war? Why are we unable to live 'mid plenty, with peace and understanding? Why . . ."

He was interrupted by the arrival of the man who had laid the

*One of the Indians of the neighboring village.

trap. When he missed the wild animals, which the Great Spirit had set free, he became angry and was about to strike the two men down when the great animator spoke:

"Tireless hunter, brave warrior, spare our lives."

"What do I care about saving *your* life? I have lost my quarry, and it's your fault. I shall eat you since I am hungry and I am the strongest."

"Don't eat us," replied Manitou. "Before the sun sets this very day, I shall present you with a fine fat buffalo, whose skin will serve to cover the nudity of my hapless friend here!"

"Why doesn't he hunt for himself, this hapless friend of yours? I want the whole buffalo—or your lives."

"Agreed."

And off he went to look for a liana which would help them climb out of the pit.

"What a scurvy creature!" said Manitou to Wabémat.

"But that's the way men treat each other here. When they are hungry, a frequent occurrence, they make no exception of brother or friend. The weak succumb to the strong, trickery triumphs over innocence. Can it be thus throughout all the land lighted by the great sun?"

"Just about," replied Manitou.

"What a destiny, to be born without weapons, without any covering, and with only two legs, doomed to an existence in a climate like this one, and to live only on the flesh of animals, who have four legs and are every bit as intelligent as we are."

"Ungrateful wretch," said Manitou, "these ten fingers that you scorn so are nevertheless far superior to the wolf's or tiger's claw. The fine sense of touch of which they are the instruments, together with their flexibility, has made them the sceptre of man's almost magic power. They are responsible for man's good fortune in being able to light and propagate fire; they are his means of having weapons, his canoe, his dwelling, his clothes. True, he has only two legs, but of all creatures, he is the most majestic, he alone commands all nature with his gaze, only he can admire the splendor of the heavens, the beauty of nature in all her glory* and elevate himself through his power of thinking toward an understanding of his inscrutable author.

*Ovid said:

> Os homini sublime dedit, coelumque tueri
> Jussit, et erectos ad sidera tollere vultus
>   (Note written to the author by Citizen Büocq.)

"The amazing perfectibility with which the Creator has endowed man's intelligence, the sublime feelings that he has put in his heart, all masterpieces of his bounty and his power, are the most precious present a father could give to his children. And after all, what is man, this vain and presumptuous being? A living atom whose generations succeed each other on earth like the shadows of clouds chased by the wind. And what of this world? A mere dot in the infinity of the universe, one of the smallest spheres in the millions of which the universe is composed.

"Yet, far superior to other creatures, who are forever bound within the narrow limits of their sphere, although, like them, he is abandoned to the rule of chance, some day he will rise to an understanding of the greatest concepts through his own might. He will subdue the elements, cross the seas, whose storms he will learn how to brave, he will improve the land and make of it a delightful home. It will depend only on him to become the artisan of his own glory and happiness.

"If his lifetime seems short, if his days seem filled with hazards and hardships, inseparable companions of life, the unquenchable spark which inspires man to act, to feel, and to think will survive till his death, will bring him, in the realm of spirits, a reward from his suffering and his virtues, or punishment for his crimes. If this law of compensation did not exist, it would be a thousand times better not to have seen the light of day, for, if he were endowed with reasoning powers, and deprived of the consolations of hope, he would be the unhappiest of creatures."

"These are strange things you are telling me," Wabémat replied. "Where did you learn all this? It seems so new."

"In the land I came from."

"Where is this land anyway? I have never heard of it. Does one have to hunt and fish in order to live, as we do in this country?"

"It rests only with you whether you will come to know it some day," answered Manitou, "and that day will be one of eternal joy and happiness, for troubles and needs are unknown in that land."

Finally the promised buffalo arrived and on leaving the pit, Wabémat said to Manitou:

"Don't go to this devourer of men; come with me."

Manitou followed him; the fire of his hearth was well kindled, but there was no kettle, for someone had put it aside. Some roots cooked under the ashes were the only food, offered to the guest.

"Why is your kettle empty and your family so naked?" Manitou asked him.

"Because the Evil Spirit always follows or precedes me, and nothing I undertake ever succeeds. Yet I never forget to offer up to him the smoke of my first pipe every day just as the sun rises."

"Have you ever seen the Evil Spirit?"

"No, never."

"Well, then, what makes you think he exists?"

"Who could ever doubt his existence when for forty-two times winter snows have squashed our wigwams; for forty-two winters the ice has carried away our canoes; packs of wolves have carried off our women and our children, while we were off hunting. Deadly epidemics have poisoned half of our villages, tempests have uprooted our forest, and the fire from on high has destroyed all. Why did there have to be men created on earth since they were born to meet nothing but misfortune in all their ways?"

"Just what is this misfortune? Have you ever seen it in your life?"

"No, I really don't know what it is like. As cunning as a squirrel, it hides itself behind the trees that I pass. But if I can see it ever, I shall certainly kill it. It is the only enemy that I should like to eat. It has made me starve so much!"

"Is it possible that you do not eat what you kill by tomahawk in war, as do your fellow men?"

"No."

"Why not?"

"Fear that you will poke fun at me prevents my knowing what to say."

"Speak freely. I am not one of your countrymen, as you know."

"Very well, I shall. Here is what my reasoning tells me every time I am gnawed by hunger and inclined to follow my neighbor's example. How can you eat your fill of a person whose tongue, like your own, might have spoken? Or of a person whose heart, like yours, could have loved wife and children. How can you bring yourself to drink the brewed flesh of a man who, had he been born on this bank of the river, would have been your neighbor, aye, your friend mayhap. Wolf never eats wolf, a fox would sooner die than eat one of his own species. And you, a man, would eat, and ravenously, too, one of your fellow men! Aren't your hate and revenge sufficiently appeased when you have spilled the blood which gave life to his body to be food for the flies? When you are starved, why don't you go into the woods and seek the orikomah, the wotta-towah, or the wennasimah? If you boil or cook them over embers, they will nourish your family.

"That is what my reasoning tells me every time my comrades start cutting up a corpse, after killing an enemy. They turn my repugnance into ridicule, call me a weak, faint-hearted Nishy-norbay, who doesn't know how to enjoy the spoils of victory. These reproaches uttered by my neighbors increase my unhappiness."

"Then you aren't a warrior?" Manitou inquired.

"Why, yes, just as good a warrior as the others: when our enemies cross the Wenowee River to attack the village, at the risk of my life, I defend the honor of my family and tribe; but when *we* must cross the river to attack *them* . . . that's different. I stay right here, with no desire to entangle myself in a quarrel which doesn't interest me. Again I am ridiculed, again they insult me in my very wigwam, but I am as unyielding as a huge rock in the river."

"Then you have never tasted human flesh, no matter how gnawing your hunger was?" asked Manitou.

"No, never. When I have been unable to catch either fish or game, I eat roots, as you notice. As long as my family likes them, I am satisfied."

"Wabémat, bless the moment when I fell into the pit, for the roots that nourish you will soon bear fruit. The time for retribution is at hand. Now which do you prefer: to wait until death, whose date is uncertain, comes to deliver you from the burden of life to enjoy the unalterable, eternal pure happiness of the spirits—or—would you rather revel in all the fullness of the happiness one can enjoy on earth beginning now?"

"Alas!" Wabémat replied, "what can you do about it, since like me, you are only the son of a mortal woman?"

"I can answer your questions," Manitou said.

"The happiness of the spirits! I've never heard of that! Is such a land far away?"

"Yes, quite far."

"Why can't I go there right away?"

"The time is not yet ripe and the other land, why it's fairly near yours!"

"Do people there die of hunger as they do here, when hunting and fishing are poor? Do men war against one another?"

"People there live in peace and plenty."

"Ah, what a fine country."

Those words made Wabémat's heart leap with joy.

"Well, then," he said, "if you can accomplish what you wanted to, make good your promise. I am so tired of my diet of herbs and my misery that I can scarcely wait to get there."

"I know an island in the Lake of Tempests (Michigan) where I shall take you and your whole family. But, before hearing my last words, bow down."

"What! Bow down before my equal!"

"Oh, I only appear to be your equal."

"Who are you anyway?"

"In the silence of the night, haven't you ever watched the glory of the heaven, and the twinkling stars which brighten and give life to the thousands of worlds just like this one which, although invisible to your eyes, move about through space? Haven't you ever admired the radiant sun in the magnificence of dawn and in the glory of her daily sunset over the lake waters? In casting your eyes over the beauty of living nature, haven't you ever felt an involuntary impulse of respect and admiration? Haven't you ever asked yourself what was the life-giving principle which animates all earthly things of the land as well as those under the water and in the atmosphere? Who is responsible for maintaining everlasting freshness and eternal youth? Who, from the most contemptible refuse, makes the elements of new reproduction? Well, Wabémat, it is I who am the life-giving universal spirit. Now judge of my power and my bounty. Without me, the order on which the very existence of the universe depends, the stability of its intricate counterbalances would soon be upset. Long since the light of the sun and moon would have been extinguished and matter would have returned to the chaos of the void and of eternal darkness whence I freed it many moons ago."

Seized with awe and respect, Wabémat bowed quaking before Agan-Kitchee-Manitou. Scarcely had his face touched the earth when the dark clouds which hid the majesty of the sun dispersed. The whistle of the wind ceased, the cry of the animals, the buzzing of insects, even the song of the birds could no longer be heard and the primeval silence of nature returned to the earth, and the great life-giving power continued:

"Since you prefer to hasten the moment of your happiness, rather than await the great day of retribution, you must cease being a man. Do you consent to that?"

"What! Cease to be what I am! What are you going to do with me anyway?"

"Do you consent, I ask you?"

"May your will be done."

"So that you will not be distracted by futile thoughts, source of the greatest part of your unhappiness, you must lose your power of speech. Do you consent?"

"Lose my power of speech? But how could I chat with my neighbors, with my wife and my children who are so dear to me?"

"Do you consent to this, I ask you?"

"All right, since your benevolence, which is a necessary companion to your power, would wish only for my happiness."

"This gift will be replaced by a series of sounds simpler but every bit as useful as speech, and although less varied, just as expressive. With these, you and yours will be able to carry on all undertakings. Just as before, you will know love, conjugal and paternal happiness, as well as sobriety, temperance, and chastity. Your children will respect you, and love you and succor you when you are old. The absence of mental anguish will take the place of enjoyment and happiness for you. You will be able to conceive, and execute intelligently, all the plans necessary to the well-being of your family and for that I will permit you to retain your memory, your foresight, and your judgment.

"You will enjoy social privileges whence come peace and repose. Misfortune will never follow nor precede your every step as it has in the past. You will love life and you will enjoy it long with neither sickness nor infirmity. Your appetites, your wants, and your tastes will always be simple and moderate. Looting and warring will always horrify you. Your pure hands will nevermore cause blood to be spilled. You will have no more enemies, nor will your descendants, as long as they stay on this island, unknown to man.

"You will be a fine architect. You will understand the principles of water power. With the help of your family, you will construct a spacious, comfortable, clean home on the water. You will have sharp words with which to defend yourself, without ever having any desire to be the aggressor. For you will love peace, retreat, and silence. You will be able to live under water as well as on land, and for that purpose I shall give you the most beautiful of furs.

"A soft, quiet light will soon replace the flaming torch of your reason, which has served only to dazzle and distract you up till now. Guided by this new light which never wavers, you will be happy, with no anxieties, wise, with no sadness, provident, without futile desires, thoughtful though sated in spirit. Only the darkness of death will extinguish this light.

"If ever you come to regret the loss of your reason, you will be able to console yourself in the thought that you have been freed forever from its errors, its illusions as well as its aberrations, for paroxysms of abysmal despair will no longer seize your soul, since you will nevermore know the frightening outbursts of delirium and revenge, the shameful fits of frenzy, nor the degrading errors of anger and madness.

"These are the foundations of the happiness which you shall enjoy, Wabémat; that happiness which your privations, your sufferings, and your abstinence from human flesh have so justly deserved. What does your heart tell you? . . . Speak."

"Powerful as you are, why, in order to achieve happiness, must I lose my identity as a human being? Is it possible that your eternal decrees have ordered that man should never know happiness! You, the creator, the organizer of all matter, the soul and the support of the universe! Give heed to your own goodness and Wabémat and his brethren will be happy. Since before calling man from the void of life, you necessarily foresaw his destiny on earth, why didn't you provide him with . . . ."

Scarcely had these words been uttered when by a sudden metamorphosis, there appeared the first family of beavers that had ever been known on earth.

After watching this new and last example of his creative power, this masterpiece of his strength and generosity, Agan-Kitchee-Manitou disappeared and has not revealed himself since.

And, in accordance with his words, this family of beavers lost no time in constructing a dam to swell the waters of the first stream that it met on the island of the Tempests (Michigan) where the beavers were suddenly transported. And on this dam, they built a spacious home, clean and comfortable, where after many vicissitudes, they finally found peace and plenty. For this island, unknown to man, was covered with many alders, birches, and willows. The family shed tears occasionally but they were tears of joy, pleasure, and gratitude when, united on the river bank, papa told of the old days of war, of want, and of misfortune. (For, by a very special favor which was limited to the first generation, the mighty Manitou wished to preserve in him the memory of man's former state.)

After many snows had passed over his head, the old beaver Wabémat succumbed in the arms of his children and in accordance with Manitou's prediction, his family was everlastingly happy, to the point where the happiness they enjoyed so long increased their number, that several families were obliged to settle on new sites of Lake Michigan's shores. From there by slow degrees, they spread throughout the northern region of the continent. Then man, enemy of all living creatures, declared war on them to cover his nudity with their fine furs, but still with some compassion and some regard for their divine origin. The result is that even today when hunters come upon a beaver colony, they always permit a certain number to escape.

Translated by the undersigned interpreter of the king for Cherokee, residing at Sinica, on the Keowee River.

June 17, 1774

Adrien O'Harrah

NOTES

Works frequently cited have been identified by the following abbreviations:

Letters *Letters from an American Farmer.* London, 1782.

Lettres *Lettres d'un cultivateur américain.* 3 vols. Paris, 1787.

Journey *Journey into Northern Pennsylvania and the State of New York.* Translated by Clarissa S. Bostelmann. Ann Arbor: University of Michigan Press, 1964.

Mantes Library at Mantes, France.

Mitchell Julia Post Mitchell. *St. Jean de Crèvecoeur.* New York: Columbia University Press, 1916.

R. Crèvecoeur Robert de Crèvecoeur. *St. John de Crèvecoeur: sa vie et ses oeuvres.* Paris: Librairie des Bibliophiles, 1883.

Rice Howard C. Rice. *Le cultivateur Américain: étude sur l'oeuvre de Saint John de Crèvecoeur.* Paris: Champion, 1932.

Sketches *Sketches of Eighteenth Century America: More "Letters from an American Farmer."* Edited by Henri L. Bourdin, Ralph H. Gabriel, and Stanley T. Williams. New Haven: Yale University Press, 1925.

Notes

Stone

Letters from an American Farmer and Sketches of Eighteenth-Century America, by J. Hector St. John de Crèvecoeur. Edited and with an Introduction by Albert E. Stone. New York: Penguin Books, 1981.

INTRODUCTION

1. Description in letter supposedly written by Crèvecoeur's father, Mitchell, 314.

2. Ibid., 707–8.

3. Ibid., 312–13.

4. *Letters*, 40.

5. See note 1, above.

6. Letter to the Duke d'Harcourt, July 27, 1787, cited by Rice, 14. See also title page of *Voyage dans la haute Pensylvanie et dans l'état de New-York* (Paris, 1801): "Par un Membre adoptif de la Nation Onéida."

7. *Lettres*, III, 3–34.

8. *Crèvecoeur's Eighteenth-Century Travels in Pennsylvania & New York, selections from the* Voyage . . . Translated by Percy G. Adams. Lexington: University of Kentucky Press, 1961.

9. Letter to Thomas Jefferson, April 24, 1785, Mantes Library.

CHAPTER I
Norman Child—British Youth

1. Reproduced in Mitchell, 307, and R. Crèvecoeur, 284.

2. According to the tax records of the *intendant royal* for the Caen area, Crèvecoeur's father bought his Pierrepont estate at a fairly late date, in 1747, when his son was already twelve, but the family must have lived there and rented the estate for some time and was very much attached to it, for the records bear this curious note: "Guillaume Jean de Crèvecoeur Esquire claims and proves that he acquired the land of Pierrepont by a contract dated 8/8/1747, for the sum of 22,000 pounds and a commission of 800 pounds. . . . And he added

232

that this was the price of love and special reasons had incited him to accept such a high price for a piece of land whose income does not correspond to the sum invested." And indeed he declared an annual income of only £650 (less than 5 percent of the capital invested), which figure was accepted by the *intendant*.

Other tax records show that Guillaume Jean de Crèvecoeur owned land in other parishes. In the parish of Mathieu (to the north of Caen), he owned a small farm ("une acre et trois vergées de terre" or, since a *vergée* was a quarter of an acre, about 2.50 acres. It is to be noted that before the adoption of the metric system in 1799, the value of an "acre" in France varied considerably from one place to another. The conversion of figures given in French acres into U.S. acres requires the use of special conversion tables such as those found in Commandant Henri Navel, *Recherches sur les anciennes mesures agraires normandes* [Caen: Jouan et Bigot, 1932]. Even then the result is only approximate.) In the parish of Robehomme (to the northeast of Caen), he owned, according to the tax records for 1737, houses and lands covering in all thirty French "acres"—i.e., about 65 U.S. acres (or 2,100 square meters) and his annual income was £725. He was by far the richest man in the parish. In Pierrepont, as was often the case, a small farm was attached to the castle. The note in the tax records referred to above also contains the following indication: "The contract gives the price of 24,800 pounds, including the commission, but there is also an income of 100 pounds sold by the contract and part and parcel of it," corresponding to the farm.

Crèvecoeur's father also owned land at Quesnel, which brought an annual income of £481, and in 1778 he bought more land at Pierrepont for £3,600 in all. He was described on this occasion as "le seigneur du lieu" (the lord of the place). In 1787, he must have once more bought some land, for he had to pay a tax of £32 representing one-twentieth ("le vingtième") of the annual income of the property he had acquired (£650).

3. The street "au Canu" is now called Demolombe Street. Canu was the name of the original owner of one of the houses on that street. Rue au Canu lay in St. Stephen's parish, but, as St.

Stephen's church was part of an abbey and did not fully func-
tion as a parish church, young Crèvecoeur was baptized at St.
John's.

4. Arthur Young, *Travels in France* (August 19–22, 1788).

5. Quoted by R. Crèvecoeur, 5.

6. After the expulsion of the Jesuits from France in 1762, the
   name of the *collège* changed to Collège du Mont, not because
   it was built on a hill, for it was not, but because the original
   building had been the Caen residence of the Abbots of St.
   Michael's Mount. Robert de Crèvecoeur, anachronistically,
   calls it Collège du Mont in his biography. In Crèvecoeur's
   time the full official name was Collège Royal de Bourbon.

7. Quoted by R. Crèvecoeur, 4.

8. "Take literature from men and you take all their humanity."
   See F. Charmot, S.J., *La pédagogie des Jésuites* (Paris: Spes,
   1943).

8a. Ibid.

8b. Ibid.

9. So Crèvecoeur probably went to Salisbury when he was only
   sixteen, and not eighteen, as all previous biographers have
   thought, misinterpreting an ambiguous indication in the letter his father sent to the British authorities, at a date unfortunately unknown, to find out if he was dead or alive. The
   document is quoted in full by Mitchell, 314 (see note 15,
   below, for a translation). The figure of eighteen given by his
   father probably refers to the duration of his exile rather than
   to his age when he left France.

10. There is a particularly apt quotation of "in terrorem," mean-
    ing "to inspire terror," in *Sketches*, 115.

11. See François de Dainville, *L'éducation des Jésuites* (Paris: Édi-
    tions de Minuit, 1978).

12. The name Mutel is given by Crèvecoeur's father in the letter
    translated in note 15, below.

13. On Salisbury in the eighteenth century, see the files of the
    Salisbury Journal and E. E. Dorling, *A History of Salisbury* (1911).

In *Martin Chuzzlewit,* chapter 5, Dickens offers a lively description of Salisbury on a market day. It is Salisbury as Dickens saw it nearly a hundred years later, but the town had changed little in the interval. It is described as a busy and somewhat rowdy place. "Mr. Pinch [one of Dickens's characters, a very mild and naïve young man] even had a shrewd notion that Salisbury was a very desperate sort of place; an exceeding wild and dissipated city."

14. *Sketches,* 52–53.

15. Mitchell, pp. 313–14, quotes the full text of this letter in the original French. Here is the translation:

A private person from the Province of Normandy begs the Government of England to procure for him the life or death certificate of the person named hereunder.

The man about whom information is being sought is called Michel Guillaume Jean de Crèvecoeur, he is a gentleman and was born at Caen, the capital of Lower Normandy; he is about 38 years old, and five feet four inches tall, he is very handsome, well shaped and well proportioned.

He is red-haired and used to wear a wig, his face is rather long, but full, though; his skin is white, but with many freckles. He has beautiful brown eyes, his eyebrows are of the same color and quite thick, his forehead is fine and broad, his nose somewhat long. His freckles are of the small kind and look like bran; they extend as far as his hands, which are covered with them. The latter are fairly large and rather thin.

He has lived abroad for eighteen years, in England for ten or eleven. He was at first the guest of the Misses Mutel, old maids of at least seventy years of age, who inhabit the town of Salisbury; through them, he became acquainted with persons who have assets in Philadelphia and in Pennsylvania and he has lived in this province of New England [*sic,* by analogy with New France] in the very town of Philadelphia for eight or nine years. He was first there as partner or assistant-manager of a merchant whose name and line of business are unknown to us and the last time we heard from him was in 1767. He must know English perfectly, at least this is what he claims. It is not known whether he is married or not, or was in the past. It is only known that, shortly after he arrived in England he was engaged to marry the only daughter of a merchant, that she died before the marriage could take place and it is owing to this event that he has obtained the interests he is now possessed of in Philadelphia.

Considerable family interests require the exhibition of the certificate which we are applying for and we hope it will be delivered at the French Ambassador's request.

This letter shows, among other things, that Crèvecoeur's father had only the haziest notions about the geography of America, since he placed Pennsylvania in New England and did not clearly distinguish the thirteen colonies from Great Britain.

16. Robert de Crèvecoeur mentions (p. 6, n. 2) a manuscript essay in French entitled "Le roc de Lisbonne" which was inserted in the manuscript of *Letters from an American Farmer*. The manuscript of *Letters from an American Farmer* is now in the Library of Congress.

CHAPTER II
French Soldier Becomes American Citizen

1. In an 1823 letter; see R. Crèvecoeur, 7.

2. In Army Archives in Paris.

3. The best account in English of the Seven Years' War is the most recent edition of Francis Parkman, *Montcalm and Wolfe* (New York: Atheneum, 1984). Parkman was sympathetic with the British, but in quoting the archives of both sides he was scrupulously honest.

4. Parkman, 212.

5. Rice, 9ff.

6. Parkman, 212.

7. Rice, 11–12.

8. R. Crèvecoeur, 14; Rice, 11.

9. Parkman, chapter 17.

10. Rice, 12.

11. Parkman, chapter 14.

12. Ibid., chapter 16.

13. *Sketches,* 172.

14. Rice, 13.

15. Mitchell, 307–9.

16. R. Crèvecoeur, 17n.

17. Rice, 14.

18. Mitchell, 89.

19. Ibid., 36–39.

20. Quoted by Bernard Chevignard, in "St. John de Crèvecoeur in the Looking Glass: *Letters from an American Farmer* and the Making of a Man of Letters," *Early American Literature,* XIX (1934), 173ff.

21. Ibid., 174 (quoted from William Smith, *Historical Memoirs 1778–1783* [Ed. W. H. W. Sabine. New York: The New York Times and Arno Press, 1971].

22. *Memoir,* quoted by Rice, 14–15.

23. *Lettres* (1784), 387f.

24. Letter to the Duke de La Rochefoucauld, July 15, 1784. Library of Mantes.

CHAPTER III
Hector St. John the Farmer

1. Mitchell, 309–10.

2. Ibid., 37.

3. Ibid., 307–9.

4. Ibid., 30.

5. Ibid., 310.

6. The authors visited the location several times.

7. Cf. Stone, 271.

8. See watercolor sketch on jacket.

9. Stone, 313–14.

10. Ibid., 299.

11. Ibid., 298.

12. Mitchell, 40.

13. Ibid., 309–10.

14. Stone, 275.

15. Ibid., 280f.

16. Ibid., 54.

17. Ibid., 236.

18. Herbert G. Gutman, *The Black Family in Slavery and Freedom, 1750–1925.* (New York: Random House, 1976).

19. Stone, 59.

20. Ibid., 76.

21. Frederick Jackson Turner, *The Significance of the Frontier in American History,* 1893.

22. Stone, 78.

23. Ibid., 79.

24. Ibid., 86.

25. Ibid., 285.

26. *Journey,* 37.

CHAPTER IV
The Nightmare Years

1. For background: J. Franklin Jameson, *The American Revolution Considered as a Social Movement* (Princeton University Press, 1926); Paul H. Smith, *Loyalists and Redcoats: A Study in British Revolutionary Policy* (University of North Carolina Press, 1964); Alfred R. Young, *The Democratic Republicans in New York* (University of North Carolina Press, 1967); Ian R. Christie and Benjamin W. Larabee, *Empire or Independence, 1760–1776* (New York: Norton, 1976).

2. Norman Gelb argues the Loyalist side in *Less Than Glory: A Revisionist View of the American Revolution* (New York: Putnam, 1984).

3. Wilbur C. Abbott, *New York in the American Revolution* (New York: Scribners, 1929), 29.

4. Ibid., 45.

5. Ibid., 68.

6. Ibid., 75.

7. Thomas Jones, *History of New York During the American Revolution* (New-York Historical Society, 1879), 2 vols, I, 18, 37.

8. Abbott, 144.

9. *New York Historical Atlases, Orange County,* No. 296, I, 83.

10. Jones, I, 218.

11. Stone, 201ff.

12. Ibid., 346–74.

13. Ralph Gray, "Down the Susquehanna by Canoe," *National Geographic,* July 1950, 73–120.

14. Stone, 375f.

15. *Sketches of Eighteenth Century America,* ed. Henri L. Bourdin, Ralph H. Gabriel, and Stanley Williams (New York: Benjamin Blom, 1972), 192ff.

16. In 1909 Thomas Campbell. the popular Scottish poet, wrote a poem about this atrocity called *Gertrude of Wyoming*. It is a highly romantic poem in Spenserian stanzas, detailing the sufferings of a young, innocent heroine, Gertrude, during the period of the massacre. It is worth mentioning here because it shows the unrealistic imagination of the Scottish poet who knew nothing about the American frontier. In an "Advertisement for the First Edition" of *Gertrude,* he says: "historians and travellers concur in describing the infant colony as one of the happiest spots of human existence. . . . In an evil hour the junction of European with Indian arms converted the territo-

rial paradise into a frightful waste." The second stanza shows how fanciful the poet was:

> Delightful Wyoming! beneath the skies
> The happy shepherd swains had nought to do
> But feed their flocks on green declivities . . .

while from morn to night they amused themselves with timbrel and flageolet.

17. Stone, 379.

18. Francis Jennings, *The Invasion of America: Indians, Colonialism, and the Cant of Conquest* (New York: Norton, 1976).

19. Rice, 136ff.

20. For a translation of the letter see chapter I, note 15.

21. Mitchell, 47.

22. Oscar Theodore Barck, *New York During the War for Independence* (New York: Columbia University Press, 1931), 53.

23. Mitchell, 47.

24. *Sketches* (Bourdin, ed.), 192n.

25. *Lettres,* I, 417.

26. Mitchell, 50.

27. Barck, chapter 5.

28. Ibid., 75.

29. Ibid., 102.

30. Abbott, 143–44.

31. Barck, 94.

32. Bernard Chevignard, "Documents pour l'Histoire de la Normandie: St. John de Crèvecoeur à New York en 1779–1780," *Annales de Normandie*, vol. 33, n. 2, June 1983, 161–75.

33. Ibid., 172.

34. Mitchell, 54; *Lettres,* I, 428ff.

35. Mitchell, 52.

36. Abbott, 208.

37. *Lettres,* I, 425–62.

38. Ibid., 345–425.

39. Ibid., 454.

40. *Annales de Normandie,* 164.

41. Ibid., 167.

42. Ibid., 170.

43. Mitchell, 51; letter in Mantes.

44. *Lettres,* I, 461.

CHAPTER V
Back to France

1. Letter to Ally, 1805.

2. Letter dated July 8, 1779, quoted by Mitchell, 54 n. 21.

3. Mitchell, 55 n. 21.

4. R. Crèvecoeur, 64 n. 2 and *Lettres,* 1:461 and 2:iff.

5. *Courier de l'Europe, Gazette Anglo-Française,* 13 (May 9, 1793): 296, in Howard C. Rice, *Le cultivateur américain* (Paris: Champion, 1932), 66.

6. Franklin's statement is quoted in the notes to the Everyman's Library edition of *Letters from an American Farmer* (1940), 236.

7. On the reception of the *Letters,* see Rice, 63–64, and Mitchell, 346–50.

8. Friedrich-Melchior von Grimm, *Correspondence littéraire, philosophique et critique,* ed. Tourneaux, 14:88. Quoted in Everyman's Library edition of *Letters,* 234.

9. Quoted by Thomas Philbrick in *St. John de Crèvecoeur* (New York: Twayne, 1970), 162.

10. *Letters of James Russell Lowell,* ed. C. E. Norton (New York: Harper, 1894), 2:30. See also the review of William Ellery Channing, *Sermons and Tracts, Edinburgh Review,* 50 (October 1829): 130–31.

11. The right of primogeniture, the application of which was meant to prevent the breaking up of large estates, was not universally recognized in France before the 1789 revolution. In Normandy, it was applied only in Pays d'Auge. Elsewhere, landed property was divided among all the male heirs according to the clauses of the will drawn up by the deceased. Female heirs were entitled only to a share of the chattels. This lack of uniformity was criticized and led to controversies among the supporters of the various systems. Thus in 1724 the Jesuits of the Collège de Bourbon staged a debate in the form of a play between six students of the top form, or *rhétorique.* Here is the argument:

> It is supposed that a foreign prince, after traveling in France, wants to follow the model of our laws in his country; one point, however, causes him some embarrassment: the division of family property about which customs vary in France from one province to another; in some places, the children divide equally, in others unequally, so that customary law in several regions gives two thirds of the estate to the firstborn; in some it gives the advantage to the youngest child; and sometimes allows the fathers and mothers to favor whichever of their children they prefer. The Prince wonders to which of these different customs he will give the preference. So those whose names follow will speak
> for an equal division
> for an unequal division
> for the firstborn
> for the youngest
> for the free choice of parents. . . .

12. R. Crèvecoeur, 294–95.

13. *Lettres,* 3:1.

14. See Chactas in *Les Natchez.*

15. Arthur Young, *Travels in France,* October 1787.

16. *Mémoires, ou souvenirs et anecdotes du Comte de Ségur* (Paris: Didier, 1845), 1:40.

16a. Ibid.

17. Mme. de Staël, *De l'Allemagne.*

18. Jean-Jacques Rousseau, *Confessions.*

19. Gouverneur Morris, *Diary and Letters,* under February 13, 1790.

20. Quoted by Hippolyte Buffenoir, *La Comtesse d'Houdetot—une amie de J. J. Rousseau* (Paris: Levy, 1901).

21. R. Crèvecoeur, 70–71.

CHAPTER VI
Farmer Becomes French *Philosophe*

1. Pierre-Louis Lacretelle, "Lettre au rédacteur du *Mercure de France,*" January 4, 1783, reprinted in *Lettres* 1:9.

2. Guillaume Raynal, *Histoire philosophique et politique des établissements et du commerce des Européens dans les deux Indes.* See book 15, chapter 15. There were seventeen editions of Raynal's work between 1772 and 1780.

3. Quoted by R. Crèvecoeur, 68–69.

4. Ibid., 73.

5. See Gilbert Chinard, *Les amitiés américaines de Madame d'Houdetot* (Paris: Champion, 1924). Franklin's letter of September 26, 1781, was also published in part by Mitchell, 65.

5a. Ibid.

6. Translated from Crèvecoeur's "Souvenirs sur Mme. D'Houdetot," quoted by R. Crèvecoeur, 74.

7. Quoted by Rice, 76.

8. Ibid., 85–86.

9. *Lettres,* 1:7–21.

10. R. Crèvecoeur, 78–79.

11. Mitchell, 83; letter in Mantes.

12. Unpublished letters in the National Archives in Paris.

13. Mitchell, 83, 87 n. 100.

CHAPTER VII
Consul in New York

1. *Lettres,* III, 4–17.

2. Wilbur C. Abbott, *New York in the American Revolution.* (New York: Scribners, 1929), chapter 11.

3. *Lettres,* III, 253.

4. Abbott, 271.

5. *Lettres,* III, 255.

6. Mitchell, 92.

7. Abbott, 281.

8. *Lettres,* III, 266.

9. Abbott, 282.

10. *Lettres,* III, 272.

11. Ibid., 17–21.

12. Ibid., 23.

13. Ibid., 32–34.

14. *Weatherwise,* No. 35 (Dec. 1982), 252–62.

15. Mitchell, chapter 11.

16. *Lettres,* III, 253.

17. Mitchell, 92.

18. Robert Seton, *An Old Family,* 262–63 (cited by Mitchell, 92).

19. May 8, 1785, *Jefferson Papers,* Library of Congress, Washington, D.C., ser. 2, vol. 74, no. 5.

20. Mitchell, 90.

21. R. Crèvecoeur, 296n.

22. *Lettres*, III, 7.

23. Ibid., 8.

24. Mitchell, 134.

25. Ibid., 128.

26. Quoted by Mitchell, 128; letter in Mantes.

27. Mitchell, 130.

28. Letter in Mantes.

29. Quoted by R. Crèvecoeur, 353, and Mitchell, 143.

30. Mitchell, 110.

31. Ibid., 217; R. Crèvecoeur, 96ff.

32. Mitchell, chapter 12.

33. Seton to the Duke de La Rochefoucauld, Jan. 6, 1784, at Mantes.

34. Crèvecoeur's letter quoted by Mitchell, 234–35.

35. Letter to the Duke de La Rochefoucauld, Nov. 5, 1784, in Mantes; quoted by Mitchell, 232.

36. Letter in Mantes.

37. Translation of letter in Mantes.

38. Rice, 34, n2.

39. R. Crèvecoeur, 122.

40. Mitchell, 136.

41. Henry Dwight Sedgwick, *Lafayette* (New York: Bobbs-Merrill, 1928), 137–44.

42. Ibid., 136.

43. *Lettres*, III, 315ff.

44. Sedgwick, 136.

45. Mitchell, 143; quotes newspaper dated Dec. 28, 1785, but Crèvecoeur left one year earlier.

46. Mitchell, 141.

47. Ibid., 145.

48. R. Crèvecoeur, 115, n1.

49. *Lettres*, III, 250.

50. *Lettres*, III, 314.

51. Mitchell, 147.

52. Brissot de Warville, *Mémoires* (1850), 411–12.

CHAPTER VIII
On Leave in France

1. Quoted by Mitchell, 147.

2. Ibid., 148.

3. R. de Crèvecoeur, 354.

4. Ibid., 118.

5. Ibid., 119.

6. Ibid., 353. There was a very favorable review in particular in *Correspondance littéraire, philosophique et critique*, ed. Friedrich-Melchior von Grimm, 14; 88–89 (January 1785):

> . . . this book [. . .] written without any method or art, but with great seriousness and much sensibility, fully carries out the object that the author seems to have had in mind, namely to make the reader love America. [. . .] You find in it trivial details, trite truths, repetitions and tedious passages, but it pleases nonetheless with its plain and candid descriptions, the expression of an honest soul deeply imbued with the sense of all domestic virtues and all the happiness that a sweet independence, assiduous labor, the affection of a dearly loved family and the enjoyment of an estate safely and legitimately owned can procure to a man.
>
> Until half of Europe becomes a province of America, as it is perhaps destined some day to be, it seems to me that, if I

were a king desirous of making my subjects happy [. . .] it would be one of the books which I would be most tempted to forbid them to read. There is hardly any that would be more calculated to encourage them to emigrate, as all Europeans seem all too inclined to do. [. . .] Some of the author's remarks on the condition and character of the savages would have delighted J. J. Rousseau; he would have learnt with infinite pleasure that several children kidnapped by the savages in wartime, when claimed back by their parents when peace returned, absolutely refused to follow them. [. . .] Refuse to believe after that, if you dare, that the natural condition of man is not civilized.

7. R. Crèvecoeur, 128.

8. Ibid., 355.

9. Ibid., 359.

10. Mitchell, 152–53.

11. R. Crèvecoeur, 134.

12. Mitchell, 155.

13. Ibid., 159.

Chapter IX
Last Years as Consul

1. *Lettres* (1784), 250f; Mitchell, 265.

2. Mitchell, 262.

3. R. Crèvecoeur, 17 n. 1.

4. R. Crèvecoeur, 12 n. 2.

5. Quoted by Mitchell, 263.

6. Translated from letter in Mantes.

7. Quoted by Mitchell, 277f.

8. Ibid., 279.

9. Translated from letter in Mantes.

10. Ibid.

11. Mitchell, 267f.

12. This forty-five-page pamphlet was published in New York and London in 1787. On pages 36–45 are translations from "Esquisse du fleuve Ohyo & pays de Kentucky," which appears in *Lettres* 3:387f. A copy of the pamphlet is in the Library of Congress.

13. *Lettres,* 3:414.

14. Mitchell, 268; R. Crèvecoeur, 304–5.

15. Ohio Company pamphlet, 38–39.

16. *Lettres,* 3:392.

17. Mitchell, 266.

18. Carl Van Doren, *Benjamin Franklin* (New York, 1941), 741.

19. *Lettres,* 2:416.

20. Quoted by Van Doren, 731.

21. Mitchell, 269.

22. R. Crèvecoeur, 142–43.

23. Translated from a report by Count de Moustier dated Dec. 25, 1788, now in the French National Archives.

23a. Ibid.

24. R. Crèvecoeur, 151.

25. Ibid., 382.

26. Correspondence on this subject has been translated from letters in Mantes.

27. The best discussion is in R. Crèvecoeur, 145–57; correspondence, 318–24.

28. *Lettres,* III, 557.

29. R. Crèvecoeur, 147–48.

30. Quoted by Mitchell, 271.

31. Quoted by R. Crèvecoeur, 153–54.

32. Mitchell, 272.

33. R. Crèvecoeur, 156.

34. Letter quoted ibid., 374–75.

35. Letter quoted ibid., 375–76.

36. Ibid., 120ff.

37. Quoted ibid., 161.

38. Ibid., 162.

39. Mitchell, 277.

40. Ibid., 279.

41. Quoted by Mitchell, 280.

42. R. Crèvecoeur, 163–64.

CHAPTER X
Surviving the French Revolution

1. Letter dated New York, April 2, 1790, quoted by Gilbert Chinard in *Les amitiés américaines de Mme d'Houdetot* (1924).

2. *Mémoires, ou souvenirs et anecdotes du Comte de Ségur* (Paris: Didier, 1845), 2:18–45.

3. William Wordsworth, *The Prelude*, book 6, ll. 344–74.

4. R. Crèvecoeur, 389.

5. Quoted by Charles Kunstler in *La vie quotidienne sous Louis XVI* (1950).

6. Gabriel Sénac de Meilhan, *Portraits et caractères du dix-huitième siècle*, quoted by Charles Kunstler in *La vie quotidienne sous Louis XVI* (1950).

7. Arthur Young, *Travels in France* (1790).

8. Ms. fragment of *A Tramp Abroad* in the Mark Twain Collection of the University of California, Berkeley.

9. *Mémoires du Comte de Ségur* (1845), vol. 1, 185.

10. *Mémoires de Brissot de Warville* (1830).

11. *Diary and Letters of Gouverneur Morris* (1970).

12. Chinard (see n. 1).

13. Quoted by J. Robiquet, in *La vie quotidienne sous la révolution* (1938).

14. Young, *Travels in France* (Jan. 12, 1790).

15. Morris, *Diary and Letters.*

16. Crèvecoeur's letters of February 10 to February 15, 1792, are to be found in the French National Archives. They are still unpublished.

17. *Diary and Letters of Gouverneur Morris.*

18. Quoted by R. Crèvecoeur, 176.

19. Letter to Ethan Allen dated July 17, 1785, quoted by Mitchell, 141.

20. The marriage of Fanny to this promising young diplomat had made Crèvecoeur very happy. Fanny, who had been traumatized by the tragic experience she had gone through as a child and who suffered from the loss of her mother and the almost constant absence of her father, was sometimes moody and difficult and a source of worry to him. His concern appears in particular in a letter sent to Crèvecoeur by his good friend Bartélémi Tardiveau on October 7, 1789. Commenting on the good effects on Fanny of a vacation in the country, he wrote: "Miss Fanny's rides on horseback, and the satisfaction she must enjoy among friends eager to entertain her, cannot but have a good effect upon her temperament and her disposition [. . .]. Her affections have been too concentrated until now [. . .] she needs to be brought out of herself [. . .] her indifference you wrongly blamed on nature [. . .]. I congratulate you in advance upon the great improvement in amiability you will find upon her return." (Quoted by Howard C. Rice in *Bartélémi Tardiveau—A French Trader in the West.* [Baltimore: Johns Hopkins University Press, 1938], 35).

21. *Mémoires du Comte Miot de Mélito* (1873).

22. R. Crèvecoeur, 182.

23. *Lettres* 3:414.

24. Ibid.

25. During the Revolution, the people in the Caen area were quite moderate in their views. Thus, in 1789, two members of the Third Estate concluded their observations on the *cahiers de doléances* (list of grievances) of the area in the following terms: "The five particular 'cahiers' and the general 'cahier' of the 'baillage' of Caen embrace many other objects; some passages present sound views, salutary reforms and a program of improvements, but let us not hurry in our quest for Good. It must grow slowly. . . ." They were in favor of a gradual evolution rather than of a revolution, and the *cahiers* of the nobility were, for their part, quite liberal in spirit. Their demands often coincided with those of the Third Estate. During the Revolution, Montagnard delegates of the Convention sent to Caen to have the Girondists arrested were themselves imprisoned for a time in William the Conqueror's castle.

There were violent crises and excesses there as elsewhere, however. In 1790, Count de Belsunce, the commanding officer of the garrison, and other officers were massacred by rebellious soldiers and the populace, who were incensed by the vituperations of Marat in *L'ami du peuple,* which represented them as dangerous enemies of the people to be disposed of. The event is alluded to in Chateaubriand's *Mémoires d'Outre-Tombe.* It has sometimes been claimed that Charlotte Corday, who went all the way from Caen to Paris in 1793 to kill Marat, was in love with Belsunce and wanted above all to avenge him. Her gesture shows how thoroughly hated the Montagnards were in Caen.

CHAPTER XI
In the Wake of Napoleon

1. On France after 9 Thermidor, see Henri Meister, *Souvenirs de mon dernier voyage à Paris (1795)* (Paris, 1910); Jacques Godechot, *La vie quotidienne sous le Directoire* (Paris, 1977); Edmond and Jules de Goncourt, *Histoire de la société française sous le Directoire* (Paris, 1899); and Marquise de la Tour du Pin, *Journal d'une femme de cinquante ans, 1788–1815,* vol. 1 (Paris, 1913).

2. Heinzmann's testimony is quoted by Jacques Godechot.

3. See Crèvecoeur's father's letters of July 29 and December 23, 1795, in R. Crèvecoeur, 390–91.

4. Quoted by R. Crèvecoeur, 205.

5. See the letter sent by Lafayette to Crèvecoeur on October 25, 1800, in R. Crèvecoeur, 397, and Rice, 38 n.3.

6. See Otto's letter to Crèvecoeur dated Paris, December 18, 1796 in R. Crèvecoeur, 391 and 211 n.1.

7. See Otto's letter to Crèvecoeur dated Lesches, October 12, 1797, ibid., 391, which refers to his *Voyage en Pensylvanie*.

8. The letter sent by Mme. d'Houdetot to Ally from Sannois on January 10, 1798, has been published in R. de Crèvecoeur, 392–93.

9. Ibid., 219.

10. Ibid., 394–97.

11. Ibid., 397.

12. The reviews published in *Le Moniteur* and *La Décade* are reprinted in R. Crèvecoeur, 308–9.

13. Ibid., 399–400.

14. On Crèvecoeur's stay in Munich, see his letters to his daughter-in-law in R. Crèvecoeur, 401–8.

15. R. Crèvecoeur, 250.

16. Ibid., 409–10.

17. Ibid., 405–8.

18. Ibid., 257.

19. Ibid., 258.

20. Ibid., 413, a letter to Manlich dated Sarcelles, September 1809.

21. Ibid., 259–60.

22. Ibid., 263–65.

23. Ibid., 265–66.

24. Ibid., 266.

25. *Mémoires du Comte Miot de Mélito,* (Paris, 1875), vol. 1.

26. Letter to Gillet de Laumont dated October 7, 1873, in R. Crèvecoeur, 411.

27. Only one of these letters is quoted by R. Crèvecoeur, 421–22.

28. The French translation of Louis's letter, originally written in English, is given by R. Crèvecoeur, 420–21.

29. Crèvecoeur's statement on the effect of Louis's "resurrection" is quoted by R. Crèvecoeur, 276.

30. The full text of this memoir about Mme. d'Houdetot is given by R. Crèvecoeur, 327–31.

31. Ibid., 277.

32. Ibid., 290–92.

INDEX

Crèvecoeur *(cont.)*
 financial difficulties of,
  58–59, 65–66, 99–100
 as fur trader, 26, 28
 heritage of, 1–3, 13, 14,
  26–27, 55, 74–75, 170–71
 high points in career of,
  174–75
 as homesick, 129
 honesty of, 100, 151, 153
 honors of, 99, 126–27, 174,
  191, 196
 humility of, 86, 100, 211
 idealism of, 214
 on ideal wife, 36–37
 illnesses of, xix, 31, 66, 103,
  105, 107, 109, 122–23,
  127, 130, 172–73
 imprisonment of, xix, 28,
  57–58, 61–64, 69, 150
 as independent, 64
 intellectual curiosity of, 4–5,
  16, 193, 200
 kindness of, 113–15
 linguistic training of, 12–13,
  16
 literary fame of, xv–xvi,
  xix–xx, 89, 117, 132
 love affairs of, xviii, 16–17
 as map maker, xvii–xviii, 11,
  21–22, 26–27, 60–61, 98,
  144
 metamorphosis of, 88–89
 military service of, xviii, 17,
  19–23, 24–25, 48, 139,
  144
 music appreciated by, 15,
  201–202
 as naturalist, 41–45
 obituary for, 210–11
 old age of, 208–10
 as open-minded, 16
 paintings by, xvii, 35

 papers and manuscripts of,
  62–63, 68–70, 93–95
 parties given by, 161
 pension application of,
  173–75
 persecution of, 50, 53,
  57–58, 96, 107
 personal tragedies of, 197,
  208–10
 petulance of, 122, 152
 physical appearance of, xv
 pride of, 64, 122
 prose style of, xvii, xxi–xxii,
  27, 73–74, 147–48
 prudence of, 33–34, 177,
  181–82
 reading enjoyed by, 16, 48
 religion of, 11, 128–29
 as sentimental, 37, 205
 skepticism of, 144
 social status of, 170–71
 as surveyor, xviii, 11, 18,
  26–27, 60–61, 66–67, 179
 travel enjoyed by, 18, 27,
  29–31, 51
 wounds of, 22
 writing loved by, 192
 as young man, 12–13, 15–18
Crommeline, Daniel, 34
Cussy, Thomas de, 8–9
Cutler, Manasseh, 159

Daily Advertiser, 161
Damas, Charles de, 149
 during French Revolution,
  163–64, 183–84
 political beliefs of, 157
Dante, 80
Danton, Georges Jacques, 180
Davies, Thomas, 70
Davis, Lockyer, 70, 94
Declaration of Independence,
 50